The Materiality of Devotion in Late Medieval Northern Europe

The Materiality of Devotion in Late Medieval Northern Europe

IMAGES, OBJECTS, PRACTICES

Henning Laugerud, Salvador Ryan
& Laura Katrine Skinnebach

EDITORS

FOUR COURTS PRESS

Set in 10.5 on 13.5 AGaramond for
FOUR COURTS PRESS
7 Malpas Street, Dublin 8, Ireland
www.fourcourtspress.ie
and in North America for
FOUR COURTS PRESS
c/o ISBS, 920 N.E. 58th Avenue, Suite 300, Portland, OR 97213.

ISBN 978-1-84682-503-3

SPECIAL ACKNOWLEDGMENT

Published with the financial support of The Scholastic
Trust, St Patrick's College, Maynooth; Bergen Museum,
University of Bergen; Department of Linguistic, Literary
and Aesthetic Studies, University of Bergen.

European Network on the Instruments of Devotion (ENID)

www.enid.uib.no

Printed in Spain by
Castuera, Pamplona.

Contents

Contributors

BARBARA BAERT is Professor in Medieval Art and the History of Christian Art, and head of the Iconology Research Group (IRG), Faculty of Arts, Katholieke Universiteit, Leuven.

ROB FAESEN is Professor at the Faculty of Theology and Religious Studies, Katholieke Universiteit Leuven, and at the Ruusbroec Institute, Faculty of Arts, University of Antwerp.

GEORG GEML is a doctoral student at the Art History Department, Faculty of Arts, Katholieke Universiteit Leuven.

BERNDT HAMM is Professor Emeritus at Friedrich Alexander Universität Erlangen-Nürnberg.

HANS HENRIK LOHFERT JØRGENSEN is Associate Professor at the Department of Aesthetics and Communication, Aarhus University.

HENNING LAUGERUD is Associate Professor at the Department of Linguistic, Literary and Aesthetic Studies, University of Bergen.

SALVADOR RYAN is Professor of Ecclesiastical History at the Pontifical University, St Patrick's College, Maynooth.

LAURA KATRINE SKINNEBACH holds a postdoctoral position financed by the Danish Council for Independent Research at the School of Communication and Culture, Aarhus University.

SOETKIN VANHAUWAERT is a doctoral student at the Art History Department, Faculty of Arts, Katholieke Universiteit Leuven.

Acknowledgments

The editors would like to thank Kristian A. Bjørkelo for his assistance during the editing of this volume. Warm thanks are also extended to the following for their very generous financial support: The Scholastic Trust, St Patrick's College, Maynooth, Ireland; and the Bergen Museum as well as the Department of Linguistic, Literary and Aesthetic Studies, both at the University of Bergen, Norway.

Some of the following contributions were first presented as papers at a five-day workshop for the European Network on the Instruments of Devotion, ENID, at the Benedictine abbey Michaelbeurn, Austria, 14–18 October 2009. We would like to thank the abbey for its kind hospitality. Thanks also to Mohr Siebeck Publisher of Tübingen for permission to translate and reprint the contribution of Prof. Berndt Hamm.

A number of individuals and institutions have most generously purveyed illustrations free of charge; Prof. Jeffrey F. Hamburger, Harvard; Marienbibliothek, Halle; Germanisches Nationalmuseum, Nürnberg; the Kupferstichkabinett, Staatliche Museen zu Berlin; Staatliche Graphische Sammlung, München; Bibliothèque du Grand Séminaire de Strasbourg. For this, we are most grateful. Sincere thanks are also due to those who have assisted in the translation of a number of these essays, namely Paul Larsen, Mary McCaughey, John Arblaster and Francesca M. Nichols.

Finally, we would like to thank the staff at Four Courts Press for their cooperation and professional assistance in preparing this volume for publication.

Henning Laugerud, Salvador Ryan & Laura Katrine Skinnebach
31 July 2015

Introduction

HENNING LAUGERUD, SALVADOR RYAN
& LAURA KATRINE SKINNEBACH

This volume explores aspects of the devotional world of late medieval northern Europe, with a special emphasis on how people interacted with texts, images, artefacts and other instruments of piety. It focuses on the materiality of medieval religion and the manner in which Christians were encouraged to engage the physical senses – gazing, hearing, touching, smelling and tasting – in their devotional practices in order to intensify the devotional experience. The contributions shed light, in different ways, on how bodily, sensory and material actions and objects were strategically applied for the purpose of reinforcing the devout sentiments of the soul and were solidly integrated into memory, which was regarded as one of the most essential faculties of human perception. In so doing, the collection brings together the ideals of medieval mystical writing and the increasingly tangible and material practice of piety character-istic of the period.

THE SENSORY AND BODILY ASPECT OF DEVOTION

The study of medieval – and particularly late medieval – devotion is a large and still expanding field. A striking feature is its fundamental interdisciplinary approach, which applies all kinds of cultural-historical perspectives, theories and methods, as is evident also in this collection of studies, both within each contribution itself, but also the collection at large. This is in line with much of the recent historiography of the Middle Ages. It is an approach that opens up new vistas on the medieval world in a kind of 'global Middle Ages', as Miri Rubin has termed it.[1]

Recent scholarly research has firmly established the body and the bodily senses as one of the most significant aspects of medieval devotional practice. The work of Caroline Walker Bynum is paramount, but other scholars such as Barbara Baert, Susannah Biernoff, Daniel Heller-Roazen and Christopher Woolgar have made important contributions to the field.[2] The body, it has been argued, was a devotional

---

[1] See Miri Rubin's historiographical reflections, with her study of Mary as a point of departure, in 'The global "Middle Ages"' in Miri Rubin, *Emotion and devotion* (New York, 2009), pp 5–43. **2** See, for example, Caroline Walker Bynum, *Christian materiality* (New York, 2011); *idem*, *Wonderful blood* (Philadelphia, 2007); and *idem*, *Holy Feast and Holy Fast* (Berkeley, CA, 1987). See also Barbara Baert, *Collected essays on 'Noli me tangere'* (Leuven, 2011); Susannah Biernoff, *Sight and embodiment in the Middle Ages* (Basingstoke, 2002); Daniel Heller-Roazen, 'Common sense: Greek, Arabic and Latin' in Stephen G. Nichols, Andreas Kablitz and Alison Calhoun (eds), *Rethinking the medieval senses* (Baltimore, 2008); *idem*, *The inner touch* (New York, 2007) and C.M. Woolgar, *The senses in late medieval England* (New Haven, CT, 2006).

instrument in its own right.[3] Because of the paradoxical nature of the relation between the human material body and the divine spiritual soul, questions concerning *how* to *deal* with the body lay at the very core of medieval theological reflection.[4] The result was, however, not a rejection of the flesh, but an attempt to embrace it.[5] Physical movements such as kneeling, lying face down on the floor, lighting a candle, and the employment of the outer senses – beholding an image, touching a rosary or the cold floor against one's face or knees, tasting the Eucharist or the words of prayer in one's mouth or the dryness following hours of recitation, smelling the sweet scent of incense and listening to names of the Virgin or words from Holy Scripture – were not merely outer expressions of the inner state of the soul, but devotional actions strategically incorporated for the purpose of affecting the soul. The practice of devotion strived towards transcending the paradoxical relation between body and soul by transforming the relation into a mutual dependence where body and soul followed each other closely, making common cause in contemplating God. Although bodily chastisement could be regarded as an attempt to suppress the material body (sometimes termed 'mortification'), it was also a way in which the close bond between body and soul became effectively and physically manifest to the self. As Bynum has stated, 'Control, discipline and torture of the flesh is, in medieval devotion, not so much the rejection of physicality as the elevation of it – a horrible yet delicious elevation – into a means of access to the divine'.[6]

According to a frequently used metaphor, the five senses were the gates to the soul. What passed through these gates affected the soul. If the gates were not sufficiently guarded by sober judgment, the soul would be engulfed by enemies, whereas a well-guarded sensory apparatus could be constructive. Medieval theories on perception acknowledged the indispensable connection between sense and cognition and thus regarded the *sensorium* as the combination of the outer sensory instruments and the inner sensory faculties. Thomas Aquinas stated that 'it is natural to man to attain to intellectual truths through sensible objects, because all our knowledge originates from the senses'.[7] The act of sensing did not merely produce passive sensory experiences, but also organized and formed the mind and senses according to medieval religious and devotional culture. In his commentary on Aristotle's *De Anima*, Aquinas also argued that when we sense something, we are changed and affected by what we sense, so that the senses become somehow *like* the objects.[8] Sensing was, then, according to this

3 Bynum, *Christian materiality*; Laura Katrine Skinnebach, 'Practices of perception' (PhD, University of Bergen, 2013).   4 Kristin B. Aavitsland, 'Incarnation: paradoxes of perception and mediation in medieval liturgical art' in Henning Laugerud, Hans Henrik Lohfert Jørgensen and Laura Katrine Skinnebach, *The saturated sensorium* (Aarhus, 2015).   5 See Bynum, *Christian materiality*; Aavitsland, 'Incarnation: paradoxes of perception and mediation in medieval liturgical art'; Laura Katrine Skinnebach, 'Devotion: perception as practice and body as devotion in late Medieval piety' in Henning Laugerud et al., *The saturated sensorium*.   6 Bynum, *Holy feast and holy fast*, p. 182.   7 ST, I, Q. 1, art. 9, quoted from Thomas Aquinas, *Summa Theologica*, ed. and trans. Fathers of the English Dominican Province (London, 1920).   8 Thomas Aquinas, *Commentary on Aristotle's De Anima*, for example Book II, ch. XII; see Thomas Aquinas, *Commentary on Aristotle's De Anima*, trans. Robert Pasnau (New Haven, CT, and London, 1999), pp 197–202. A good example of this can be found in bk VI of Augustine's

view, the process by which the senses were changed by what they sensed.[9] Beholding an image of the Virgin and child, for example, was thought to have a beneficial effect on the soul. Devotional objects – images, prayer books, rosaries, prints, amulets – were central to devotion because of their ability to mediate the divine and affect the senses and, thus, the soul in a positive manner. Lecherous or explicitly violent sights and other sinful uses of the senses were, on the contrary, regarded as unfavourable or even as outright works of the devil. Sensing was indeed not a 'natural' practice, but distinctly culturally defined.[10]

Such embodied devotional practices were closely connected to memory and mnemotechnical practices. Memory worked on different but completely interlaced levels, structured, as it was, around a set of visual concepts and figurations that incorporated the whole *sensorium*. In the practice of devotion, memory was operationalized through the practice of bodily and mental actions; bodily positions, sensory absorption of objects and devotional circumstances were, in an almost physical manner, *imprinted* on memory. Through this memory, it was thought, the self would be transformed into a living image of Christ.[11]

THE MATERIALITY OF LATE MEDIEVAL RELIGIOSITY

As the present volume illustrates, medieval devotion – mysticism and more ordinary devotions alike – exhibited a deep and profound awareness of the essential importance and, consequently, devotional potential of materiality. It should be underlined that materiality, in the medieval conception of *matter*, was regarded as anything but static or dead. On the contrary, as Bynum has argued, 'the basic way of describing matter – default language, so to speak, into which theorists tended to slip – was to see it as organic, fertile and in some sense alive'.[12] When dealing with medieval materiality – or matter – we need to go beyond the ostensible exteriority; the sensory world was not regarded as superficial but as immanently spiritual and the senses were able to 'see through' the surface of things and perceive their inner essence or quiddity, as Aquinas argued; 'Thus that which is the object of our intellect is not something existing outside sense objects, although intellect apprehends the quiddities of things differently from the way they are in sense objects'.[13] This also applied to objects and artefacts created by man; their devotional significance was due to the fact that the distinction between

---

Confessions in which he relates the cautionary tale of his friend Alypius, who was beset by a craving for the gladiatorial games and chose to attend one of the contests. Upon witnessing one gladiator fall wounded, the sight of the blood spurting from the gladiator's body drove Alypius into a frenzy of excitement and Augustine comments that Alypius thereby 'suffered a more grievous wound in his soul than the gladiator he wished to see had received in his body': *Confessions*, trans. Maria Boulding OSB (New York, 1997), pp 108–9. **9** Thomas Aquinas, *Commentary*, bk III, ch. I, pp 291–9. **10** See the discussion in Hans Henrik Lohfert Jørgensen: 'Sensorium: a model for medieval perception' in Henning Laugerud et al., *The saturated sensorium*. **11** See Henning Laugerud, 'Memory: the sensory materiality of belief and understanding in late medieval Europe' in Henning Laugerud et al., *The saturated sensorium*. **12** Bynum, *Christian materiality*, p. 30. **13** Thomas Aquinas, *Commentary*, bk III, ch. 8, p. 357.

materiality and spirituality was, in itself, porous. What we may regard as absolute dichotomies were, in a medieval context, absolutely interlaced. Body and soul, inner and outer, interiority and exteriority, materiality and spirituality were reciprocally intertwined; the one could not exist without the other; and medieval men and women were well aware of this. As a result, modern enquiries into the religious culture of the medieval period face a number of challenges regarding the way we approach the very texture of devotion. Bynum touches the heart of matter when she states that 'until we understand medieval art in a new way – until we see how it plays with, uses and interrogates materiality – we will not understand what it is that we need to explain'.[14] And the same could be said with regard to all other aspects of devotional practice; the incorporation of perception, memory, the senses and the body.

THE INTERLACED SENSORIUM

The present volume offers different perspectives on medieval materiality, but one specific characteristic will shine through; the practices involved with or involving materiality were – as will be shown – somehow *interlaced*. Body and soul were like two sides of a coin; it was impossible to see both sides at the same time, but it was equally impossible to use only one side as payment. In spite of their paradoxical nature, body and soul were inseparable and mutually constitutive. The five outer sensory instruments were interlaced in a similar manner. No one would disagree about the existence of five distinctive senses whose sensory abilities were distributed to mouth, ears, eyes, nose and skin. But in *practice* their abilities could not be separated equally neatly. Theological texts and devotional guides dealing with the senses were well aware of the amorphous perimeters between them. Senses could interact – as when seeing was regarded as a form of touch – or take each other's place – as when the Eucharist was tasted with the eyes (*manducatio per visum*) – or senses could be made to flit from one sense to the other – as when a visual object was transformed into a candle that conveyed new sensory information.

The practice of devotional sensing – incorporated as it was through repeated performance of bodily and mental exercises – was fundamentally connected to the medieval understanding of signs and meaning. As Henning Laugerud states in his contribution, signs were *polysemous*, almost inexhaustible because of the fallen state of man.[15] The Bible itself had to be interpreted and understood as containing meaning on many levels.[16] In the Middle Ages human understanding could not be reduced to a single truth. Understanding was a continuous practice; Truth was in God, not in man. A single sign could, then, convey a whole world of meanings that were all intricately interlaced and yet concentrated around the truth of God. Materiality – both

14 Bynum, *Christian materiality*, p. 52.   **15** Laugerud, this volume, p. 60ff.   **16** See especially Susan Boynton and Diane J. Reilly (eds), *The practice of the Bible* (New York, 2011).

natural and created props – mediated by the senses, could open the doors of memory and trigger unending trails of reflection. Isidore of Seville (*c.*560–636) introduced his 'De Pictura' ('On Pictures') in *The etymologies* by stating that 'a picture is an image representing the appearance of some object, which, when viewed, leads the mind to remember'.[17] When looking at an image of Christ on the Cross, for example, all of the different aspects related to Christ and the Cross would spring to the mind. Even the most basic sign could be unfolded to signify whole worlds, something that may be illustrated by one of Julian of Norwich's visions in which she experienced how she was given a small object about the size of a hazelnut:

> And in this he showed me something small, no bigger than a hazelnut, lying in the palm of my hand, as it seemed to me, and it was round as a ball. I looked at it with the eye of my understanding and thought: What can this be? I was amazed that it could last, for I thought that because of its littleness it would suddenly have fallen into nothing. And I was answered in my understanding: It lasts and always will, because God loves it; and thus everything has being through the love of God.[18]

The small object does not tell Julian anything in itself, but *through* her reflection on its being (the *eye* of her *understanding*), a whole new world of understanding is opened. From the little insignificant object she is led further to an insight of tremendous depth, namely about the nature of the love of God that is the reason for all being.

Such signs or *vestiges* triggered the physical appreciation that led further to imagination where signs were processed and made comprehensible according to the individual devotional level. In her recent study of the religious imagination in the Middle Ages, Michelle Karnes states that as 'the last of the sense faculties, imagination made a unique contribution to the process by which sensory knowledge became intellectual apprehension'.[19] Far from serving to denigrate medieval piety, Karnes links the period's (affective) meditations on events in Christ's life to an Aristotelian notion of imagination. For her, these meditations should not be regarded as solely affective; more often than not (especially in the devotional writings of St Bonaventure) 'affect and intellect are proportionate and interdependent'.[20] St Bonaventure himself states that 'imagination assists understanding'.[21]

Karnes underlines her point by elaborating on the role imagination plays in the

---

17 'Pictura autem est imago exprimens speciem rei alicuius, quae dum visa fuerit ad recordationem mentem reducit', *Etymologiae*, bk 19, ch. 16. Here cited after (English trans.): *The etymologies of Isidore of Seville*, ed. and trans. Stephen A. Barney et al. (Cambridge, 2006), p. 380. Latin text: Isidore of Seville: *Etymologiarvm sive Originvm*, vol. II (ed. W.M. Lindsay) (Oxford, 1951 [1911]), Lib. XIX, XVI; 5. **18** Julian of Norwich: *Showings*, long text, ch. five. Here quoted from Julian of Norwich: *Showings*, trans. E. Colledge and J. Walsh (Mahwah, NJ, 1978), p. 183. **19** Michelle Karnes, *Imagination, meditation and cognition in the Middle Ages* (Chicago, 2011), p. 4. **20** Ibid., p. 16. **21** See the prologue to his *Lignum Vitae*. Here quoted from St Bonaventure, *Mystical Opuscula*, trans. Jose de Vinck (Paterson, NJ, 1960), p. 98.

movement from the corporeal to the non-corporeal. She quotes the twelfth-century pseudo-Augustinian *Liber de spiritu et anima*, which states that 'when the mind wants to rise up from the lower to higher things, we first meet with sense, then imagination, then reason, then intellection, and understanding, and at the top is wisdom'.[22] Mary Carruthers has characterized theological 'pictures' such as those produced by Opicinus de Canistris (1296–*c*.1353), Hugh of St Victor (*c*.1096–1141) and Hugo de Folieto (*c*.1100–74) as mnemonic rebuses that have very little in common with modern diagrams. They are not image-for-word rebuses in the ordinary meaning of the word. They are *imagines rerum*, designed to call to mind the framework of a composition that each individual should ponder and elaborate further. 'They provide "places" as it were, for memorial "gathering", *collatio*'.[23] Signs provided places for further exploration and through one single sign the whole mystery of Christianity could be comprehended. Signs provided little doors of perception that could lead the way further to transcendent experiences. Thus, a vast hinterland of meaning lay embedded in each single picture, object or movement.

From a rhetorical point of view, the function of signs was to consolidate meaning in the minds of the devout. All expressive aids were able to do this, but they did it in different ways; signs differed according to *how* they helped store information in the mind and how *effectively*. The importance of storing information in the mind was closely connected to the position of *commemoration* in medieval culture. According to the New Testament, Christ, during the Last Supper, requested his disciples to remember his sacrifice '*hoc facite in meam commemorationem*'.[24] The biblical events belong to the past and cannot be experienced first-hand. In order to keep faith and memory alive it was of crucial importance that the past was constantly commemorated through the rituals and ceremonies of the Church that recalled the actions and deeds of Christ and left images and traces of the past in the minds of the faithful. The event was fundamental in liturgical celebration where the sacrifice of Christ was commemorated in such a way that it became present, the liturgical dimension called *anamnesis*. At the same time, medieval culture relied heavily on memory; whereas people today have the possibility of storing information in books and other media that we can consult if needed, medieval people had to rely on a combination of books (which were only accessible for the few), images (the medieval democratic medium per se) and what they were able to store in their own memories. This has led Mary Carruthers to argue that medieval culture was basically a culture of memory; *memoria* was one of the cornerstones of medieval education and this is clearly mirrored in the material culture of the period where learning was designed to aid the mind in forming and maintaining heuristic formats that were both spatial and visual because this was thought to be the best way to memorize.[25]

---

22 *Liber de spiritu et anima*, PL 40:786C. Quoted in Karnes, *Imagination*, p. 26.   **23** Mary J. Carruthers, *The book of memory* (Cambridge, 1990), p. 254.   **24** Luke 22:19.   **25** Carruthers, *The book of memory*, esp. p. 32.

THE ANTHOLOGY

In their own distinctive ways, the eight contributions in this volume address many of the scholarly concerns highlighted above.

Berndt Hamm's contribution concerns the understanding of the mediation of grace in the later Middle Ages, where we can find an intensified representation of the holy and that which sanctifies. This he describes with his key concept of 'proximate grace' (*nahen Gnade*), an understanding that Grace was immanent and close to man. This is, in Hamm's view, closely linked to new forms of mediality of the fifteenth and sixteenth centuries, where also the new printing technologies played an important role.

Rob Faesen focuses on the thirteenth-century poet and mystic, Hadewijch of Amsterdam's (Eucharistic) Visions, usually numbered 7–8. Faesen suggests that the two visions should be seen as one, and shows how the latter (8), which has remained relatively enigmatic in recent scholarship, may be interpreted in light of the former (7). Hadewijch analyses the different aspects of the union with Christ, the climax being the 'union without difference'. In this contribution, Faesen proposes a new hypothesis, which focuses on the physicality both of Christ and of Hadewijch ('without difference'). The visual and the theological aspects thus become mutually clarifying.

The questions raised in **Henning Laugerud**'s contribution concern what the visionaries of the Middle Ages saw. In other words, how do visions appear to medieval visionaries, and in their accounts? And not least, how are we to understand what the visionary sees? Visions are by definition visual acts and have to do with *seeing* in one sense or another. Visions are inner or outer *images* of transcendental, holy or divine beings, which appear in a manner that human beings can see, and represent an experience that transports them away from their immediate surroundings and places them in contact with the next world. During the Middle Ages visions and the literature regarding visions were an essential element of Christianity, both as practice and experience, yet also in a dialogue with and part of theological speculation. This contribution explores the relationship between visions, images – both exterior physical and interior mental images – and memory.

Salvador Ryan, in his contribution, explores the motif of Christ, lover of the soul, a theme that was very popular in late medieval mystical writing and, indeed, more broadly in devotional literature. Some of this literature depicts the relationship between Christ and the individual Christian soul while using a host of sensuous, carnal and even eroticized imagery. While often associated with the writings of female (but not exclusively female) religious mystics in England and on the Continent, Ryan draws attention to instances in which remarkably similar imagery appears in the lesser-known religious verse of fifteenth- and sixteenth-century Irish bardic poets. This is especially the case in Irish poetry concerning Christ's passion and poems that emphasize devotion to Christ's wounds.

Laura Katrine Skinnebach's contribution takes as its point of departure the biblical story of the Transfiguration of Jesus in the presence of three of his disciples. The story describes how the disciples come to understand the nature of Jesus as the Son of God as a result of a change in the appearance of Jesus that leads to a shift in their mode of perception. Skinnebach argues that the theme of transfiguration lies as an undercurrent in the practice of devotion and descriptions of devotional experiences. Body, senses and objects were incorporated into the practice of devotion through a combination of different devotional actions, through which the mind and body of the pious practitioner went through a transformation that left him or her enlightened.

In their joint contribution, **Soetkin Vanhauwaert** and **Georg Geml** take a close look at the so-called *Johannesschüssel*, an object with a close relation to the cult of relics. On the one hand, the sculpture has been seen as a substitute for the head-relic of John the Baptist that was brought to Amiens in the aftermath of the Fourth Crusade. On the other hand, many *Johannesschüsseln* contained relics themselves. This is not very surprising as many of these examples meet the ideal image of a reliquary: they are made of gold and silver, and precious materials were believed to be essential for a reliquary. However, there are several *Johannesschüsseln* that contained relics and were nonetheless made of wood without any precious materials, not even gemstones. As this observation challenges the common understanding of reliquaries, the contribution examines the materiality of the *Johannesschüssel* as reliquary and asks the following questions: What was it that made the wooden *Johannesschüsseln* worthy? Were these sculptures intended to contain a relic or did they become reliquaries at a later date? Did the materials used change the perception of the reliquary? And finally, did the relic define the sculpture?

In her essay, **Barbara Baert** revisits the Quattrocento iconography of the Annunciation from the standpoint of the senses. She argues that the devotional *Bildakt*, the interchange between the image and its beholders, in this period becomes unlocked through the pictorial (self-) reflections on the *sensorium*. In Tuscan Quattrocento interpretations of the theme especially (for example, Filippo Lippi) we can find an argument for how the *performative* interchange is built upon new insights in the optics, upon certain convictions about the role of the ear (hearing), and even upon intuitions regarding taste and smell. By integrating this *sensorium*, seen as a complex and chiasmic osmosis (that is, seeing as hearing), into the iconography, a new devotional and sensous relationship between image and beholder was established. Hence, in this essay Baert contributes to the 'hermeneutic of the senses in iconology'.

The *mediation* and *instrumentalization* of perception has most often been thought of as a marker of secularized modernity and of the disenchanted modern alienation of sensory experience. In contrast to this post-human assumption, **Hans Henrik Lohfert Jørgensen** employs late medieval devotional instruments to argue that the human *sensorium* was always already mediatized and organized by the cultural practices and cultic images through which its religious world-view and beliefs were shaped. The Christian *hagiosensorium* produced a world of holy perception through its multimodal media of cult and devotion.

1 Types of grace mediality in the late Middle Ages[1]

BERNDT HAMM

MEDIALITY AND THE IMMEDIACY OF PROXIMATE GRACE

Many links between certain changes in the understanding of grace and new usages of religious media can be observed in the fifteenth and early sixteenth centuries. Noticeable are the phenomena of intensive representation of that which sanctifies, saves and redeems, phenomena converging under the key concept of 'proximate grace', which appeared as a response to intensified conceptions of the nearness of satanic power and celestial punishments, thus from a 'proximate disgrace'.[2] At the same time we encounter new forms of mediality, i.e. new modes of a symbol-based mediation and agency in every communicative practice through which divine grace approaches humanity and through which humanity searches for the way to salvation. The representation of proximate grace and the development of new forms of mediality were in close interrelationship and reinforced each other.[3] The development of new ways of articulating the proximity of grace, for example indulgences and meditations on the Passion of Christ, led to a corresponding popularization and multiplication of visual and textual media including xylographic and typographic printmaking;[4] conversely, this innovative dynamic influenced the mediated forms of communication and the ways in which one qualitatively imagined the content of proximate grace in the fifteenth and early sixteenth centuries: as spatially and temporally illustrated, really present, immediately experienced, spiritually and sensorily encountered, effortlessly accessed, easily reached, spiritually perceived and felt, definitely available and at all times retrievable and even cheaply obtainable grace – to name some of the most

---

1 This contribution was first published in German as 'Typen Spätmittelalterlicher Gnadenmedialität' in Berndt Hamm, Volker Leppin and Gury Schneider-Ludorff (Hrsg.): *Media Salutis: Gnaden- und Heilsmedien in der abendländischen Religiosität des Mittelalters und der Frühen Neuzeit* (Tübingen, 2011) by the publishers Mohr Siebeck.   2 This essay (the German version) is a revised and expanded version of the contribution 'Die Medialität der nahen Gnade im späten Mittelalter' in Carla Dauven van Knippenberg, Christian Kiening and Cornelia Herberichs (eds), *Die Medialität des Heils im späten Mittelalter* (Zürich, 2010), pp 21–59. For the typical late medieval view of 'proximate grace' and 'proximate disgrace', see Berndt Hamm, 'Die nahe Gnade' in Jan A. Aertsen and Martin Pickavé (eds), *'Herbst des Mittelalters'?* (Berlin, 2004), pp 541–77; Berndt Hamm, 'Die Nähe des Heiligen im ausgehenden Mittelalter: Ars moriendi, Totenmemoria, Gregorsmesse' in Berndt Hamm, Klaus Herbers and Heidrun Stein-Kecks (eds), *Sakralität zwischen Antike und Neuzeit* (Stuttgart, 2007), pp 185–221; Berndt Hamm, 'Naher Zorn und nahe Gnade' in Christoph Bultmann, Volker Leppin and Andreas Lindner (eds), *Luther und das monastische Erbe* (Tübingen, 2007), pp 111–51.   3 Peter Schmidt, 'The multiple image' in Peter Parshall et al. (eds), *Origins of European printmaking* (Washington, DC, 2005), pp 37–56; German ed.: Peter Schmidt, 'Das vielfältige Bild' in Peter Parshall et al. (eds), *Die Anfänge der europäischen Druckgraphik* (Nürnberg, 2005), pp 37–56.   4 For xylographic printmaking, see Peter Parshall, *Die Anfänge der europäischen Druckgraphik.* For typographic printmaking, see especially Falk Eisermann, *Verzeichnis der typographischen Einblattdrucke des 15. Jahrhunderts im Heiligen Römischen Reich deutscher Nation*, 3 vols (Wiesbaden, 2004).

important facets. Grace was something within the range of anyone who strived for salvation. But what is particularly characteristic about spiritual immediacy is precisely that it is connected to the wealth of inventiveness and shaping of mediated expression with spiritual mediation of seeing and beholding, reading and hearing, touching, tasting and smelling, moving, standing and kneeling, the activation of the body and the bodily senses in conjunction with the spiritual mobilization of the imagination, cognition, memory, reflection and understanding, as well as the affective sensations and feelings through which the devotion of the graced person reached its goal.

Late medieval conceptions of proximate grace thus connect the ideal of maximum possible immediacy, a type of proximity of the sacred, with new perspectives of medial contact points between God and man and with new medial strategies of intensive contact. Proximity and mediality condition each other. This applies even for late medieval mysticism, in so far as it popularizes new possibilities of an unmediated experience of the redemptive nearness of God for unlearned lay men and women as well, with the inclusion of vernacular sermons and texts, the development of new possibilities of expression in the vernacular, the representation of mystical piety through pictures and chanting and the corresponding mass media such as copying and printing. These forms of mediality make possible and facilitate the direct contact of the soul with grace and salvation. If one understands the interrelationship of immediacy, conceptions of mediation and perspectives of mediated presence,[5] then there is the obvious consequence that one must speak about the proximate grace of the late Middle Ages as an event of mediation, and the other way around: of the mediality of salvation as a programme of proximate grace. Thus the following discussion concerns simultaneously the phenomenology of the varieties of proximate grace as well as a typology of diverse forms of grace mediality.

GRACE MEDIALITY AND THE IMMEDIACY OF ETERNAL BLISS

To do this task justice, a brief clarification of the relationship between the concepts of grace and eternal bliss is necessary. Bliss itself is the eternal, heavenly glory where there is no longer any mediation, but only the spiritual immediacy of the vision of God and the hearing of heavenly music. This is a collective event, similar to the graded tiers in an opera house and according to the widespread medieval idea, devoid of the individual touch which characterizes life on earth, hell and purgatory. In the widest sense, grace is that which is identical with God's power, guiding men to their heavenly goal of eternal glory, and yet it also protects them and their community from worldly harm. The term 'grace' (*gratia*) is associated with all possible conceptions, expectations and offers of goodness, love and compassion, blessing, freedom, liberation, salvation, sanctification and strengthening, help and protection. What is meant here is primarily

---

5 See Christian Kiening (ed.), *Mediale Gegenwärtigkeit* (Zürich, 2007).

and causally the essence and realm of God, i.e. God the Father, Jesus Christ and the Holy Spirit, but also in a derivative way the co-operation of Mary and the saints and all possible manifestations of grace such as the Holy Scriptures and the liturgy, the sacraments and sacramentals, relics and indulgences. While heavenly bliss consists in pure immediacy to God, grace and the way to heaven is characterized by a mediation of grace bound up with signs, so that the mediation of salvation can be thematized only by speaking of the mediation of grace. My further considerations point to the question of how diverse notions of the immediate working of grace for human beings and their unmediated access to grace are combined with diverse conceptions of grace mediality. It will be shown that concepts like 'proximity' and 'nearness', insofar as they relate to the journey of the pilgrim to heaven, the *homo viator*, can never be meant absolutely, but rather only relatively, as applying to a lesser closeness and a growing distance from saving grace.

PICTORIAL MEDIA FOR MEDITATIVE REPRESENTATION: THE ACTIVATION OF LOVE

In order to concretize this and focus on the proclaimed typology of the mediation of grace, I come to the first example, which shows how a direct contact between the devout soul and the divine saviour was imagined (fig. 1.1).

It is a copper engraving made in the year 1467 by the famous master with the initials E.S., who probably worked in the Upper Rhine region.[6] A large heart with Tau-shaped cross beams above it is to be seen in the central axis of the leaf. It is surrounded by putti holding the instruments of the Passion (*arma Christi*). In the wide-open wounds of the heart stands a blessed, naked Christ child, who in his left hand has a long banner with the inscription 'He who carries Jesus in his heart, is bestowed at any time with eternal joy'.[7] The leaf is full of semantic references to a dense, late medieval fabric of texts and pictures, all of which express the near-presence of the saving holiness of grace. In fact, the citation is similar to a text line from the highly visual and mystical theology of the German Dominican friar, Henry Suso (d. 1366).[8]

This representation of the infant Jesus is reminiscent of other single-sheet prints, the so-called New Year sheets, which show a naked Christ child, and on the banner convey New Year's greetings to the beholder. Thus on a woodcut from Ulm from the same period (pl. 1) a Christ child is to be seen with a lucky-bird (*Glücksvogel*) in his

---

6 The Christ child inside the Heart, single-sheet copper print on paper, 16 x 11.4cm; copy: Berlin: Kupferstichkabinett, Collection of drawings and printed graphics, figure and description by Holger Jacob-Friesen in Staatl. Kunsthalle Karlsruhe (ed.), *Spätmittelalter am Oberrhein, Maler und Werkstätten, 1450–1525. Ausstellungskatolog* (Stuttgart, 2001), p. 137 n. 55.   **7** 'Wer ihs in sinem herczen tret dem ist alle zit die ewig froed beraeit.'   **8** See Heinrich Seuse, *Horologium sapientiae* 1, 14: 'Ceterum ex his, o sapientia aeterna, hanc mihi summam colligo, quod quicumque aeternam salutem et praemiorum magnitudinem desiderat habere …, debet te Iesum, Iesum inquam crucifixum, iugiter in pectore suo portare.' Quoted according to the edition by Pius Künzle, *Heinrich Seuses Horologium sapientiae* (Freiburg, 1977), pp 493, line 24; 494, line 3.

1.1 Master E.S., The Christ child inside the heart. Single-sheet copper
print, 1467. Andreas Heese, Staatliche Museen zu Berlin.

hands[9] and the scroll underneath reads: 'My name is Jesus, that is true and I offer myself to you for a good year. And whoever holds me with love in his heart, to him I will offer myself in his final suffering'.[10] This formulation can be understood as a clarification of a parallel expression in the sentence observable on the E.S copper print sheet; 'To hold Jesus in the heart' means to love him from the heart; and whoever does this, according to the promise of Jesus, is 'bestowed at any time with eternal joy'. Ultimately heavenly bliss has come so close to him that it will always be waiting for him whenever the hour of death comes ('his final suffering'). The two sheets therefore articulate an intimate proximity of grace between Jesus and the soul: whoever loves Christ and – as visually expressed on the sheets – takes the Son of God into his heart and thus offers it as a birthplace and a crib for the Christ child, to him Jesus will offer himself at the end of his life in order to directly guide his soul to eternal bliss.[11]

With the message of countless late medieval single sheet prints, which combine pictures and texts, in mind, one can speak of a 'formula of reciprocity'. The texts present a conditional regularity, which is always formulated according to the 'he-who pattern' (*Wer-der-Muster*), by which an individual who gives something specific will receive something specific in return.[12] Both my examples are concerned with a firm conditional relationship prescribed between Christ and the soul: whoever, through his lifetime, is conditioned and prepared through the love of Jesus is bestowed with eternal bliss. Through this a rule for salvation is formulated, foundational for the whole of late medieval theology and piety: only one who at the end of his life dies in the state of love for God and in return is loved by God, is accepted to eternal bliss and saved. This active love of the individual involves the pain of a true and heartfelt contrition over the sins committed – a contrition that is the core of a true pentitence. All theologians are united in the view that such love and contrition are not just generated through the sinner himself, but rather are always the result of the working of God's grace in the soul. By pouring his sanctifying grace into man's heart, God awakens all emotions of the heart such as love, devotion, painful humility and joyful hope, placing the sinner's soul in an immediate relationship with salvation. This spiritual-affective immediacy to the divine Trinity moves and activates the powers of the human soul. When touched by grace, the individual experiences himself as a subjective participant who contributes to his own movement towards eternity: he himself loves and he himself carries Jesus in his heart.

The essential question is, however: through which forms of mediality is this

---

9 New Year's greetings with the Christ child, coloured single-sheet woodcut on paper, 36.5 x 25.5cm probably Ulm, about 1460–75; copy at Marienbibliothek Halle B n. 3; figure and description by Johannes Trippsin Cecile Dupeux et al. (eds), *Bildersturm* (Bern, 2000), p. 222 n. 75. **10** 'Ich haiß ihs das ist wăr: Und gib mich uch zŭ aim gŭte Jar/ Und wer mich Im herczen lieb haut [=hat] Dem gib ich mich an siner lesten năt.' **11** For the context of the contemporary Christ child devotion, see Johannes Tripps in Dupeux, *Bildersturm*, p. 223 n. 76. **12** See Sabine, *Text-Bilder und ihre Kontexte* (Zürich, 2011), pp 274–7. Griese appropriately talks about 'wer-Formeln' or 'he/she-who-formulas', proposing a contract between the spectator and the depicted image: 'wer etwas bestimmtes tut, erhält dafür etwas bestimmtes'.

graceful love conveyed to human beings? One possibility is meditation (*meditatio*). The two images are aimed at the meditative visualization of the childlike and suffering Saviour. Owing to the efforts of an expansive popularizing ministry, diffusing mysticism and a theology of inner piety, meditative immersion into the incarnation and passion of Christ became one of the chief media of grace and salvation of the late Middle Ages. Meditation is fundamentally defined as a sign-based medium that serves to communicate intensified proximity of grace as it aims to represent the cognitive-commemorative, imaginative and affective presence of the salvation story through word, text, images and music. The meditating person should incorporate the redemptive works of Christ spiritually into himself and allow them to become the inner reality of his heart. He can do this because God himself reaches down in compassionate condescension to the person in misery and into his world of sensible signs, and so through the closest possible proximity the gap between God and his sinful creature has been bridged.

THE INCARNATED REDEEMER AS A MEDIUM OF GRACE

The whole late medieval imagination of the proximity of grace thus presupposes the Christological turn of the twelfth and thirteenth centuries, i.e. the often-described shift from the visual representations of Christ as *Majestas Domini*, to the incarnated redeemer who is indentified both as Saviour and as pitiful human child in a crib as well as wooing bridegroom who lovingly embraces the poor individual. From the time of Peter Abelard (1079–1142) and Bernard of Clairvaux (1090–1153) onwards, the closely present saviour, the Christ child and the 'Man of Sorrows', develop into media of grace and salvation per se. In view of the present attempt to establish a medial typology, this Christological dimension would henceforth represent the first type of grace mediality, laying the basis for all other forms of grace mediality: God comes through the Incarnation and Passion and thus through the medium of the bodily saviour in the most intimate somatic-spiritual communication to people of all time.

This mediality of Christ is, in its essence, a broken mediality, because the heavenly Son of God approaches humans in need of salvation under a form in contrast to his divine glory; not in magnificence, but rather in bitter shame.[13] It is a contrast that is forcefully expressed in countless late medieval texts as, for example, when the sorrow of Mary lamenting her dead Son is formulated with words like: 'Oh sunshine, eternal light, how you have become extinct! Oh utter wealth, how do you appear in great poverty! O joy delightful, how has your face become so wretched!'[14] However, it is

---

13 The Franciscan monk Stephan Fridolin, in his principal work, *Der Schatzbehalter*, from 1491, gave an impressive description of this concept of opposition as the key to the interpretation of the passion and the structuring principle of passion descriptions: see Petra Seegets, *Passionstheologie und Passionsfrömmigkeit* (Tübingen, 1998), pp 218–25. **14** 'O sunnen glantz ein ewigs licht wie bistu erloschen. / O hoher reichtum wie scheinestu so in groszer armut. / O wunne wunniglich wie ist dein antlitz so iemerlich.' Excerpt from the lamentation of

exactly this miserable form of Jesus that is valid as a medium of grace; the mediated brokenness both denies immediacy of the pure divinity of God and makes possible the closest, most immediate, intimate contact to the divine saving power of Christ.

MEDITATION SYMBOLS OF CHRIST'S PROXIMITY OF GRACE: NUDITY,
THE OPENING OF THE BODY, HEART WOUND, BLOOD ATONEMENT,
CONDESCENSION, EMBRACING AND TOUCHING

Certain symbols were used to highlight the maximum possible immediacy and proximity in this world. Noticeable at first is the symbolism of the bodily nakedness of the Christ child and the Christ of the passion. They symbolize not only the stripping of all worldly goods, poverty and misery, but also the real humanity and tangible proximity of God's saving holiness.

Another important symbol of the unmediated close contact is the opening of Christ's body through the wounds of the crucifixion, especially through the alleged heart wound, which represents the side-wound inflicted by the lance of a Roman soldier to the already dead Jesus (Jn 19:34).[15] This wide open wound, which we have already seen on the engraved copper sheet of the Master E.S. (fig. 1.1) symbolizes the wound of Christ's love. Out of love, the incarnated God lets himself be wounded for the sake of sinful humanity; and through the outer opening of his body, inner love emerges visibly and sacramentally to the outside through blood and water. When man, through meditation, contemplates the side-wound of Christ as the external manifestation of the love of Christ, his own heart is also wounded out of love, and tortured by the pain of contrition. That which affected Christ in a movement from the inside to the outside now reaches the individual from the outside to the inside, so that he, as a lover, carries the crucified and wounded Christ as well as the childlike redeemer in his heart. The open heart wound on the copperplate with the child Jesus, therefore, simultaneously symbolizes the saving sidewound of Christ and the love wound of every graced heart. A coloured single-sheet woodcut (pl. 2) from the same period, around 1470,[16] again demonstrates this encounter occurring between the wounded

---

Mary on an illustrated and coloured single-sheet woodcut (paper), 37.5 x 27.5cm, by Michel of Ulm, about 1465–75; copy at the Boston Museum of Fine Arts, William Francis Warden Fund, inv. no. 53. 359; Schreiber no. 986m; figure and description by Richard S. Field, *Exhibition catalogue: Die Anfänge der europäischen Druckgraphik*, pp 236–8, no. 69; see also the detailed interpretation by Sabine Griese, 'Bild – Text – Betrachter' in Nikolaus Henkel et al. (eds), *Dialoge* (Tübingen, 2003), pp 315–35, here pp 323–6; Griese, *Text-Bilder*, pp 126–51. For this prayer preserved in several versions from the fifteenth and sixteenth centuries with the openings words 'O du ausfließender Brunnen', see, in addition to Griese, the paper by Gisela Kornrumpf, 'O du uzvliezender brunne' in *Die deutsche Literatur des Mittelalters. Verfasserlexikon*, 6 (Berlin, 1987), cols 1268–72. One version of the prayer has been preserved in the devotional book 'Die himmelische Fundgrube' by Johannes von Paltz (ed. p. 226, 1–18) discussed further below (see n. 17, below).   **15** See Thomas Lentes, 'Nur der geöffnete Körper schafft Heil' in Christoph Geissmar-Brandi and Eleonora Louis (eds), *Glaube, Hoffnung, Liebe, Tod.* (Klagenfurt, 2nd ed. 1996), pp 152–5.   **16** Christ child inside the heart. Coloured single-sheet woodcut print on paper, 7 x 5.5cm, Upper German; copy: Albertina, Graphische Sammlung, Vienna, inv. no. 1925/317; Schreiber no. 807; figure and description by Jean Wirth, *Glaube, Hoffnung, Liebe Tod*, pp 148f. For further representations of the open side-

Christ and the wounded soul: the Christ child in the heart, which has been opened by the lance, is recognizable as the redeeming Christ of the passion through the symbols of his suffering, the scourging and the rods, and the four bloody hand- and feet-wounds; what is in focus is, thus, the birth of Christ in the soul as the painful birth of compassion.

Late medieval textual guides for meditation on the passion are the explanatory contexts of such condensed representations of opened bodies and hearts. Thus in a German guide for meditation on the passion from 1490, attributed to the Augustinian hermit from Erfurt, Johannes of Paltz, and distributed in numerous copies, one finds the following prayer model for meditating on the side-wound of Christ: 'O dear Lord, I thank you that you let your holy side be opened. I beg you, break open my sinful heart and let me rest in your holy side. And pray one Our Father in love'.[17] Typical is how Paltz stresses the mirror image for the opening and breaking open: on the part of Christ and on the part of the human being. Also typical is how, in his visual language, not only does Christ move into the open heart of the person, but also, conversely, the meditating person by love moves into the loving heart of Christ and there finds peace – a common interpretation of the Song of Songs verse 2:14 about the dove nesting inside rock cavities ('*foramina petrae*').[18] Based on the meditation of the five wounds of Christ, Paltz presents the entire Passion of Christ as a spiritual mine with open galleries through which the meditating person moves and approaches the gold ore of God's grace.[19]

The entire treatise is hence called 'The heavenly treasure trove' 'Die himmlische funtgrub' ('Fundgrube' being a technical term for 'mine'). A handwritten copy of the treatise originating from Cologne and dated to 1508 contains many costly miniatures,[20] of which the first one is a plate displaying the five isolated wounds of Christ (pl. 3), presented before the eyes of the beholder as media of salvation to be absorbed through meditation.[21]

---

wound and Christ's isolated heart, see pp 140f, 144–7, 150–5.   **17** 'Ach liber herr, ich dank dir, das du dir list dein heilige seiten aufprechen. Ich bit dich, brich auf mein sundiges herz und gib mir zu ruen in deiner heiligen seiten. Und bet ein Vatter unser in die libe.' Johannes von Paltz, *Die himmlische Fundgrube*, ed. Horst Laubner et al., in *Paltz, Opuscula* = Paltz: Werke 3 (Berlin and New York, 1989), pp 155–284, here p. 225, 12–14. No fewer than eighteen Upper German and three Lower German printed editions of the 'Himmlische Fundgrube' (printed in Leipzig, Nuremberg, Magdeburg, Augsburg, Erfurt, Strasbourg and Cologne) as well as twelve secondary manuscripts, are known from the period between 1490 and 1521.   **18** See, for example, Paltz, *Himmlische Fundgrube*, pp 204, 4–11 (with reference to the sermon on the Song of Songs by Bernard of Clairvaux). As for the tradition (going back to Pope Gregory the Great and the Venerable Bede) of associating the rock cavities with the wounds of Christ, see Paltz, *Himmlische Fundgrube*, n. 14.   **19** See ibid., p. 204, 1–3: 'Von der himelischen funtgruben. Das heilig leiden Christi ist ein goltgrub und mer dan ein goltgrub. Dise funtgrub oder genad hat vil stollen, da durch man mag eingan.' For the late medieval and early modern use of the metaphor of the spiritual mine, see Volker Honemann, 'Bergbau in der Literatur des Mittelalters und der Frühen Neuzeit' in Karl Heinrich Kaufhold and Wilfried Reininghaus (eds), *Stadt und Bergbau* (Cologne, 2004), pp 239–61, here pp 246–8.   **20** For this manuscript (private property), see the description in the edition of the *Himmlische Fundgrube*, pp 187–92 (manuscript j); colour plates showing the twenty-one miniatures of passion scenes, after p. 200. For the attribution of the miniatures to the Master of the St Bartholomew altarpieces in Cologne, see pp 190–2.   **21** Ibid., fig. 2 (description p. 188).

The body of Christ opened by wounds and the open heart of the beholding and contemplating person symbolizes the closest possible proximity of grace in a mutual and joyful love, a penetrating being-present and being-united in the heart of the beloved. A Benedictine 'Nonnenmalerei' from Eichstätt from the late fifteenth century depicts how the soul of a Benedictine nun is intimately united with her wooing bridegroom in the open heart of the Passion (pl. 4).[22] The opening of the hearts through love and pain is a visual mediation of the mystery of the Passion as a union of God and man already experienced in this life as a foretaste of heavenly bliss.[23]

Other symbolic representations of grace mediality modelled on Christ's passion should be briefly mentioned here. Connected to the symbolism of nakedness and the opening of the wounded body are other symbols: the symbol of the atoning blood, which those in need of salvation receive through seeing, touching and drinking;[24] the symbol of condescension with which the crucified Christ comes down off the cross and searches for the nearness of human beings; and the symbol of embracing, with which Christ surrounds human beings in love. These three symbols of proximate grace are combined in the famous legendary vision of St Bernard of Clairvaux, which is often portrayed in the late Middle Ages, as in the case of a South-German woodcut from around 1450 (pl. 5).[25] Noticeable above all is how this archetype of Bernard is taken up in a meditative and visionary-contemplative way in female monasteries and transformed accordingly into images. A particularly telling example is a miniature of a book of hours from the late fifteenth century (pl. 6) that probably originates from the Dominican convent of St Margaret and Agnes in Strasbourg.[26] The sheet, which

22 The image depicts a nun in the heart of the crucified Christ. Coloured pen and ink drawing on parchment, 8.4 x 7.4cm; Eichstätt: Benediktinerinnenabtei St Walburg, inv. no. A3; figure and description by Maria Magdalena Zunker, in Frank Matthias Kammel (ed.), *Spiegel der Seligkeit: Privates Bild und Frömmigkeit. Katalog zu Ausstellung 'Spiegel der Seligkeit. Sakrale Kunst im Spätmittelalter'* (Nuremberg, 2000), pp 201–3, no. 36; see also Zunker, 'Spämittelalterliche Nonnenmalereien aus der Abtei St Walburg. Versuche einer Deutung' in ibid., pp 97–116, here pp 109–12. For a monograph dedicated to the paintings from the Walburg convent, see Jeffrey F. Hamburger, *Nuns as artists* (London, 1997); for this image, see esp. pp 101–36.   **23** See Christoph Burger, 'Mystische Vereinigung – erst in Himmel oder schon auf Erden?' in Berndt Hamm and Volker Leppin (eds), *Gottes Nähe unmittelbar erfahren* (Tübingen, 2007), pp 97–110. For the necessary distinction between different concepts of *unio* related to grace in earthly life in the fifteenth century, see the contribution by Berndt Hamm, '"Gott berühren": Mystische Erfahrung im ausgehenden Mittelalter. Zugleich ein Beitrag zur Klärung des Mystikbegriffs' in ibid., pp 111–37, here pp 111–15 and Barbara Steinke, '"Den Bräutigam nehmt euch und habt ihn und verlasst ihn nicht, denn er verlässt euch nicht." Zur Moral der Mystik im Nürnberger Katharinenkloster während des 15. Jahrhundets' in ibid., pp 139–64.   **24** For the monastic mysticism of the twelfth century, see, for example, Peter Damian (d. 1072): Vita Romualdi 31 (PL 144, 938 A/B) and about it, Bernard McGinn, *Die Mystik im Abendland*, 2 (Freiburg i. Br., 1996), pp 222ff. Peter Damian cites Romuald's personal experience with God during his time at his beloved hermitage at Fonte Avellana: 'I often witnessed in direct visions of my mind Christ attached with nails to the cross and I avidly received his dripping blood with my mouth'. 'Saepe cernebam praesentissimo mentis intuitu Christum clavis affixum, in cruce pendentem, avidusque suscipiebam stillantem supposito ore cruorem.' Here again, stress is put on the closest possible experience with Christ in a meditative and contemplative 'communio' of seeing, touching and drinking, one of the numerous and vivid examples of what late medieval literature and figurative art were able to transmit.   **25** Vision of St Bernard of Clairvaux, coloured single-sheet woodcut print on paper, 28.2 x 20.4cm, work of Jörg Haspel of Bibrach; copy in Vienna, Albertina, Graphische Sammlung, inv. no. 1930/133; Schreiber no. 1271; figure and description by Jean Wirth, *Glaube, Hoffnung, Liebe, Tod*, pp 266f., and by Tarin Tebbe, *Spiegel der Seligkeit*, p. 207, no. 41.   **26** A Dominican

has been pasted into the book, shows a nun in a Dominican habit who is not only passively embraced by the stooping and blood covered Christ, but actively – similar to Bernard on the woodcut – embraces Jesus with arms outstretched. It is a reciprocal giving and receiving of self-sacrificial love and it is exactly in this sense that the inscription formulates the appeal of Jesus: 'O my child, give me your heart, to alleviate my great pain! Embrace me in your arms, so that I am forever in your mercy!'[27]

The physical and mental image of embracing and touching is the most intensive medium for expressing the experience of the close proximity of salvation in personal encounter with God, an experience that is possible already during earthly life. Images of kissing and tasting also belong to this category of tactile symbolism. No other physical sense can express the immediacy, intimacy, interiority and familiar nearness of the personal contact to salutary sanctity as clearly as touching and tasting.[28] They are therefore particularly suited for articulating the desire of a mystical piety for experiences of God's immediacy, presence and close proximity. The loving embrace and touch portrayed on the Bernard woodcut and the nun miniature are, of course, to be understood in a spiritual, mental, affective and emotional sense. Yet as corresponding texts from female monasteries show, there is also a somatic, experiential dimension included in this contact.[29] All featured pictures until now, beginning with the copper engraving of Master E.S. (fig. 1.1), aim at making present internally the redeeming passion and birth of Christ in the realm of meditational contact, integrating a contemplative internalization of the images by means of imagination.

THE BASIC MEDIALITY OF CHRIST, MARY, SAINTS AND ANGELS
(FIRST TYPE OF GRACE MEDIALITY) AND THE RELATED MEDIALITY
OF PARTICIPATION (SECOND TYPE OF GRACE MEDIALITY)

At this point, I would like to return to my venture to establish a typology of grace and salvation mediality. As a mediality of the first type, I referred to the redemptive event

nun embracing the Christ of the passion, miniature on paper, pasted into a prayer book, 14.8 x 11cm, probably the work of a nun from the convent; Strasbourg, Bibliothèque du Grand Séminaire, MS 755, fo. 1; figure and description by Philippe Lorentz, in Dupeux, *Bildersturm*, pp 264ff, no. 114. It is noteworthy that in spite of the intensity of the embrace, the blood streaming from the martyred body does not stain the nun's hands or her white habit. An ink drawing, probably from a Cistercian monastery in lower Rhineland dating to the first half of the fourteenth century, offers a remarkable parallel; Cologne, Schnütgen-Museum, inv. no. M 340; figure and description by Karin Tebbe, in *Spiegel der Seligkeit*, pp 206ff, no. 40; Hamburger, *Nuns as artists*, pp 1ff with fig. 1, colour plate 1 (opposite p. 134) shows Bernard of Clairvaux and a nun kneeling below the bleeding body of the crucified Christ. Although Bernard and the nun closely gather around the legs of Christ, their hands and garments remain unstained by the blood. Tebbe pertinently remarks that the spheres of reality between Christ and the devotional figures remain formally separated and that although the scene reveals a closeness and intimacy to Christ, it nevertheless explicitly stresses the spiritual nature of this vision. The contemplative attitude of Bernard and the nun in the image is supposed to be transferred to the beholders' meditative and contemplative way of dealing with the redeeming and purifying passion of Christ. **27** 'O myn kint gib mir din hertz so wurt gemiltert myn grosser smertz entpfo mich jn din arm dz ich mich dyn ewigclich erbarm.' **28** See Hamm, 'Gott berühren', esp. pp 125–9. **29** See ibid., p. 122f., and Steinke, *Bräutigam*, p. 143.

of Jesus Christ, the grace and salvation mediated by the redeemer, who in his condescension, through the Incarnation and suffering, humbles himself to join the misery
of human beings, as it was relived in Bernard's visions and meditations. From a
medieval perspective, this was the fundamental event of communication and contact
between God and sinful humanity, the basic mediality of salvation. This first type of
mediality also included the gracious cooperation of Mary, the saints and the angels.
Through their compassion and through their holiness conformed to the passion, they
constitute together with Jesus the fundamental mediality of grace and protection from
which the other types of salvation mediality are derived.[30] From this essential and basic
mediality, this fundamental communication of proximate grace, I distinguish a
salvation mediality of the second type, which may be referred to as participation
mediality, provided it concerns the bestowal and appropriation of proximate grace.
Meditation may be found at this medial level; because of its system of symbols and
semantic references, meditation is a participation medium, through which the basic
mediality of gracious sanctity is bestowed upon the meditating person who actively
and subjectively appropriates it, finding not only the sanctifying, protecting and
saving power of Christ, but also that of Mary, the saints and the angels. It is through
meditation that man obtains their saving favour, their protecting companionship and
their intercession before God.

PARTICIPATION MEDIA: THEIR DIFFICULT AND EASY ACCESSIBILITY
(EXAMPLES: BIBLE, SACRAMENT OF PENANCE, HOLY COMMUNION,
RELICS, INDULGENCES, THE VERA ICON, AND IMAGO PIETATIS)

At this second level of mediality, meditation is evidently only one among several other
important media that all serve to communicate grace and salvation, often in combination and linked together with meditation: for example, Holy Scripture, the
sacraments and sacramentals, sermons, indulgences, grace-related images and relics,
the apostles' creed or prayers. An exception is the Eucharist, since here, in the real
presence of the body of Christ, the basic mediality of salvation and participation
mediality converge: eating and drinking the true body of Christ creates the closest
possible proximity to grace which fully overcomes each temporal and spatial distance
from Golgotha (*anamnesis*). It needs to be emphasized, however, that these participation media do not *eo ipso* provide for a mediality of proximate grace, that is, for an

---

30 I especially refer to the so-called medieval 'Repräsentationsfrömmigkeit' or 'piety of representation' which
basically reveres the representation of the presence of Christ *per modum repraesentationis* of the saints and their
followers. Together with Christ, the representatives therefore become mediators of salvation: see Volker Leppin,
'Repräsentationsfrömmigkeit. Vergegenwärtigung des Heiligen in der Frömmigkeit des späten Mittelalters und
ihre Transformation in der Wittenberger Reformation' in Mario Fischer and Margarethe Drewson (eds), *Die
Gegenwart des Gegenwärtigen* (Freiburg i. Br. and Munich, 2006), pp 376–91; Leppin, 'Christus nachfolgen –
Christi Nähe erfahren – Christus repräsentieren. Zur Glaubenswelt Elisabeths von Thüringen', *Zeitschrift für
Kirchengeschichte*, 118 (2007), 320–35.

easily accessible and available grace in unmediated reach of those in need of help. This may occasionally be the case, but it is not necessarily so.

For those in the Middle Ages with no or limited knowledge of Latin, the Bible was a difficult medium of salvation. However, in the later Middle Ages, vernacular biblical texts included in German language Pericopae books or Plenaries were easily available and readable.[31] For the period between 1473 and 1523, over fifty German printed editions of Pericopae translations with their glossaries have been counted.[32] Priestly absolution through the sacrament of penance is sometimes presented by theologians, preachers and confessors as a grace not easily obtained if, on the side of the penitent, true contrition (*vera contritio*) is understood as a necessary condition for the validity of the sacrament. The problem is, above all, that a person willing to confess can never be sure that his remorse over his sins is truly contrition out of love or not. On the other side there is – especially under the influence of Scotist teaching – the opposite position which advocates that the sacrament of penance is a medium of easily accessible grace. Those theologians stipulate that the necessary precondition for an effective absolution is not a perfect, true contrition. Through subsequent priestly effect of the sacrament of penance the attrition can be elevated to the higher level of the true *contritio*.[33] In this way, even the most evil sinner, provided that he does what is in his power to do, can be saved sacramentally – a dimension of proximate grace, which the aforementioned Erfurt theologian, Johannes von Paltz, led to in the anthemic statement: 'God the Lord is more merciful and generous through the priests than through himself ..., since God works more benefits through the mediation of the priests than without them, and without the priestly office he would save only very few (*paucissimi*)'.[34]

The problem of the validity of true penitence, i.e. of true contrition, complete confession and the serious intention to improve, shows how difficult access to Holy Communion, to participation in the real presence of the Christ in the Eucharist, could be made through the required condition of the right preparation and the worthiness of the recipient.[35] In principle, the problem that arose with the participation mediality

31 See Heimo Reinitzer, and Olaf Schwencke, 'Plenarien' in *Die deutsche Literatur des Mittelalters. Verfasserlexikon*, 7 (1989), cols 737–63; Nigel F. Palmer, *Bibelübersetzung und Heilsgeschichte* (Berlin, 2007). **32** See Paul Pietsch, *Ewangely und Epistel Teutsch* (Göttingen, 1927). **33** See Valens Heynck, 'Zur Lehre von der unvollkommenen Reue in der Skotistenschule des ausgehenden 15. Jahrhunderts', *Franziskanische Studien*, 24 (1937), 18–58; Berndt Hamm, *Frömmigkeitstheologie am Anfang des 16. Jahrhunderts* (Tübingen, 1982), pp 275–84. **34** 'Ex quibus sequitur, quod dominus deus est magis misericors et liberalior per sacerdotes quam per se ipsum loquendo non quantum ad naturam suam, sed quantum ad effectum et exhibitionem, quia plura beneficia exhibet mediantibus sacerdotibus quam sine ipsis; quia sine ministerio sacerdotum paucissimos salvaret ...'. Johannes von Paltz: *Coelifodina*, ed. Christoph Burger and Friedhelm Stasch: Werke 1 (Berlin, 1983), p. 264, 6–10. For Paltz's doctrine of attrition and the pastoral impetus for facilitating access to salvation for the large number of sinners, see Berndt Hamm, 'Wollen und Nicht-Können als Thema der spätmittelalterlichen Bußseelsorge' in Berndt Hamm and Thomas Lentes (eds), *Spätmittelalterliche Frömmigkeit zwischen Ideal und Praxis* (Tübingen, 2001) (*Spätmittelalter und Reformation. Neue Reihe* 15), pp 111–46, here pp 114–22. **35** See the discussion in late medieval Eucharistic treatises and sermons about the correct preparation and worthiness – presupposing true contrition – for redemptive reception of communion; for example, Antje Willing, *Literatur und Ordensreform im 15. Jahrhundert* (Münster, 2004).

of the Middle Ages was which quality and activity, efforts and worthiness are required of people so that they can be made partakers in grace-treasuries of Christ and the saints, because always and in differing ways the objective presence and power of bestowal of the medium is combined with the subjective component of appropriation as a prerequisite.

Relics and indulgences, too, could be all but easily accessible media of present grace. A striking example is the famous veil of Veronica. The relic of the veil on which, according to late medieval belief, was the real impression of the suffering face of Christ, commonly known as the *Vera Icon*, was preserved in the old St Peter's Basilica in Rome.[36] In order to visit the relic, pilgrims journeyed from 'beyond the mountains' to Rome, and obtained there, as was documented in the majority of the many different historical sources that puts a figure on it, a papal indulgence of 12,000 years and even more.[37] This was a very distant tangible relic of Jesus and therefore a remote grace, which was only attainable through hardships. Through the immeasurable number of replicas made of this most sacred and widespread image of cult and grace in medieval Western Europe, the *Vera Icon*, together with the working of indulgences, became a mass-medium of proximate grace. The worshipper thus no longer had to come to the original image; rather the picture came to him.[38] Countless people could look at this image of the suffering face of Christ in churches and private spaces or on many replicated single-sheet prints. They could contemplatively impress the *Vera Icon* onto their souls and obtain the promised indulgence through devotional prayer in front of the image.[39] A coloured woodcut print from Ulm dating from about 1482 (pl. 8),[40] demonstrates well the stereotypical combination of the *Vera Icon*, prayer and the promise of indulgences.[41]

---

36 For the legend of the veil (*sudarium*) of St Veronica and the history of its imagery, see Parshall, *Die Anfänge der europäischen Druckgraphik*, pp 313f., no. 100. **37** For the most frequent quotation of 12,000 years and more, for example '12,000 years of indulgence and 12,000 quarantines [quarantine = unit of 40 days]', see Nine Robijntje Miedema, *Die römischen Kirchen im Spätmittelalter nach den 'Indulgentiae ecclesiarum urbis Romae'* (Tübingen, 2001), pp 326f. (n. 17), 368, 374f., 378–80, 382, 385. **38** See Gerhard Wolf, 'Das Paradox des wahren Bildes' in Wirth, *Glaube, Hoffnung, Liebe, Tod*, pp 430–3. **39** For the quantity of this *Vera Icon* indulgence at a remote location from Rome, see Nikolaus Paulus, *Geschichte des Ablasses am Ausgang des Mittelalters* (Darmstadt, 2nd ed., 2000), p. 250: 'Für ein Gebet zum heiligen Antlitz wird öfters ein Ablaß von 10000 Tagen verheißen, den Johann XXII erteilt haben soll. Bisweilen ist auch von 10000 Jahren die Rede, zudem von 6000 Jahren, die einem Papst Eugen zugeschrieben werden. In einem Holzschnitt [s. Anm. 39/40, Abb. 8] wird erklärt: "So fil sind gegeben tag applas und karen [Einheiten von 40 Tagen] disem gebet, das ich sy hie nit künd wol begriffen." Der Herausgeber von'Jubilacio animae' verheißt für die Verehrung des Veronikalbildes 30000 Jahre und 12720 Tage. Der Ablaß von 30000 Jahren wird in verschiedenen Schriften auf Papst Silvester zurückgeführt.' ('A prayer to the holy face would most often release 10,000 days of indulgence, an amount supposedly connected to John XXII. Occasionally, however, 10,000 years is mentioned, or even a grant of 6,000 years attributed to a Pope named Eugen. Nikolaus Paulus mentions a certain woodcut in which it is stated that performance of the prayer will result in an "incomprehensible" number of days of indulgence. ("So fil sind gegeben … wol begriffen."). The editor of "Jubilacio animae" states that veneration of the Vera Icon is worth 30,000 years and 12,720 days of indulgence. Different sources connect this latter amount of indulgence to Pope Silvester'), see p. 250. **40** The face of Christ on the veil of Veronica, coloured single-sheet woodcut on paper, 12.9 x 11.2cm, printed by Konrad Dinckmut, copy: Germanisches Nationalmuseum Nürnberg, Inv. no. H 96; figure and description by Peter Schmidt, in Parshall, *Die Anfänge der europäischen Druckgraphik*, pp 240–2 n. 71. **41** The typographic prayer

The reproduction of the *Vera Icon* was a typical phenomenon of the transfer of grace, as is also to be observed in other Roman images mediating grace, which also guaranteed a certain number of indulgences. They were copied and distributed in the West.[42] One of them is the so-called *Imago pietatis*, a mosaic icon preserved in the Roman church of Santa Croce in Gerusalemme, a portrait of the dead 'Man of Sorrows',[43] which, in the fifteenth century, was included in and widely distributed as part of many and varied representations of the Mass of St Gregory[44] – as, for example, the Epitaph of the nun Dorothy Schürstab (pl. 7) which, in 1475, was installed in the chapel of the Dominican cloister of St Katharina in Nürnberg.[45] This image of the *Imago pietatis* was given a high rank since it was seen as the authentic and realistic visual representation of the 'Man of Sorrows' in the legendary revelation to Pope Gregory I (590–604), during the celebration of mass in Santa Croce. As in the case of the replicas of the *Vera Icon* – which incidentally is also represented on the Schürstab epitaph together with the *Imago pietatis* – the relocation of the image of the Mass of St Gregory evoked the real presence of the martyred Christ and transported it

text 'Grist siestu hailiges antlit' includes a plea before the face of the redeemer to protect the worshippers from sin's' harmful consequences and to guide them to the heavenly fatherland where amidst the blessed community they may expect to reside before the face of the redeemer. According to Schmidt (see n. 40, above) this is a transcript of an abridged version of a Latin hymn going back to the fourteenth century with the title 'Salve sancta facies' attributed to Pope John XXII (1316–34). It allegedly was also this pope who had linked the devotional contemplation of the veil of Veronica and the recitation of the prayer 'Salve sancta facies' with the aforementioned indulgence grant (see n. 40, above). The short version goes as follows: 'Salve sancta facies / nostri redemptoris, / in qua nitet species / divini splendoris, / inpressa panniculo / nivei candoris / dataque Veronicae / signum ob amoris. // Salve decus saeculi, / speculum sanctorum, /quod videre cupiunt / spiritus coelorum; / nos ab omni macula / purga vitiorum / atque nos consortio /junge beatorum. // Salve nostra gloria / in hac vita dura, / labili et fragili, / cito transitura; / nos perduc ad patriam, / o felix figura, / ad videndam faciem, / quae est Christi pura. // Esto nobis, quaesumus, / tutum adjuvamen, / dulce refrigerium / atque consolamen, / nobis ut non noceat / hostile gravamen, / sed fruamur requie/ omnis dicat: amen.' Text according to Franz Mone Xaver, *Lateinische Hymnen des Mittelalters*, 1 (Freiburg i. Br., 1854), repr. Aalen 1964, pp 155f. no. 119; for the tradition of the prayer hymn, see Falk Eisermann, 'Medienwechsel - Medienwandel. Geistliche Texte auf Einblattdrucken und anderen Überlieferungsträgern des 15. Jahrhundert' in Wolfgang Harms and Michael Schilling (eds), *Das illustrierte Flugblatt in der Kultur der Frühen Neuzeit. Wolfenbütteler Arbeitsgespräch 1997* (Frankfurt a. M., 1998), pp 35–58, here pp 41–3. The indulgence promise (as cited by Paulus in n. 39, above) stands out by its vagueness and is very unusual. It points to an enormous reprieve of temporal punishment for sins without specifying any quantity, as otherwise expected. There are, however, parallels; see, for example, Miedema, *Die römischen Kirchen*, p. 368, stating an immeasurably large indulgence in connection with the display of Veronica's veil.   **42** See also, for example, the replicas of the famous devotional image at the Santa Maria del Populo church in Rome, showing the half figure of a Madonna holding the Christ child in her arms and presenting the indulgence prayer *Ave Sanctissima Maria*. For single-sheet prints of this image/text dating to the end of the fifteenth century, see Griese, 'Text-Bilder', pp 300–9; for a corresponding presentation displaying devotional image, prayer and indulgence assurance on a triptych painting from Augsburg dating to the 1490s, see exhibition catalogue (Germanisches Nationalmuseum Nürnberg): *Martin Luther und die Reformation in Deutschland* (Frankfurt a. M., 1983), p. 49 n. 418 (Hartmut Boockmann). For more examples, see Gerhard Wolf, *Salus Populi Romani. Die Geschichte römischer Kultbilder im Mittelalter* (Weinheim, 1990).   **43** See Hans Belting, *Das Bild und sein Publikum im Mittelalter* (Berlin, 2000), esp. pp 66f. and fig. 14 (p. 65).   **44** See Esther Meier, *Die Gregorsmesse* (Cologne, 2006); Andreas Gormans and Thomas Lentes (eds), *Das Bild der Erscheinung* (Berlin, 2007).   **45** Master of the Velden altar, epitaph of Dorothea Schürstab (d. 1475) showing St Gregory's Mass, painting on fir wood, 128 x 92cm; Germanisches Nationalmuseum Nürnberg, Gm 521; see also Hamm, 'Die Nähe des Heiligen', here pp 197–219.

everywhere. The mass production and distribution of these images – which worked almost sacramentally, attributed, as they were with indulgence guaranteed by church law – served to secure that the passion's treasures of grace were everywhere present. The indulgence inscription on the Schürstab epitaph promised, therefore, to all devout spectators of the Nürnberg image, the same indulgence that was obtained by pilgrims to the Basilica of Santa Croce in Rome.[46]

FACILITATING OR AUXILIARY MEDIALITY
(THIRD TYPE OF GRACE MEDIALITY)

With this mention of the spatial and medial transfer of the distant and arduously accessible Roman grace to a near, effortlessly available, local grace, we have already approached the subject of the third type of salvation mediality. It is presented very clearly in the reproductions of the *Vera Icon*, and the *Imago pietatis*. While the mediality of the second type, which I have termed 'participation mediality', included a way to salvation that could be difficult and even elitist, the third type of mediality makes grace and salvation generally easily accessible. Hence it is perhaps best described as a facilitating or auxiliary mediality of grace, although the label is far less important than the medieval appreciation of this particular, third type of mediality. We have already encountered it in all the aforementioned single-sheet print images and painted miniatures. When beholders had images of the childlike and suffering redeemer, his open heart, his wounds, his blood and his contiguous embrace, supplied with an instructive, appealing and guiding inscription in German placed before their eyes, it facilitated a meditative and commemorative devotion of the heart, and an inward contemplative and loving self-immersion in the treasures of grace from Christ. In itself, meditation, as the activity of the human spirit, can be a highly demanding participation medium, an arduous path to heaven. Through images and their inscrip-

---

46 The indulgence inscription following widespread standard formulations begins with the words: 'Wer dise figur kniennd ert mit einem pater noster und ave maria, der hat von der erscheinung, die sant gregorius erschain in ainer kirchhen, dy heist portacrucis, den selben ablas der selben kirchen, des ist 30,000 iar ablas …' ('He who honours on his knees this figure with a Paternoster and an Ave Maria will receive through the appearance which St Gregory received in the church with the name "Porta crucis" [i.e. Sante Croce in Gerusalemme] the same indulgence of the same church which is tantamount to 30,000 years indulgence'). This is followed by the pledge of several minor indulgences for those who in the same way devotedly pray before the epitaph, i.e. a remission of twenty years by two popes, forty days by forty-three bishops, and two hundred days by thirty additional popes (see the transcription by Hamm, ibid., p. 201 n. 54). In view of the popularizing diffusion and close visualization of this 'Roman grace', it is interesting to note that many single-sheet prints from the same period, of which some are older than the epitaph itself, render exactly the same combination of Gregory mass and indulgence pledges, often with the habitual formulations 'He who honour this figure on his knees' etc. However, the sheets diverge significantly regarding the expected number of prayers, the popes and bishops, and the indulgences: see the excellent overview by Gunhild Roth, 'Die Gregoriusmesse und das Gebet "Adoro te in cruce pendentem" im Einblattdruck. Legendenstoff, bildliche Verarbeitung und Texttradition am Beispiel des Monogrammisten d. mit Textabdrucken' in Volker Honemann et al. (eds), *Einblattdrucke des 15. und frühen 16. Jahrhunderts* (Tübingen, 2000), pp 277–324.

tions, however, meditation was made easier. There are three steps of mediality: first, the mediality of salvation through Jesus Christ as mediator; second, the mediality of meditation as subjective participation in the Christ event; and third, the material-technical mediality of an available image sheet, to present as closely as possible, the meditative contact between the soul and Christ's grace. In an analogous way, the example of the *Vera Icon* (pl. 8) shows the three steps of mediality: the mediation of the suffering of Christ represented by his tortured face, the medium of the veil of Veronica with the impression of the suffering face of Christ and finally the medium of the pictorial reproductions of the veil.

EXAMPLES OF EASY ACCESS TO APPROXIMATE GRACE:
ELEVATION OF THE HOST, EXHIBITION OF RELICS, OSTENSORIES,
SPIRITUAL PLAYS, ACTING IMAGES, SONGS

The third type of facilitating and auxilliary mediality has, then, a lot to do with the materiality of images and texts and with the physicality of seeing, the use of other bodily senses and physical activity such as walking or kneeling. With the word 'seeing' one thinks for example of the Elevation of the Host commonly celebrated in the later Middle Ages, which urged the faithful to visual forms of devotion and facilitated an effortless communion of the eye (*Augenkommunion*) through the daily mass;[47] or one thinks of the large displays of relics (*ostensio reliquiarum*) in Munich/Andechs, Nürnberg, Augsburg, Regensburg and other places[48] or of the many presentations of relics in precious ostensories[49] that made easier the unmediated visionary contact to the bones of the saints. Through seeing and hearing, believers were captivated by the late medieval spiritual spectacles[50] or the dramatic use of 'movable images' during mass.[51]

The sensory medial staging of proximate grace – in a similar fashion as late

---

47 See Peter Browe, 'Die Elevation in der Messe' in *Bonner Zeitschrift für Theologie und Seelsorge*, 8 (1931), pp 20–66; repr. in *Die Eucharistie im Mittelalter* (Münster, 2003), pp 475–508. **48** See Hartmut Kühne, *Ostensio reliquiarum* (Berlin, 2000). **49** See Bruno Reudenbach, 'Heil durch Sehen. Mittelalterliche Reliquiare und die visuelle Konstruktion von Heiligkeit' in Markus Mayr (ed.), *Von Goldenen Gebeinen* (Innsbruck, 2001), pp 135–47. **50** See Bernd Neumann, *Geistliches Schauspiel im Zeugnis der Zeit*, 2 vols (Munich, 1987); Dorothea Freise, *Geistliche Spiele in der Stadt des ausgehenden Mittelalters* (Göttingen, 2004). **51** See Johannes Tripps, *Das handelnde Bildwerk in der Gotik* (Berlin, 2nd ed., 2000); see also the image examples and explanations in the section 'Handelnde Bilder im Kirchenjahr' in Dupeux, *Bildersturm*, pp 218–43 nn 74–92, for example, p. 235 n. 86, figure and description by Johannes Tripps: painted paschal grave chest from St Martin in Baar (around 1430), today in Zug (CH), Museum in der Burg; the function of such and other saintly grave chests are known, since the first third of the fourteenth century, to have been used for storing the host and a figurine of the crucified Christ (with movable arms) in the Easter liturgy between Good Friday and Easter Sunday. The rite often involved figurines of custodian angels holding candles and placed around the chest. The chest containing the Christ figurine remained open for devotion until the evening of Holy Saturday, while choirboys kept vigil around the grave. During service on Easter Sunday, a cross was taken out from the chest and placed in an upright position on the crucifixion altar to symbolize the resurrection of Christ. Instead of the cross, a figurine of the risen Christ could also be used. Today the figurine of the grave chest from Baar is lost.

medieval songs, which were spread through manuscripts and prints in convents, lay communities with a resemblance to monastic life such as the *Devotio Moderna*[52] or even as read and sung in the common parish mass – aided the meditative and devotional realization of salvation. A good example of such medial function of songs is the German spiritual chant, 'A Ship comes loaded' ('*Es kommt ein Schiff geladen*'),[53] which originates from the Dominicans, perhaps from Johannes Tauler and which thematized and popularized the typical late medieval devotion to the Christ child. In a translation from around 1450[54] the last two strophes (excluding the Marian refrain) go as follows:

> He lies in the crib,
> the lovely, pretty child.
> He has become our brother,
> he must be praised …
> So whoever will kiss the child
> on his red lips,
> will receive from him a great joy
> at this very hour.

> *Es liget in der kribben,*
> *das liebe hubsche kindelin.*
> *Es ist unser broder worden,*
> *gelobet muß es sin […].*
> *So wer das kint wilt kussen*
> *fur sinen roten munt,*
> *der enphohet groessen glusten (empfängt große Lust)*
> *von im zu der selber stunt.*[55]

Typical for the late medieval humanized image of Christ is how the Incarnation is established as the evident reason for the divine proximity: because Christ has become the 'brother' of human beings, he can become their dear child, beloved and bridegroom. Instantaneously and effortlessly and not only in the afterlife, but rather 'at this very hour' he can bestow them with beatifying bliss and joy. The mediality of a

---

52 See, for example, Ulrike Hascher-Burger, *Gesungene Innigkeit* (Leiden, 2002); Christoph Burger, 'Late medieval piety expressed in song manuscripts of the modern devotion' in Ulrike Hascher-Burger and Hermina Joldersma (eds), *Music in the spiritual culture of the modern devotion* (Leiden and Boston, 2009), pp 19–35; *idem*, 'Auf dem Wege ins himmlische Vaterland. Ein neu entdeckter Zyklus von Liedtexten aus dem niederrheinischen Chorherrenstift Gaesdonck' in Rudolf Suntrup and Jan R. Veenstra (eds), *Himmel auf Erden/Heaven on Earth* (Frankfurt a. M. et al., 2009), pp 23–56.   53 See the account of the song's tradition by Reich Christa in Hans Jakob Becker et al. (eds), *Geistliches Wunderhorn* (Munich, 2001), pp 60–8 n. 4.   54 Staatsbibliothek Berlin Preußischer Kulturbesitz Ms. germ. oct. 53 (most probably from the Strasbourg Dominican monastery *St Nicolaus in undis*).   55 Hans Jakob Becker et al. (eds), *Geistliches Wunderhorn*, p. 62.

humanized and incarnate God who descends down to the crib is linked to the mystical-meditative internalizing mediality of spiritual kissing and the sensory-material mediality of what is diffused through the written, read and sung hymns – the threefold mediality of proximate grace.

THE POPULARIZING DYNAMICS OF FACILITATION MEDIALITY AND PRINT TECHNOLOGY

When emphasizing the corporality, materiality and sensory perceptibility of the third type of mediality, then, it must first and foremost be noticed how cumulative, combining and reproductive this mediality appears, with a strong impetus towards popularization. In this way the late medieval processions and short local pilgrimages to the 'proximate grace' of devotional images, relics and miraculous hosts only a few kilometres away were combined with collective activities of walking, singing and praying, of bending low and kneeling before the shrine and touching it devoutly.[56] At these blessed locations, one could obtain devotional sheets, a blessed image, a depicted relic or letters of indulgence and then one could take such easily accessible sources of grace home and activate them through daily prayer.[57]

The enormously reproductive and popularized media phenomena of xylographic and typographic printmaking, especially after 1470/80, perhaps best illustrates this third extremely innovative and powerful mediality. In this respect, one could further investigate the mass-produced letters of indulgence and indulgence instructions, as recorded by Falk Eisermann,[58] or investigate the theological guides on piety written in vernacular language – as for example the 'Zeitglöcklein' of Brother Berthold[59] or the

---

56 For the increase in late medieval pilgrimage sites, for instance in Alsace (at the end of the fifteenth century there were about two hundred), see Dupeux, *Bildersturm*, p. 246; a similar phenomenon of increased piety in the same period is also observable in the region of actual Bavaria, this time through a marked upsurge in the number of saints, whose names are tied to specific areas, boroughs or devotional places. Cults of relics and proclamation of miracles led to the formation of local pilgrimage sites as well as processions (for example, St Achahildis at Wendelstein near Nuremberg, or St Radegundis at Wellenburg near Augsburg); see Berndt Hamm, 'Theologie und Frömmigkeit im ausgehenden Mittelalter' in Gerhard Müller, Horst Weigelt and Wolfgang Zorn (eds), *Handbuch der Evangelischen Kirche in Bayern*, I (Von der Anfängen bis 1800) (St Ottilien, 2002), pp 159–211, see pp 186–8. **57** See the examples of pilgrim miniatures, badges and so-called 'Schluckbildchen' in Dupeux, *Bildersturm*, p. 246, nos 95–7; p. 250, no. 101; p. 253, no. 104; pp 256f., no. 107–9. As for the function of the 'Schluckbildchen', Dominik Wunderlin (ibid., p. 257) explains that they consisted of small, devotional images, sometimes coloured and approximately stamp-sized and printed in series on larger sheets. Each image measured between 5 and 30mm in height. The buyer of such images was intent to make sure that the sheet had been conse-crated previously by a cleric who, if possible, had been in direct physical contact with the original cult object concerned. In case of failing health, an image could be separated from the sheet and ingested orally just like medicine by either a human or even a domestic animal. Help and protection were thus sought from the saints depicted on the images through somatic internalization. Proximate grace could therefore also inherit the form of something physically ingested. **58** See Falk Eisermann, 'The indulgence as a media event: developments in communication through broadsides in the fifteenth century' in Robert Swanson (ed.), *Promissory notes on the treasury of merits* (Leiden, 2006), pp 309–30. **59** See Sabine Griese, 'Das Andachtsbuch als symbolische Form. Bertholds Zeitglöcklein und verwandte Texte als Laien-Gebetbücher' in Rudolf Suntrup, Jan R. Veenstra, Anne Bollmann (eds), *The mediation of symbol in late medieval and early modern times* (Frankfurt a. M., 2005), pp 3–35.

aforementioned 'The heavenly treasure trove' of Johannes of Paltz – which offer meditations and prayers for laity in well-measured portions and functional, reader-friendly layouts. Such short edificatory texts could go through ten or even twenty editions in a few years.[60] Finally, however, I turn once again to the illustrated single-sheet texts, which, in my opinion, best made use of the new medial opportunities of a combined, reproduced, inexpensive and also popularized proximate grace.

AN EXEMPLARY SINGLE-SHEET WOODCUT: THE TWO DIMENSIONS OF EXTERNALITY AND INTERNALITY OF GRACE, INDIVIDUAL ACTION AND THE POWER OF GRACE, CLERICAL MEDIATION OF GRACE AND AUTONOMY FROM THE HIERARCHY

A single-sheet woodcut from southern Germany dating from about 1480 (pl. 9)[61] is a good example. The image depicts the scene of Calvary. The text beside the picture formulates a prayer to Christ of the passion, which begins with a supplication 'O you dearest Lord Jesus Christ! I ask you by your all surpassing love, with which you have dearly loved the human race when you, oh heavenly king, were hanging on the Cross with divine love, with a very gentle soul, with very sad gestures, with troubled senses, with pierced heart, with broken body, with bleeding wounds …'[62] After further illuminating descriptions of the character of the Lord's sufferings, the prayer articulates the plea 'O Thou dearest Lord Jesus Christ! In the same love, through which your passionate heart has been pierced, I beg you to show mercy on my enormous number of sins and condescend to give me a good, blessed end of my life and also a clear, joyful resurrection, for the sake of your great mercy, you who with God the Father and the Holy Spirit live and reign forever and eternally. Amen'.[63] Next follows the incitement to pray a *Pater Noster* and an *Ave Maria*. Then follows the announcement of an indulgence for worshippers: Pope Benedict XII (1334–42) gave all those who, with right contrition and sorrow over their sins, and as often as they devoutly speak the above-mentioned prayer, so many years of indulgence, like wounds on the suffering body of

---

60 For the seven German and seven Latin printed editions of the 'Zeitglöcklein' between *c.*1488 and *c.*1500 (and an undetermined number of editions from the sixteenth century), see Griese, 'Das Andachtsbuch', pp 29f.; for the twenty-one printed editions of the 'Himmlische Fundgrube' between 1490 and 1521, see n. 17, above. **61** The crucified Christ between the two thieves. Single-sheet woodcut print on paper with text printed in xylography, 35.2 x 25.3cm, copy: Munich, Staatl. Graphische Sammlung, inv. n. 118.124; Schreiber n. 964. See Sabine Griese, 'Dirigierte Kommunikation. Beobachtungen zu xylographischen Einblattdrucken und ihren Textsorten im 15. Jahrhundert' in Harms Schilling (ed.), *Das illustrierte Flugblatt*, pp 75–99, here pp 91–4. **62** 'O Du aller-liebster herr ihesu criste Ich bit dich durch die übertreffenlich liebe / durch die du hast liebgehabt das menschlich Geslecht / da du himlischer künig hiengest an dem Creütz / mit götlicher liebe / mit gar senffter Sele / mit gar traurigem geperd / mit betrübten Sÿnnen / mit durchstochem herczen / mit durcherslagnem leib / mit plutigen wunden …'. **63** 'O du allerliebster herr ihesu Christe / in derselben lieb dadurch dein inprünstigs hercz durch-sniten ward / Bit ich dich / Daz du mir seÿest gnedig / über die menig meiner sünd / vnd geruchest mir zugeben ein guts seligs ennde meines lebens / vnd auch ein clare fröliche vrstend / durch deiner grossen parmherczigkait willen / der du mit Got dem vater / vnd dem heiligen Geist / lebest / und regnirest ymer vnd ewigclich. Amen.'

Christ (according to the common belief there were in all 5,490 wounds).[64] This indulgence permit was confirmed by several other popes. The sheet brings together in an exemplary way the three types of mediality that I have indicated: the fundamental mediality of Christ as redeemer, the participation mediality of prayer and indulgences and the facilitating, auxiliary mediality of a printed sheet. This woodcut furnishes the persons seeking instruction and protection with an ideal model prayer and at the same time a particularly advantageous form of indulgence to be retrieved from the sheet at any moment whether on the road or at home and as often as desired.

At the same time the sheet reveals a characteristic late medieval understanding of proximate grace as two-dimensional: on the one side this grace is a protecting and saving holiness, which lies beyond the human sphere. It is the grace of the mercy of God, the agency and representation of Christ and the intercession of Mary and the saints. She (Mary) is in fact invoked in the model prayer mentioned above: 'I beg you, that you will look with mercy on the enormous number of my sins'. Indulgence is another typical variant of this outside, protective grace. On the other side, the proximity of grace becomes evident in that it works in individuals and accomplishes in them a new quality of devotion (*devotio, pietas*), love, contrition and gratitude, as a necessary counterpart to the external dimensions of grace. Without this inner correspondence, the external promise, the outside assurance of forgiveness, protection and salvation from God, Christ, Mary, the saints and the angels would be completely ineffective and empty.

The two-dimensionality between externality and internality corresponds to the former type of two-sidedness which has already been discussed in connection with the so-called 'formula of reciprocity': whoever has a particular spiritual attitude and does something specific will receive something specific in return. This latent contractual structure lay beneath the whole sense of the function of proximate grace. In countless varieties of instructing, exhortatory or consoling messages, the same idea is conveyed: grace is very close; it is, so to speak, directly at the door, just before the door of your heart or your house; you need not do much, but the minimum necessary you must and can do, in order to obtain grace.

This palpable contract structure that shines through here is fundamentally a manner of applying the flexible axiom of later medieval theology: God does not deny his grace to those who do what they can ('*homini facienti quod in se est deus non denegat gratiam*').[65] This action, required from a sinful person, consists of both an internal

---

64 This is the popular number given in the 'Vita Jesu Christi' of Ludolph of Saxony, which probably represents the most widespread devotional book of the late Middle Ages: see Arnold Angenendt et al. (eds), 'Gezählte Frömmigkeit', *Frühmittelalterliche Studien*, 29 (1995), pp 1–71, here p. 45; Griese, 'Dirigierte Kommunikation', p. 94 n. 47. **65** According to late scholastic theology, the rule may also have the following wording: 'Homini facienti quod in se est deus infallibiliter dat gratiam'. In his first lecture on Psalms (1513–15), Luther still approvingly refers to this sentence in explicitly mentioning the structural framework of the divine contract and union (*pactum*): 'Hinc recte dicunt doctores, quod homini facienti quod in se est deus infallibiliter dat gratiam, et licet non de condigno sese possit ad gratiam preparare, quia est incomparabilis, tamen bene de congruo propter

activity of the heart and a particular form of external activity. Our passion-sheet gives a good impression of how indulgence was tied to contrition, sorrow and devotion as well as recitation of the formulated prayer. In addition to the prayer, the previously mentioned Schürstab epitaph from Nürnberg (pl. 7) also prescribes the bodily devotion of kneeling: 'Whoever honours this figure (of the 'Man of Sorrows') on his knees and honours him with a *Pater Noster* and *Ave Maria*' is granted a certain number of years and days of indulgence.[66] Also a real kiss can be demanded as a condition. So, for example, on a southern German single-sheet woodcut of the side-wound of Christ from the later fifteenth century (pl. 10)[67] an indulgence of seven years is promised to whoever kisses the wound of Christ on the sheet 'with contrition and sorrow, also with devotion, as often as he does this'.[68] The typical *Totie(n)s-quotie(n)s* pledge (each time, when … the grace of the indulgence is received) was therefore integrated in the formula of reciprocity.[69] Such indulgence pledges clarify, like the many prescriptions of indulgence letters, the contract-like two sides of proximate grace[70] – in this case guaranteed by popes and bishops.[71] This structure was basic for all late medieval medial communication regarding salvation. It is inherent to the late medieval partici-pation mediality, that the objective-external performance and bestowal of grace is connected with the subjective side of the interior and operative appropriation of grace. In addition to this, the experience of suffering is included in this reciprocal structure of mediating salvation, a message which in unlimited variations comes down to the

---

promissionem istam dei et pactum misericordie'. *Martin Luther Studienausgabe*, ed. Hans-Ulrich Delius, 1 (East Berlin, 1979), pp 89, 30–91:3 (on Ps 113, 1): see Heiko A.Oberman, 'Facientibus quod in se est deus non denegat gratiam. Robert Holcot OP and the Beginnings of Luther's Theology', *Harvard Theological Review*, 55 (1962), 317–42; Berndt Hamm, *Promissio, pactum ordinatio, Freiheit und Selbstbindung Gottes in der scholastischen Gnadenlehre* (Tübingen, 1977), pp 378–83.   **66** See n. 46, above. For the numerous different variants of the formula prescribing the actions of the pious and grieving individual before the *Imago pietatis*, see Hamm, 'Die Nähe des Heiligen', p. 202 n. 55.   **67** The side-wound and the true length of Christ, single-sheet woodcut print on paper, c.1484–1500, 12 x 8.8cm, copy: Munich, Staatl. Graphische Sammlung, inv. no. 63. 248; Schreiber no. 1795: see Peter Schmidt, 'Beschrieben, bemalt, zerschnitten: Tegernseer Mönche interpretieren einen Holzschnitt' in Honemann et al. (eds), *Einblattdrucke*, pp 245–76, here pp 260 and 273, fig. 11. For a very similar coloured woodcut print, see exhibition catalogue: *Origins of European printmaking* (see n. 3, above), pp 258–60, no. 78 (with bibliography).   **68** The left-hand-side text reads: 'Das ist die leng und weitte der wunden Christi, die im in sein h[eilige] seitten gestochen war an dem crüß. Wer die mit reu und laid, auch mit andacht kusset, als offt er das thuet, hat er 7 iar ablas von dem Bapst Innocentio [VIII, 1484–92].' The right side of the text reads: 'Das creißlein [Kreuzlein], das in der wunden Christi stet, zu 40 maln gemessen, das macht die leng Christi in seiner menschait. Wer das mit andacht kusset, der ist den tag behiet vor dem gächen [jähen] doth [sudden death] und vor eim schlag' – As for the notion of 'real presence' of the representation referring to the original length and width of the side-wound and the true length of Christ's body, here rendered in a reduced scale, see, in addition to Schmidt (ibid.), also Hamm, 'Die nahe Gnade', here pp 551–4.   **69** For the 'totie(n)s—quotie(n)s'—formula, see Paulus, *Geschichte*, pp 258–60; Christiane Neuhausen, *Das Ablaßwesen in der Stadt Köln* vom 13. bis zum 16. Jahrhundert (Cologne, 1994), pp 52 and 79–81.   **70** See Johannes von Paltz (1504) who states that with the indulgence letters (*confessionalia, litterae indulgentiales*) divine grace itself had struck a deal (*pactum*) with man, urging him to carefully pay attention to its contents: 'Facit enim divina clementia pactum nobiscum in istis litteris, quod velit nos certissime exaudire secundum tenorem litterae', Paltz, *Supplementum Coelifodinae*, ed. Berndt Hamm: Paltz: Werke 2 (Berlin, 1983), p. 48, 17–19. See also Hamm, *Frömmigkeitstheologie*, pp 268 and 291. **71** See the reference to Pope Innocent VIII (n. 68, above) and to Pope Benedict XII and 'other popes' or various popes and bishops (n. 46, above Schürstab epitaph).

statement 'The more you suffer and as willingly as you suffer, the closer Christ comes to you'.[72]

The intention of facilitating access to grace was to reach both sides of the agreement, and so thence also to support human efforts (i.e. '*facere quod in se est*'). It will not only make the external dimensions of grace such as the pardon of guilt and punishment easily accessible, but also aid people in cultivating important spiritual dispositions. For the discussed woodcut, this means that through the contemplation of the Golgotha scene and the recitation of the pre-formulated prayer as well as the *Pater Noster* and *Ave Maria*, the sinner can attune himself effortlessly to the daily inner devotion of humility and remorse. A daily routinization of proximate grace thus took place through seeing and vocal praying, acquiring a spiritual *habitus*. Instructions, practices and attuning through texts, pictures and melodies are integral elements of the facilitating mediality of salvation.

Finally, it is important to stress that the mediality of proximate grace can obtain its particular quality of close sanctity either with or without assistance from the ecclesiastical hierarchy.[73] Two of the above-presented pictures show how women, a Benedictine (pl. 4) and a Dominican (pl. 6), stand in direct physical contact with Christ – a meditative incident, which although it does not exclude the context of a priestly mediation, nevertheless represents an event of contact, without the participation of the hierarchy. What is presented here was also directly expanded in the late Middle Ages to the practice of meditation among laymen and laywomen. A lot of vernacular manuscripts, single-sheets and printed writings give attention to their developing need for a more internalized and private devotion.[74] These meditative, mystical or

---

72 See, for example, the following aphorism, which, according to the so-called 'Tösser Schwesternbuch' (mid-fifteenth century), a Dominican nun called Anna Von Klingnau had pinned to her spindle, reading: 'Ie siecher du bist, ie lieber du mir bist. / Ie verschmächter du bist, ie necher du mir bist. / Ie ermer du bist, ie gelicher du mir bist.' These comforting words uttered by Jesus declare that her hardship assured her of her closeness as well as her resemblance to him; text according to Ferdinand Vetter (ed.), *Das Leben der Schwestern zu Töß beschrieben von Elsbet Stagel samt der Vorrede von Johannes Meier und dem Leben der Prinzessin Elisabet von Ungarn* (Berlin, 1906), pp 37, 15–17. On this passage from the 'Tösser Schwesternbuch' and its influence on an Ulm single-sheet woodcut, see Griese, *Text-Bilder*, pp 134–8 and 147–50. **73** See n. 68, above, especially the depictions of the Mass of St Gregory (fig. 9), which emphatically allude to the ecclesiastical hierarchy. Such representations of institutionalized sacredness helped to link the notion of grace proximity to the authority of the offices held by the popes, cardinals and bishops. **74** See, for example, the marked shift towards mystical and theological compilations in German at the Benedictine monastery of Tegernsee after 1445. These literary texts aimed to reach beguines and female members of the Munich bourgeoisie who showed a spiritual disposition towards the *vita contemplativa* and an interest in German mystical literature. It was an anonymous monk from Tegernsee, however, probably none other than the renowned and versatile Bernhard of Waging, who had undertaken the German translations of the Sermons on the Song of Songs by Bernard of Clairvaux. Among them was also a group of German-language, mystical texts on pastoral care that probably again were intended for the same, semi-religious and lay, female membership. These, too, had probably been translated from Latin to German, or rather assembled from different originals and new additions by the same Bernhard of Waging to form entirely new treatises. These texts in fact illustrate well how women towards the end of the Middle Ages, and through the mediation of learned clerics themselves, had become able to attain an independent care of their own spirituality: see Werner Höver, *Theologia Mystica in altbairischer Übertragung* (München, 1971), pp 1–135 (for the beguines pp 120–35), pp 272ff; Christian Bauer, *Geistliche Prosa im Kloster Tegernsee* (Tübingen, 1996), pp 137–59 (evidence for

near-mystical demands for a greater immediate intimacy with God were independent of priests to communicate proximate grace.[75] Hence also a specifically female directness and immediacy of grace arose in relative independence from the male-controlled mediation of salvation.[76]

INTER-CONNECTIONS BETWEEN OBJECTIVITY/SUBJECTIVITY, EXTERIOR/INTERIOR, BESTOWAL/APPROPRIATION OF GRACE

Finally, it should once more be emphasized how the three types of mediality are related to different fields of tension and furthermore how these fields are interrelated in specific ways. Of particular note here is the unsettled relationship between objectiveness and subjectiveness, externality and internality, as well as bestowal and appropriation of grace and salvation. The media of participation already spoken of above may belong either more to the side of grace-bestowal or more to the side of grace-appropriation: sacraments, sacramentals, relics, grace images or indulgences are therefore media of bestowal whose grace-generating forces are particularly linked to dimensions of objectivity and externality, bestowing the receiving individual from the outside with a trans-subjective presence of holiness. On the other hand, meditation or prayer are media of appropriation that essentially are related to individual activity, interiority and subjectivity. The facilitating and auxiliary character of the third type of grace-mediality may be linked to both, external and objective bestowal of grace on the one hand and subjective and interior appropriation on the other.

How problematic and sometimes misleading such references to compositions are – bestowal, receptivity, objectivity, outward orientation and appropriation, activity, subjectivity, interiority – becomes evident when one considers, for example, that meditation and prayer are essentially constituted through their medial connection to something external; they depend on the basic grace mediality of Christ, Mary, the saints and the angels, deeply rooted as it is in the pre-defined sign structures of Holy Scriptures, liturgy, piety forming texts and images. Conversely, the trans-subjective and external bestowal-character of grace-mediality, for example the sacraments, aims directly at the subjective moment of personal appropriation and acquisition. The intention is to form the inner devotion of the person, which subsequently reflects back to the bodily existence of the exterior person and his devotional praxis of *imitatio*

Bernhard of Waging as the anonymous translator; the Munich laywomen pp 150–3). For a profile of female monastic spirituality in the fifteenth century, see, for example, Barbara Steinke, *Paradiesgarten oder Gefängnis* (Tübingen, 2006). **75** See Volker Leppin, 'Mystische Frömmigkeit und sakramentale Heilsvermittlung im späten Mittelalter', *Zeitschrift für Kirchengeschichte*, 112 (2001), pp 189–204. **76** See, for example, Anne Bollmann, 'Een vrauwe te sijn op mijn selfs handt. Alijt Bake (1413–55) als geistliche Reformerin des innerlichen Lebens' in *Ons Geestelijk Erf*, 76 (2002), pp 64–98. For the divergences between the protective and domesticating standpoint of monastic pastors on the one hand and tendencies of female mysticism towards immediate access to salvation on the other, see Werner Williams-Krapp, '"Dise ding sint dennoch nit ware zeichen der heiligkeit." Zur Bewertung mystischer Erfahrungen im 15. Jahrhundert', *Zeitschrift für Literaturwissenschaft und Linguistik*, 20, Heft 80 (1990), 61–71.

Christi within an external social structure. Hence the medial path leads from outside to inside and from inside to outside, interlocking objectivity and subjectivity; passivity of the receiving person and activity of the self-acting and liberated person.

From the theological perspective of the late Middle Ages, such interlocking and interrelation occurs mainly because the divine medium of the Holy Spirit enables grace to be habitually and actually present in the soul of individual persons. An external force becomes an individual's sanctity; the objective bestowal of grace affects the subjective appropriation. The result is that the sanctified person may only be moved to the bliss of eternal life if it happens in corporation with the dynamics of the Holy Spirit and the infused grace. Hence, for all three types of grace mediality, there is a characteristic correlation between an objective-external dimension of bestowal and a subjective-inner one of appropriation. Thus, the redeeming mediality of Christ the saviour and mediator links in a trinitarian way with the inspiration of the Holy Spirit of God and Christ reaching into the interiority and subjectivity of the heart. To clarify with an example: poverty and suffering are fateful mediations of God's grace with which he calls the individual into imitation of the poor Christ of the passion. It is the Holy Spirit, however, who gives him the capacity to internally appropriate these media of participation and to make them fruitful by being ready and willing to accept poverty and suffering in love, gratitude and contrition from the hand of God.

It is characteristic of the late medieval period that many devotional media – for example, single-sheet prints – foster an internalization, individualization and privatization of the sacred and so simultaneously remain in close connection with the multifaceted trans-subjective, objectifying, institutional and communal forms of ecclesiastical and cultic mediality of grace. In this way, the emphasis can either shift to the side of interiorization or to the side of exteriorization of devotional life.

THE DIVERSE FORMS OF THE MEDIAL PRESENCE OF GRACE

In my study of the medial types of proximate grace, I have concentrated on the Christological mediality, and through this especially on the immediate presence of the body of Christ – a central but, at the same time, only narrow facet of the wide medial spectrum of the very diverse phenomena of grace representation. In addition, for example, one could also speak about liturgical innovations and new architectural, spatial conceptions of an intensified presence of grace. Phenomena of grace representations may also be investigated from a perspective of social history, especially with respect to certain religious communities, fraternities and urban or rural communities; or one could examine the proposed typology with regard to Mary, the saints and the angels. It was my intention, however, to identify a Christological paradigm and to find out the concrete interacting relationships of chosen texts and images and whether a general media typology is applicable to all late medieval manifestations of increased spiritual grace and salvation proximity.

THE REFORMATION: CONNECTIONS BETWEEN THE EXCLUSIVE
MEDIALITY OF CHRIST AND 'PURIFIED' MEDIALITY OF PARTICIPATION

In connection with the Reformation, the difference between the three types of grace mediality is no longer applicable. One can even say that the differences between the periods are brought to the fore by the reformers' turning from the structures of mediality mentioned above. The Reformation indeed strengthens the characteristic dynamization of proximate grace in the late Middle Ages. It takes over, albeit in a forced way, the combination of proximate grace with the new multiplying technologies of typographical printing. And it also exacerbates a late medieval and especially humanist critique, which works against many reifications of facilitating mediality such as indulgences,[77] relics, revered hosts and cultic images.[78] Even radical-mystical conceptions of the soul's pure spiritual immediacy to God beyond all pictorial and sacramental mediality remain present within some branches of the Reformation.[79] Nevertheless, for the Reformation in general, the use of the category 'facilitating mediality' as a whole is meaningless. When grace and salvation are now gratuitously obtainable and every active involvement of individuals is ruled out, no facilitation is needed.

The participation and facilitation mediality of the late Middle Ages operates, as I have shown, always within the coordinates of the two-sidedness of divine grace and human cooperation and sets as a scale of comparison always the challenging way to heaven, graded through satisfaction and merits. While the Reformation basically breaks with this model and this two-sided conception of grace mediality, there remains only a reduced, reinterpreted and biblically purified mediality of participation, which is concerned and connected exclusively with the redeeming mediality of Jesus Christ – the sole and exclusive mediator: as a pure bestowal without admixture of human activities that pertain to salvation.

In this way through every type of reformed grace mediality, the intention shifts to the fullness of salvation without gradations in the unmediated contact-proximity of the sinful person: through the biblical word of salvation in the vernacular Holy Scriptures, through sermons, sacraments, church hymns and catechism the sinner is placed in the redeeming Christian community.[80] Thus the basic salvific mediality of

---

77 See, for example, Wilheim Ernst Winterhager, 'Ablasskritik als Indikator historischen Wandels vor 1517. Ein Beitrag zu Voraussetzungen und Einordnung der Reformation', *Archiv für Reformationsgeschichte*, 90 (1999), 6–71; Berndt Hamm and Michael Welker, *Die Reformation. Potentiale der Freiheit* (Tübingen, 2008), pp 33f., 62f. **78** See Norbert Schnitzler, *Ikonoklasmus – Bildersturm* (Munich, 1996); Guy P. Marchal, 'Das vieldeutige Heiligenbild' in Peter Blickle, André Holenstein et al. (eds), *Macht und Ohnmacht der Bilder* (Munich, 2002), pp 307–32. **79** Compare George Hunston Williams, *The radical Reformation* (Philadelphia, 1962); Steven E. Ozment, *Mysticism and dissent* (New Haven, CT, and London, 1973); Gudrun Litz, *Die reformatorische Bilderfrage in den schwäbischen Reichsstädten* (Tübingen, 2007), pp 56–62 (Kaspar von Schwenckfeld and Sebastian Franck). **80** See within Reformation circles, for example, John Calvin, who differentiates between the salvific, priestly mediation office of Jesus Christ, the inner mediality of the Holy Spirit and the external media of the Church. For the latter (in bk 4 of the *Institutio Christiane religionis* dating to 1559), see the title of bk 4: 'De externis mediis

Christ and participation mediality coincide in the current process of justification and the facilitation mediality disappears.[81]

Translated by Paul Larsen, Mary McCaughey and Laura Katrine Skinnebach.

vel adminiculis, quibus Deus in Christi societatem nos invitat et in ea retinet'. Joannis Calvini, *Opera selecta*, ed. Petrus Barth, Guilelmus Niesel, 5, 3rd ed. (Munich, 1974), pp 1, 3–5. In this last part of the *Institutio*, Calvin develops his understanding of church offices and sacramental theology.   **81** However, Calvin's external *media salutis*, which in a sensitive way are all instruments of the Holy Spirit and thus allow us to participate in the saving community of Christ, can arguably be taken for auxiliary or facilitating media (see the term *adminicula* in n. 82, below) in as far as the external word of God and the sensitive sacramental signs of the church come in to support the restricted capacities of human nature: see *Institutio* 4,1,1, ibid., pp 1, 10–15: 'But as our ignorance and sloth (I may add, the vanity of our intellect) stand in need of external help, by which faith may be begotten in us, and may increase and make progress until its consummation, God, in accommodation to our infirmity, has added such aids and secured the effectual preaching of the gospel, by depositing this treasure within the Church.' 'Quia autem ruditas nostra et segnities (addo etiam ingenii vanitatem) externis subsidiis indigent, quibus fides in nobis et gignatur et augescat et suos faciat progressus usque ad metam, ea quoque Deus addidit, quo infirmitati nostrae consuleret; atque ut vigeret Evangelii praedicatio, thesaurum hunc apud Ecclesiam deposuit.'

2 The Body of Christ and the union 'without difference': Hadewijch's Eucharistic *Vision 7–8* reconsidered

ROB FAESEN

The thirteenth-century poet and mystic, Hadewijch, occupies an important position in European mystical literature. Indeed, along with her contemporary Beatrice of Nazareth (1200–68), she was the first person to write mystical texts in the vernacular. Although she is almost entirely unknown as a historical figure, her work is extant: poems (actually songs), letters and descriptions of visions, all in Middle Dutch.[1] This oeuvre exerted enormous literary and mystical-theological influence on John of Ruusbroec (*c*.1293–1381). In his standard work *Geschichte der Abendländische Mystik*, Kurt Ruh described Hadewijch's book of visions as 'the first and at the same time greatest collection of personal visions of heaven and God in the vernacular'.[2] The cycle of visions – written to a single addressee – is a description of Hadewijch's personal growth from spiritual immaturity to maturity.[3] What this means is explained at the very beginning of the book: the cycle begins on the octave of Pentecost, when she receives communion, for she was sick from desire for the joyful union with God (*Vision 1*). She receives this union, and the subsequent visions reveal the breadth and consequences of this union to her. Hadewijch's spiritual maturity increases as she comes to understand the fullness of what this union means.

Halfway through Hadewijch's book of visions, we find a pivotal moment, namely the seventh vision, which forms a literary unity with the eighth. In this Eucharistic vision, Hadewijch describes the various aspects of union with Christ based on her experiences. The climax in her description is union 'without difference'. The second part (*Vision 8*) has remained relatively unclear in recent studies, in part due to misinterpretations of the first part (*Vision 7*). In this contribution, I present a new hypothesis, which will clarify how the humanity and embodiment of both Hadewijch and Christ are of enormous value in the aforementioned unions with God.[4]

---

1 No biographical information about Hadewijch has been transmitted: see Rob Faesen, 'Was Hadewijch a Beguine or a Cistercian?' (2004), pp 47–64. Generally, one may assume that she lived in the Duchy of Brabant during the first half of the thirteenth century. It is clear from her work that she was familiar with courtly culture and with Cistercian spirituality.   2 'Die erste und zugleich die großartigste Sammlung persönlicher Himmels- und Gotteschau in der Volkssprache' in Kurt Ruh, *Geschichte der Abendländische Mystik*, Band II (München, 1993), p. 191.   3 As is evident in the last vision: see Hadewijch, *Visioenen*, ed. van Mierlo, 1 (1924), pp 163–4, lines 110–24.   4 The first part of this essay (the discussion of the seventh vision) is a revised version of part of my article on 'Deification in Hadewijch' in *A companion to Hadewijch* (Leiden, in preparation).

DESIRE TO KNOW CHRIST'S HUMANITY

The liturgical context of this vision is a hermeneutical key to understand the development of the vision's content. Hadewijch says the events occurred on the morning of Pentecost, during the singing of Matins in the church.

Te enen cinxen daghe wart mi vertoent inde dagheraet. Ende men sanc mettenen inde kerke ende ic was daer.[5]	On a certain Pentecost Sunday, I had a vision at dawn. Matins were being sung in the church and I was present.

Pentecost is the liturgical feast that celebrates the descent of the Holy Spirit upon the apostles and the Virgin Mary. In the tradition of William of Saint-Thierry (*c.*1085–1148), Hadewijch conceived of the Holy Spirit as the complete and mutual love of the Father and the Son, a love in which the human being shares. This liturgical celebration may thus be referred to as the deification of the human person through participation in the Trinitarian life of Christ. Indeed, that is what some of the preceding visions suggest. The first vision occurs on Trinity Sunday, when Hadewijch receives communion – i.e. *communio* with Christ. In the second vision, which occurs on an Easter day, she receives communion and Christ shows her the love unity between the Father and the Son. With respect to the content of the visions, this sets the tone and the later visions explore this point of departure. As mentioned above, one of the crucial aspects of spiritual growth as described in the visions is whether (and if so, how) human beings can actually participate in the life of the Trinity.

After this introductory passage, Hadewijch describes her own inner condition. She states that she has an intense desire to experience Christ's humanity fully:

Ende mijn herte ende mijn aderen ende alle mine lede scudden ende beveden van begherten. Ende mi was – alst dicke heeft gheweest – soe verwoeddeleke ende soe vreseleke te moede dat mi dochte, ic en ware minen lieve ghenoech ende mijn lief en vervulde minen nyet, dat ic stervende soude verwoeden ende al verwoedende sterven. Doe was mi van begherliker minnen soe vreseleke te moede ende soe wee dat mi alle die lede die ic hadde sonderlinghe waenden breken ende alle mine aderen waren sonderlinghen in arbeiden.	My heart and my veins and all my limbs trembled and quivered with eager desire and – as often occurred with me – such madness and anxiousness beset my mind that it seemed to me that, if I did not content my Beloved, and if my Beloved did not fulfil my desire, I would go mad and going mad I would die. On that day my mind was beset so anxiously and painfully by desirous love that all my separate limbs threatened to break and all my separate veins were in travail.

---

5 For the Middle Dutch text, I follow the critical edition of Hadewijch's works: Hadewijch, *Visioenen*, ed. van Mierlo, pp 74–91. English translations are from Hadewijch, *The complete works*, trans. and intr. Columba Hart (1980), pp 280–4 (slightly modified by me). For the text in the oldest manuscript, see pl. 12. The transition from one column to the next in the manuscript is indicated in our text with a single vertical line (|); the transition from one page to the next with a double line (||).

Die begherte daer ic doe in was, die es ontseg-
gheleke enegher redennen ocht yemens die ic
kinne. Ende dat selve dat icker af segghen
mochte ware onghehoert vore alle die die
minne nye en bekinden | met begherten
werken ende die vore minne nye bekint en
waren. Aldus maghicker af segghen: ic
begherde mijns liefs te vollen te ghebrukene
ende te bekinnenne ende te ghesmakene, in
allen vollen ghereke, sine menscheit
ghebrukeleke mitter miere, ende de mine daer
in te ghestane ende starc te wesene in onghe-
brekelecheiden te valne, dat ic hem weder dat
onghebrekeleke ghenoech ware, suver ende
enech ende in allen te vollen ghereke ghenoech
te doghene in elker doghet. Ende daer toe
woudic van binnen dat hi mi met siere
godheit in eneghen gheeste ghenoech ende al
ware dat hi es, sonder ontbliven.

The longing in which I then was cannot be
expressed by any language or any person I
know, and everything I could say about it
would be unheard-of to all those who never
apprehended love with the activity of desire,
and whom love had never acknowledged as
hers. I can say this about it: I desired to
have full fruition and knowledge and taste
of my Beloved, in all aspects; [to enjoy,
know and taste] his humanity with mine,
and [I desired] that my humanity would
hold its stand therein and would be strong
enough, in order not to fall short, so that I
could content him without falling short: to
suffer sufficiently in all virtue, purely and
uniquely and in all aspects. To that end I
desired that for me he would be all that he
is, with his divinity, in the unity of spirit,
without withholding anything.

At a cursory glance, this is a rather strange statement. Considering that Jesus
Christ's humanity is exactly the same as that of any other human person – including
Hadewijch – it is surprising that she would want to 'experience his humanity'. If we
bear in mind, however, that to Hadewijch, Jesus Christ's humanity primarily evokes
his suffering, the statement is not so surprising, and the addition 'be strong enough
not to fall short' is also very fitting. In the *Sixth Letter*, for example, she states that the
crucified Christ fulfils the law of love, which human beings fail to do constantly.[6]

In other words, Hadewijch indicates that complete human participation in the life
of the Trinity consists in being a human in the same way Christ was human, namely
to the ultimate consequences of suffering-in-love. This is the only way to experience
complete love, 'love without a why' (*minne sonder waeromme*):

Want die ghichte coesic meest, boven alle
ghichten die ic ye ghecoes: dat ic ghenoech
ware in allen groten doghene. Want dat es dat
volcomenste ghenoech doen, te wassene god met
gode te sine. Want dats doghen ende pine,
ellende ende in groten nuwen vernoye te sine,
ende dat al laten comen ende gaen sonder
vernoyen, ende el en ghenen smake daer af te
hebbene dan soete minne ende helsen ende
cussen. Aldus begherdic dat mi god ware hem
mede ghenoech te sine.

For above all the gifts that I ever longed for,
I chose this gift: that I would give satisfaction in all great sufferings. For that is the
most perfect satisfaction to grow up in order
to be God with God, namely suffering,
pain, misery and living in great new grief of
soul, and to let everything come and go
without grief and to experience nothing else
of it but sweet love, embraces and kisses. In
this sense I desired that God give himself to
me so that I might content him.

---

6 Hadewijch, *Brieven*, ed. van Mierlo (1947), pp 67–8, lines 324–43; the absoluteness of the commandment of
minne (love) is emphasized in Hadewijch's *Twelfth Letter*; see *Brieven*, ed. van Mierlo, pp 108–9, lines 151–73.

GROWING REALIZATION OF UNION WITH CHRIST (*VISION 7*)

Hadewijch then describes the response she receives to her desire. She first, however, provides a form of prelude, which announces that this will actually occur. An eagle flies towards her from the altar. The symbol is clear. This is an image of John the Evangelist, who functions as an 'announcer' of the union. This is not surprising, considering that the fourth Gospel contains the passage that refers to this deifying union (Jn. 17:21–2).[7]

Doe mi aldus vreeseleke te moede was, doe versaghic vanden outare comen ghevloghen te mi enen are die groet was. Ende hi seide mi: 'Wiltu een werden, soe ghereide di.' Ende ic stoent op || mijn knien, ende mijn herte gheberde vreseleke dat enechleke te anebedene, na sine werde werdecheit — dat doch mi onghereet ware, dat wetic wel, wet god altoes, te minen wee ende te minen sware. Ende gheen aer keerde, segghende: 'Gherechte here ende moghende, nu tone dine moghende cracht dijnre enecheit te eneghene, na ghebruken dijns selves.' Ende hi keerde hem weder ende seide te mi: 'Die ghecomen es, hi comt weder, ende daer hi nye en quam, daer en comt hi niet.'	As my mind was thus beset with anxiety, I saw a great eagle flying toward me from the altar, and he said to me: 'If you wish to become one, make yourself ready.' I fell on my knees and my heart beat intensely to worship that [= the unification] uniquely, according to its true dignity – which was impossible for me, as I know well, and as God knows, always to my woe and to my grief. And the eagle turned back and spoke: 'Just and mighty Lord, now show of your unity the great power to unite according to your enjoyment.' Then the eagle turned around again and said to me: 'He who has come, comes again; and where he never came, he comes not.'

The eagle not only announces the union, while it urges Hadewijch to prepare herself for it, but it also provides a Christological explanation of the union. It turns to the altar – i.e. to Christ – and says: 'Just and mighty Lord, now show of your unity the great power to unite, in the enjoyment of yourself'. It is Christ's unity (the *unio hypostatica*) that has the power to unite, namely to draw Hadewijch into the same union. Finally, the eagle turns around again and addresses itself to Hadewijch: 'He who has come, comes again; and to whatever place he never came, he comes not'. This statement, which appears enigmatic at first,[8] should probably best be understood as a reference to the 'middle coming of Christ',[9] the coming of Christ in the present, which

---

7 Hadewijch says that this is the 'loveliest word' that God ever revealed: see *Brieven*, ed. van Mierlo, p. 201, lines 319–20 ('Not that glory was lacking to him at any hour, but he wished, when he had drawn all things to himself, to glorify them with him; also he then said: 'I will, Father, that they may be one in us, as you, Father, in me and I in you.' This is the loveliest word of his love that God ever revealed – of all the words anyone reads in Scripture').
8 It was later repeated by John of Ruusbroec in his *Spiritual espousals*, ed. Joseph Alaerts (1986), p. 473, lines b1637–b1638. One possible interpretation may be that Christ only makes his presence known in loving relationship, see Hugh of Saint-Victor, *Sic familiaris est Deo charitas, ut ipse mansionem habere nolit, ubi charitas non fuerit* ('Charity is so intimately related to God that God refuses to make his dwelling where there is no charity') De laude charitatis, in *L'oeuvre de Hughes de Saint-Victor*, ed. H.B. Feiss and P. Sicard (1997), p. 198.
9 See Bernard of Clairvaux, *In priore quidem in terris visus est et cum hominibus conversatus est. (…) In posteriore vero videbit omnis caro salutare Dei nostri, et videbunt in quem transfixerunt. Medius occultus est, in quo soli eum in seipsis vident electi, et salvae fiunt animae eorum. In primo ergo venit in carne et infirmitate, in hoc medio in spiritu*

does not differ essentially from the coming in the past (namely the Incarnation). Indeed, that is what Hadewijch then witnesses:

Doe quam hi vanden outare, hem selven toenende alse een kint. Ende dat kint was van dier selver ghedane dat hi was in sinen yersten drien jaren.	Then he came from the altar, showing himself as a child, and that child was in the same form as he was in his first three years.

The fact that Hadewijch mentions the age of the infant Jesus is an indication that she saw him as an *infans* – an expression, incidentally, that is also used in William of Saint-Thierry's description of Bernard's youth vision. The young Bernard saw Christ born in the present: 'He appeared to him as though born anew of his virgin mother: the still speechless Word (*verbum infans*), the most beautiful in form of the children of humankind'.[10] This is the first step in the union of the human person with God, and it concerns human reality as such: the Son of God became *human*, and continues to do so in the present.

The next step is sacramental. Christ now no longer has the form of a child, but of an adult man:

Ende hi keerde hem te mi waert ende nam uter ciborien sinen lichame in sine rechte hant, ende in sine slinke hant nam hi enen kelc, die sceen vanden outare comende, maer ic en weet wanen hi quam. Daer mede quam hi, in die ghedane des cleeds ende des mans dat hi was op dien dach doen hi ons sinen lichame iersten gaf, also ghedane mensche ende man, soete ende scoene ende verweent ghelaet tonende, ende also onderdanechleke te mi comende alse een die eens anders al es. Doe gaf hi mi hem selven in specien des sacraments, in figuren, alsoe men pleghet. Ende daer na gaf hi mi drinken uten kelke, ghedane ende smake alsoe men pleghet.	He turned toward me and took in his right hand from the ciborium his body, and took in his left hand a chalice, which seemed to come from the altar, but I do not know where it came from. With that he came in the form and clothing of a man, as he was on the day when he gave us his body for the first time, looking like a human person and a man, wonderful and beautiful, with a glorious face, and coming to me so humbly as someone who wholly belongs to another. Then he gave himself to me in the shape of the sacrament, in its outward form, as the custom is, and then he gave me to drink from the chalice, in form and taste, as the custom is.

Hadewijch specifies: 'coming to me humbly, as someone who wholly belongs to another'. This is an important detail. Hadewijch's 'definition' of Trinitarian *minne* ('high love', *hoghe minne*) is: 'the one for the other' (*deen vor dander*),[11] the Father and

---

et virtute, in ultimo in gloria et majestate ('During his first coming, the Lord appeared on the earth and he kept company with the people. (…) Upon his return, however, 'all flesh will behold the salvation of God, they will look upon the one whom they have pierced' (Lc 3, 6; Jo 19, 37). The middle coming is concealed, only the elect experience it inwardly, and their souls are healed. Therefore, at his first coming, the Lord appeared in the flesh and in weakness, in the middle he comes in spirit and in strength, and at the last he comes in glory and majesty'): *Sancti Bernardi opera omnia* IV, ed. J. Leclercq and H.M. Rochais (1963), p. 188.   **10** *Apparuit ei quasi iterum ante oculos suos nascens ex utero matris virginis Verbum infans, speciosus forma prae filiis hominum, et pueruli sancti in se rapiens minime jam pueriles affectus. Persua sum est autem animo eius, et nobis nonumquam dicere consuvit quod eam credat horam fuisse dominicae nativitatis*: William of Saint-Thierry, *Vita Prima Sancti Bernardi*, in *Guillelmi a Sancto Theoderico Opera Omnia* VI, ed. Paul Verdeyen (2010), p. 35.   **11** *Letter 1*, ed. van Mierlo, p. 17, line 35.

the Son are essentially and totally given to the Other (neither is oriented towards himself) and in this way, they are one in the Spirit – that is the essence of the Trinity. When Hadewijch states in the first vision that she desires to be united to God, this means: united to this Trinitarian love. Having come to this point, Hadewijch witnesses that Christ actually loves thus, that this love constitutes his existence, and in such a way that it even becomes externally visible. It is in this spiritual form that Christ gives her communion in two forms. The emphasis of the 'normality' of this communion ('as is the custom') is striking. The sacramental participation in Christ's life by no means differs from the sacramental life of every other communicant.[12]

In a third step, Hadewijch feels in *her* own body how Christ's spiritual attitude of total self-giving is felt in *his* own body:

Daer na quam hi selve te mi ende nam mi alte male in sine arme | ende dwanc mi ane heme. Ende alle die lede die ic hadde ghevoelden der siere — in alle hare ghenoeghen, na miere herten begherten — na miere menscheit. Doe werdic ghenoeghet van buten in allen vollen sade. Ende oec haddic doe ene corte wile cracht dat te draghene.	After that he came himself to me, took me entirely in his arms, and pressed me to him. And all my members according to their humanity felt his [members] – as to their satisfaction, as my heart had wished. Then I was given satisfaction, outwardly and fully, and for a short while I had the strength to bear this.

Considering the context, *in alle hare ghenoeghen* ('as to their satisfaction') refers to Christ's limbs, though grammatically, *hare* may of course also refer to Hadewijch's limbs. Hadewijch scholars generally tend to prefer the latter interpretation, leading to the assumption that *ghenoeghen* is used to express enjoyment and satisfaction. When one reads this passage in light of the description of Hadewijch's desire at the beginning of *Vision 7*, this interpretation does not appear entirely convincing. Indeed, she states there that she desires to taste Christ's humanity in her own being, i.e. to suffer, as a human being, everything that Christ suffered and not to fall short. She now describes how Christ impresses his suffering upon her, not only partially, but entirely as he experienced it.[13] Indeed, the Middle Dutch word *ghenoeghen* may also mean 'to satisfy', 'be sufficient', *satis-facere*. Although Hadewijch does not say so explicitly, this appears to be strikingly similar to receiving the stigmata. Francis of Assisi is the earliest person known to have received the stigmata (in September 1224, on Monte Alverno), but two women from the same period and region as Hadewijch – namely Elisabeth of Spalbeek (d. *c.*1266) and Ida of Leuven (d. *c.*1300) – also received the wounds of Christ in their bodies.[14]

---

12 One must note, however, that receiving the Eucharist was not part of the customary devotional practice of the majority of the faithful in Hadewijch's period and region. Desiring frequent communion, a characteristic of many mystical women in Hadewijch's milieu, was considered highly unusual, and often met with considerable opposition. In some cases, priests simply refused to administer the Eucharist: see Alcantara Mens, *Oorsprong en betekenis* (1947), pp 232–42. **13** This is also the reading of Esther Heszler, *Der mystische Prozeß* (1994), p. 57. **14** See Alcantara Mens, *Oorsprong en betekenis*, p. 227.

It is precisely because this point is often misinterpreted that the meaning of *Vision 8* becomes obscure, which (as we shall see) is presented as a clarification of Hadewijch's experiences here. The most common interpretation in the secondary literature on this point is that the vision describes a physical embrace between Hadewijch and Christ, which gives Hadewijch physical pleasure. This reading, however, undermines the inner consistency of the text. The basic theme in fact concerns the fundamental issue of how the *human* might participate in the life of *God* – which is a life of absolute love, love 'without a why' (*sonder waeromme*). Is humanity as such capable of experiencing this love? Hadewijch realises that this was possible for the person of Jesus Christ, the God-man, and she desires that it might also be possible for her. But it seems to her that the suffering he bore (as a consequence of his absolute love), is impossible to bear for a human being as such. Christ makes her feel it, however, and for a brief time, she even has the strength to bear it.

In this experience she feels the reality of Christ in her own body. In the following step, however, Christ enters her human reality to such an extent that she no longer experiences him outside herself:

Maer saen in corter uren verloesic dien sconen man van buten, in siene, in vormen, ende ic sachene al te niete werdene ende alsoe sere verdoiende werden ende al smelten in een, soe dat icken buten mi niet en conste bekinnen noch vernemen ende binnen mi niet besceden. Mi was op die ure ochte wi een waren sonder differencie.

But soon, after a short time, I lost that manly beauty, outwardly in the sight of his form. I saw him completely come to nought and so fade and dissolve in one, that I could no longer recognize or perceive him outside me and I could no longer distinguish him within me. Then it was to me as if we were one without difference.

This step is, however, not the deepest experience. That is only fulfilled in the next and last step, namely when Hadewijch completely 'disappears' *in* Christ:

Hier na bleef ic in enen vervaerne in mijn lief, dat ic al versmalt in heme ende mi mijns selves niet en bleef. Ende ic wart verwandelt ende op ghenomen inden gheeste ende mi wart daer vertoent van selker hande uren.

After that, I remained in a passing away in my beloved, so that I wholly melted away in him and nothing of myself remained to me. And I was transformed and taken up in the spirit, and I received a vision about such moments.

The important point here is, of course, that Hadewijch says that 'nothing remained to me of myself'. That which is fundamentally *minne* (*hoghe minne es: deen vore dander*, 'high love is: the one for the other') has now become her own inner reality. Nothing in herself is oriented to herself. In this way, she is drawn into the Spirit, the mutual love of the Father and the Son. At this point, her union with Christ is complete, without difference (*sonder differencie*). In her humanity, she experiences the same radical suffering as Christ, and she is drawn up into the Trinitarian unity of love. By grace, she is given what God is by nature.

HUMANITY AS A 'MOUNTAIN' FOR THE ENCOUNTER WITH GOD (*VISION 8*)

The vision Hadewijch then receives, as she herself indicates, is a clarification of the preceding experience, an experience of humanity in union with God.[15]

Ic sach enen groten berch die hoghe was ende breet ende van onseggheleker scoender ghedane. Tote dien berghe ghinghen .v. weghe hoghe staen, die alle dien edelen berch ‖ op ghinghen ten hoechsten sittene dat daer boven was. Maer si ghinghen hoghe ende noch hoghere ende meer hoghere ende alder hoghest, soe dat hi selve die hoechste was gheheel ende dat hoechste wesen selve. Ende ic wart op ghenomen ende wart ghevoert op dien berch. Daer saghic een anschijn van eweleker ghebrukenessen daer alle die weghe in inden ende daer alle die ghene die de weghe volbrachten .i. in worden.	I saw a great mountain, which was high and broad and of unspeakably beautiful form. Five ways went steeply upward to the mountain. They all led to the highest seat of the noble mountain, which was there on high. But they went high, and higher, and still higher, and to the highest, so that the summit was the highest of all and the highest being himself. And I was taken up and led upward to the mountain. There I saw a countenance of eternal fruition, in which all the ways terminate, and in which all those who have followed the ways to the end become one.

In this visionary clarification of her experiences, she sees a mountain, and at its pinnacle 'a countenance of eternal fruition'. Evidently, the mountain is a universal symbol for religious experience, and the mountain's peak symbolizes the theophany. Consequently, we must question the way this might be a (visionary) clarification of what Hadewijch had previously described.[16] A patristic text by Hilary of Poitiers (*c.*315–67) may offer some insight in this regard:

Necesse est in his, quae caelestia sunt, maxima atque sublimia sub montis nomini opiniari. Et quid sublimius Christo? Quid excelsius Deo nostro? Mons autem eius est illud, quod ex homine corpus adsumpsit, in quo nunc habitat et sublimis et excelsus super omnem principatum et potestatem et omne nomen. (…) Si rego requiei nostrae spes omnis in Christi est corpore et cum in montem sit quiescendum, montem non illud possumus intelligere quam corpus, quod suscepit e nobis, ante quod deus erat et in quo deus est et per quod transfiguravit corpus humilitatis nostrae conformatum corpori gloriae suae, si tamen et nos vitia corporis nostri cruci eius confixerimus, ut in eius corpore resurgamus.[17]	When we speak of celestial matters, the word 'mountain' necessarily represents the highest and most sublime. And what is more sublime than Christ? What is higher than our God? His mountain is the human body he assumed, in which he now resides and is elevated above all principalities and powers and above every name. (…) Therefore, when the hope of our rest is fixed entirely on Christ's body and we take rest on the mountain, this must be understood as the body he received from us. Previously, he was God. In that body, he is God, and through that body he will transfigure our humble bodies and make them equal to his glorified body, if indeed we unite the weakness of our bodies to his cross, and resurrect in his body.

15 The manuscript used for the critical edition, and upon which the modern translations are based, divided the two visions at this point. *Vision 7* and *Vision 8* are, however, one continuous text, as the editor indicates (see *Visioenen*, ed. van Mierlo, p. 79, note to lines 97–9). **16** This theme is not treated extensively by Joris Reynaert, *De beeldspraak van Hadewijch* (1981). **17** 'Tractatus in psalmum XIV', *S. Hilarii Episcopi Pictavensis Tractatus Super Psalmos*, ed. Antonius Zingerle (1891), pp 87–8.

This appears to correspond to Hadewijch's description in *Vision 7*, namely the experiential awareness of what it meant for Christ to be human. The mountain refers to his humanity and its various aspects (i.e. the various 'paths').

In what follows, it is revealed that she has a guide for four of the five paths, and that the fifth path – which is not actually a path, but the mountain as such – is revealed to her by God himself. First, however, the guide – a champion of (loving) humanity – speaks:

Ende een die mi daer op voerde toende mi hem selven. Ende alse ic daer op was, seide hi te mi: 'Sich hier hoe ic ben kimpe ende rijcleec ghenen ghewareghen anschine, dat al dore siet ende doer licht den volcomenen dienste, dat volleidet ende leret diviniteit ende vroetheit, ende rijcheit gheeft aller ghebrukenessen van allen vollen consteleken smake. Ic ben ghetoent kimpe. Siet dat mine sierheit es alse al verwin-nende ende moghende derre dinc die al es daer die hemel ende die helle ende die erde vore dienen. Ende ic ben dese weghe hoghest op comen ende gheleide di. Ende ic ben dijn gherechte orconde vanden vieren. Ende den vijften — die dine es — dien saldi orconden de gherechte god, die hem di sendde ende die hem di sent.'	Someone who led me upward showed himself to me, and when I was on high, he said to me: 'Behold how I am the champion and of high rank for this true countenance, which sees through the depths of all things and irradiates perfect service, leads to perfection, teaches both the science of God and wisdom, and gives the riches of all fruition, of all the taste of full cognition. I have the appearance of a champion. See that my beauty is that of one who conquers everything and has in his power that thing for which heaven, hell and earth serve. I have ascended on these ways to the highest. I guide you. And I am your trustworthy witness for the four [ways]. The fifth way – which is yours – will be made known to you by the just God, who sent you this way, and sends it to you.'

Hadewijch then beholds the divine countenance at the summit of the mountain, by which she means Christ in his divinity, as she explains later in the text:[18]

Ende doe toende hi mi voert dat onseggheleke scoene anschijn. Ende dat was ane te siene alse ene groete viereghe vloet, widere ende diepere dan die zee. Ende doe hoerdic ene grote stem|me uter vloet sprekende te mi: 'Comt ende wes selver die overste wech, .i. inden wesenne diere volcomen in sijn, die met corten uren alle langhe uren vervolghen. Dijn grote darven van minnen heeft di ghegheven den oversten wech in mijn ghebruken, daer ic van ane beghinne diere werelt na hebbe ghehaect, dattu dicke met swaren begherten ontgouden heves ende noch sels'.	Then he showed me that ineffably beautiful countenance, which was in appearance like a great fiery flood, wider and deeper than the sea. And out of the flood, I heard a great voice, saying to me: 'Come, and be yourself the highest way. And be one with those who are perfect in it, and who with short hours retrieve all the long hours. Your great privation of love has given you the highest way in my fruition. I have longed for this from the beginning of the world, and you have often paid for it with painful desire, and you will yet pay for it'.

---

18 This is apparent, for example, from the fact that he says 'by this way I went forth to my Father to you and to those who are yours, and I came back again, from you and those who are yours, to my Father' ('*daer mede ghinc ic ute, te minen vader, te di ende ten dinen, ende quam weder van di ende vanden dinen te minen vader*', lines 46–9).

In other words, Hadewijch receives a divine confirmation that she has experienced complete love, in the way Christ desired from the moment of creation. She experienced it specifically in her 'great privation of love' (*grote darven van minnen*), which is the highest manner 'in my [= Christ's] fruition' (*in mijn ghebruken*). This corresponds to what Hadewijch had written earlier, at the beginning of *Vision 7*, where she indicated that she considered the only human way to participate in God's life to be: 'suffering, pain, misery and living in great new grief of soul, and to let everything come and go without grief and to experience nothing else of it but sweet love, embraces and kisses' (*doghen ende pine, ellende ende in groten nuwen vernoye te sine, ende dat al laten comen ende gaen sonder vernoyen, ende el en ghenen smake daer af te hebbene dan soete minne ende helsen ende cussen*).[19]

Christ then explains the four forms of human pain in love (i.e. the four paths that lead upward, but are not the pinnacle itself).[20] The most striking passage in this explanation is the following:

Ende want du eneghe dine karitate van allen met mi enech heves bracht ende du mi in derre uren berurende waers met miere naturen weghe, die ic quam ende ghinc, soe orcondic di met gherechten orconde daer ic mede ben mijns vader waerheit, ende mijn vader orconde mi dattu best die overste wech ende dien metti heves bracht daer ic na hebbe ontboden met minen verhoelnen weghe.	And because you alone placed your charity for all men in unity with me, and because you touched me in this hour with the way of my nature, which I came and went, I bear to you the true witness, with which I am the truth of my Father – and my Father bears witness to me – that you are the highest way and have brought with you this way, which I have awaited in my hidden ways.

The crucial element here is that Hadewijch is told that she is the only person who 'placed your charity for all men in unity with me'. In other words: there was no qualitative difference between the way she loved as a person – human charity – and the way Christ loves, to which Christ refers as the 'way of his nature', i.e. his divine nature, which is hidden (*verhoelen*), but revealed in his human nature.

This is an important point for a correct understanding not only of Hadewijch's

19 Hadewijch provides an enlightening explanation of this in her *Letter 16*: 'You must also live in joyful hope and strong confidence that God will allow you to love him with that great love wherewith he loves himself, Three and One, and whereby he has eternally sufficed to himself and shall so suffice eternally. In contenting him with that love, all the denizens of heaven are and shall be eternally engaged. This is their occupation, which never comes to an end; and the incompletion of this blissful fruition is yet the sweetest fruition. According to this, men on earth must strive for it with humble hearts and realize that, as regards such great love, and such sublime love, and this never-contented Beloved, they are too small to content him with love.' ('*Ghi sult oec leuen hoghe in hope van staerken toeuerlate, dat v god gheuen sal hem te minnen met dier groter minnen daer hi hem seluen mint driuoldich ende enich, ende daer hi hem seluen met ewelike ghenoech heuet gheweest ende eweleke sijn sal. Met diere minnen hem ghenoech te doene, daer ouer sijn alle hemelsche onledich ende eweleke selen sijn. Dat es hare ambacht, dat nummermeer voldaen en wert. Ende dat ghebreken van dien ghebrukene dat es dat suetste ghebruken. Hier na selen staen die ertsche met oetmoedegher herten, ende selen dat weten dat si te soe groter minnen ende te soe hogher minnen ende enen onghenoeghenden lieue alte cleyne sijn omme ghenoech te doene met minnen*') *Brieven*, ed. van Mierlo, pp 131–2, lines 9–23.   **20** I shall not discuss them in this contribution, but I refer here to lines 41–77.

mystical theology, but of the development of medieval theology as such. Indeed, it is well known that in the period Hadewijch wrote, a debate was raging concerning a passage of Peter Lombard's *Sentences*, in which he had stated that the love with which human beings love God is no different from the love with which the Father loves the Son, namely the Holy Spirit, a view he shared with one of his influential fellow students, William of Saint-Thierry:

[1] *Iam nunc accedamus ad assignandam missionem Spiritus Sanci qua invisibiliter mittitur in corda fidelium. Nam ipse Spiritus Sanctus qui deus est ac tertia in Trinitate persona (…) a Patre et Filio ac se ipso temporaliter procedit, id est mittitur ac donator fidelibus. Sed quae sit ista missio sive donatio, vel quomodo fiat, considerandum est.* [2] *Hoc autem ut intelligibilius doceri ac plenius perspici valeat, praemittendum est quiddam ad hoc valde necessarium. Dictum est quidem supra et sacris auctoritatibus ostensum quod Spiritus Sanctus amor est Patris et Filii, quo se invicem amant et nos. His autem addendum est quod ipse idem Spiritus sanctus est amor sive caritas, qua nos diligimus Deum et proximum; quae caritas cum ita est in nobis ut nos faciat diligere Deum et proximum, tunc Spiritus Sanctus dicitur mitti vel dari nobis, et qui diligit ipsam dilectionem qua diligit proximum, in eo ipso Deum diligit, quia ipsa dilectio Deus est, id est Spiritus Sanctus.*

[1] Let us now proceed to set out the sending of the Holy Spirit, by which he is invisibly sent into the hearts of the faithful. For the same Holy Spirit, who is God and the third person in the Trinity (…) proceeds in time from the Father and the Son and his own self, that is, is sent and given to the faithful. But we must consider what the sending or giving is, or rather how it occurs. [2] In order that this may be taught more intelligibly and perceived more fully, a certain premise must be made which is very necessary to this end. It has been said above, and it has been shown by sacred authorities, that the Holy Spirit is the love of the Father and the Son by which they love each other and us. It must be added to this that the very same Holy Spirit is the love or charity by which we love God and neighbor. When this charity is in us, so that it makes us love God and neighbor, then the Holy Spirit is said to be sent or given to us; and whoever loves the very love by which he loves his neighbor, in that very thing loves God, because that very thing is God, that is, the Holy Spirit.[21]

By the thirteenth century, however, many theologians had concluded that, despite the enormous respect they had for the master, he was thoroughly mistaken on this point.[22] Indeed, according to these authors there is a clear distinction between the contingent love a human being has for God, and the eternal transcendent love of the Trinity. Moreover, if the love of the human being for God were in fact to be the Holy Spirit, one could no longer claim that it is *human* love for God. Wouldn't this opinion thus undermine the value and freedom of humanity?

In light of this discussion, the passage from Hadewijch analysed above is particularly relevant. Indeed, the Eucharistic vision describes how she experienced that she is *in* Christ, and Christ is *in* her, and that they thus experience the same love (*minne*).

---

21 *Sententiae*, liber primus, dist. 17, ed. Stephanus Brown and Gedeon Gál (1970), pp 141–2, trans. Giulio Silano, p. 88, cf. also *Sent*. I, dist. 10, 3; *Sent*. III, dist. 32, 1.   22 See Edouard-H. Wéber, 'Elements néoplatoniciens en théologie mystique' (1986), pp 196–217.

Christ now confirms that her charity (*karitate*) was manifested in unity with him. Hadewijch's experience thus corresponds to the theology of William of Saint-Thierry and Peter Lombard, and not to the thirteenth-century rejections of their thought.

After a formal confirmation of this unity,[23] the abovementioned point of discussion is raised again explicitly, in Hadewijch's concluding conversation with her guide:

Ende ic quam weder int ghemoet dies gheests die mi daer brachte, ende ic vrachede hem: 'Kimpe, here, hoe sidi gheciert uwen hoghen orconde daer gi mi toe leidet, ende niet en volleidet?' Ende hi seide mi wie hi was. Daer na seide hi te mi: 'Ic orconde u die .iiij. weghe ende volleide. Daer in bekinnic mi ende die tide verwinnic. Ende den viften gaf u die ghetrouwe dien ghi ontfingt daer ic niet en ben. Want doen ic mensche levede haddic te lettel || minnen met affectien, ende volghede den scarpen rade vanden gheeste. Daer bi en mochtic niet beruert werden te also enegher minnen, want ic der edelre menscheit groet onrecht dede dat ic hare dier affectien buten hilt.'

And I came again in the mind of the spirit who had brought me there, and I asked him: 'Lord champion, how did you receive the high marks of honor, so that you led me but not to the end?' He told me who he was. After that he said to me: 'I bear witness to you concerning the four ways, and lead you completely. In these I recognize myself, and I conquer those times. But the faithful gave you the fifth way, which you received, and where I am not. When I lived as a human person, I was too little affected by love, and I followed the severe council of the spirit. For this reason, I could not be moved toward such a unified love, since I was unjust to the noble humanity by not letting it be affected in this way.'

Ende hi seide: 'Kere weder in dine materie, ende laet bloyen dine werke, ende stucken van onghenaden sijn di nekende, want du best kerende alse al verwinnende, want du al verwonnen heves.'

And he said: 'Return again into your material being, and let your works blossom forth. The blows of disgrace are drawing near to you, since you return as a victor over all. Indeed, you have conquered all.'

Doen quamic in mi selven also ene nuwe harde sereghe, ende emmermeer wesen sal, tote dien daghe dat ic daer weder in valle daer ic doe af keerde.

Then I came back to myself as someone in new severe pain, and so I shall remain, until the day that I happen to be there where I came from.

In this short concluding conversation with the guide, Hadewijch explicitly asks why – despite the fact that he is a 'champion' – he could not lead her to the pinnacle of the mountain. His response has given rise to considerable speculation in the secondary literature, especially because Hadewijch never mentions her guide's name. These speculations are often influenced by the suggestions made by the influential editor Jozef van Mierlo, who notes on this point: 'From these words we may conclude that the man was a theologian, and probably too strictly intellectualist'.[24] This obser-

---

23 In the lines 87–108. **24** 'Uit deze woorden zou mogen besloten, dat die man een theologant zal geweest zijn, waarschijnlijk te streng intellectualist', p. 91 n. to line 117. Various hypotheses have been formulated concerning the identity of this figure Hadewijch does not name (although she knew his name). For example, Columba Hart (p. 328) suggests it may refer to Peter Abelard. Considering his condemnation at the Council of Sens, it is improbable that Hadewijch would refer to him as a 'champion'. See the overview in *Das Buch der Visionen*, ed. Gerald Hofmann, II (1998), pp 130–2. Van Mierlo incorrectly interpreted *den scarpen rade vanden gheeste* as intel-

vation is, however, not entirely germane. It is important to examine the guide's precise words: as a person he has followed the severe and painful councils of the Holy Spirit (*ic volghede den scarpen rade vanden gheeste*) – in other words: not only the pleasant aspects of love, but also its pains and burdens – but rejected the complete union of *minne* (*daer bi en mochtic niet beruert werden te also enegher minnen*) by keeping humanity outside this union. The guide thus made a clear distinction (and even division) between the human experience of love and the divine unity of love in the Trinity. The guide now regrets it (Hadewijch suggests that he has died), and realizes that he did humanity a great injustice (*ic der edelre menscheit groet onrecht dede dat ic hare dier affectien buten hilt*). The guide was a champion in submitting to the greatest pains and heaviest burdens of human love for God, but he ultimately rejected the possibility of sharing fully in the Trinitarian unity of love. Hadewijch, by contrast, did allow this,[25] and consequently she was able to ascend to the top of the mountain, and contemplated the divine countenance at the height of her being. Examined in the context of the thirteenth-century scholastic debate on the identification of love and the Holy Spirit, Hadewijch's text of *Vision 7–8* is a radical, unfashionable confirmation of the complete participation in the life of Christ, and his unity of love with the Father (i.e. the Holy Spirit).

CONCLUSION

The theme of union with God – and the precise nature of such union – is central to Hadewijch's book of visions. Hadewijch describes the development of spiritual maturity as she gradually acquires new spiritual insights. *Vision 7–8* is at the centre of this development, and its focal point is the value of humanity. Is it possible, as a human being, to share completely in God's life? Hadewijch realizes that this would imply being human as Christ was human, and consequently she longs for an experience of Christ's humanity, of which his suffering is evidently the hardest experience. From her perspective, if she could not fully experience what Christ experienced in his humanity, she would not be able to share in the fullness of his love – the Trinitarian love, which is God.

She is given a response in three steps. First, she reflects on the Incarnation: he willingly assumed humanity. Second, she reflects on the Sacrament: he gives himself in the Eucharist. Third, she reflects on mutual indwelling, when Hadewijch experiences Christ living *in* her, and especially that she lives *in* him.

lectualism; Hadewijch would probably have referred to reason (*redene*) instead of spirit (*gheeste*) if that had been her intent: see Rob Faesen, *Begeerte in het werk van Hadewijch* (2000), p. 238. John of Ruusbroec used exactly the same expression, referring to Christ (*Spiritual Tabernacle*, ed. Th. Mertens (2006), p. 614, line 471), and he certainly does not imply that Christ was an intellectualist.   **25** It is notable that Christ tells her that she is the 'only person' to experience this, as it indicates how unusual the vision is. The question of her position being theologically unfashionable requires further research, in relation to the development of spiritual literature in the thirteenth century.

In order for this to become even clearer to her, she receives a visionary clarification. She is shown a mountain that symbolizes her humanity, with God's countenance at the summit. The paths leading up the mountain represent different forms of pain, rejection, darkness and desolation. The most important point, however, is that the ultimate goal (at the 'top of the mountain') is full participation in Christ's life. A loving human (the mountain) and perfect divine love (its summit) are *distinct*, but not *separate* realities.

At the end of the vision, this insight is contrasted with the view that these two realities are fundamentally separate. Hadewijch's guide on the mountain – whoever he might be – represents this view. He did not flinch from the most difficult consequences of his humanity, and is thus called 'champion', but he ultimately rejects the most profound experience of union with God. At the very end of the vision we read that the guide regrets having committed such injustice against noble humanity.

Hadewijch's *Vision 7–8* offers a fundamental reflection on the religious and mystical significance of humanity, and is a bold witness of Christian humanism. Indeed, if Hadewijch's guide were to be right – and Hadewijch appears to suggest that most people would agree with him – the ultimate consequence would imply that union with God would necessarily entail a reduction or even destruction of humanity. Hadewijch experiences that this is not the case, however, and her position is of great importance for Christian culture.

Translated by John Arblaster

3 'And how could I find Thee at all, if I do not remember Thee?' Visions, images and memory in late medieval devotion[1]

HENNING LAUGERUD

INTRODUCTION

The theme of this essay is the relationship between visions, images – both exterior physical and interior mental images – and memory. *Visions*, per definition, involve a visual act and have to do with *seeing* in one sense or another. The Latin word *visio*, in English *vision*, underscores that it has to do specifically with visualizing something. Visions are inner or outer *images* of transcendental, holy or divine beings that appear in a manner that human beings can see, and represent an experience that transports them away from their immediate surroundings and places them in contact with the next world, or divine existence.[2]

During the Middle Ages visions and the literature regarding visions were an essential element of Christianity, both as practice and experience, yet also in a dialogue with and part of theological speculation. St Thomas Aquinas (1225–74), for example, discusses visions and their reality repeatedly and claims that one who has a glorified body (*corpus glorificatum*), i.e. Christ, has the power to be seen when he wishes, and to be invisible when he does not wish to be seen.[3] He asserts that Christ can, on occasion, appear in bodily form in order to reveal himself to the whole world – such as on the Day of Judgement – or to reveal himself to a specific individual.[4] These visions are thus not imaginary or necessarily visible only to the inner eye. Christ can reveal himself to human beings physically and in the flesh. Visions can also represent actual physical appearances. In the Holy Scriptures angels are often described as appearing in such a way that everyone can see them. This proves, according to St Thomas, that such apparitions were seen with the physical eye, which means that the object seen existed *outside* the person who saw it, and consequently in principle could be seen by everyone.[5] The deceased can also show themselves to humans in order to

1 With my gratitude to Rob Faesen, Kristin Bliksrud Aavitsland and Jan Schumacher for comments on earlier drafts of this essay. The quote is from St Augustine, *Confessions*, bk 10, see n. 64. **2** Sylvie Barnay, 'Vision, visionary' in André Vauchez (ed.), *Encyclopedia of the Middle Ages* (Cambridge, 2000), pp 1526–7. Visions and dreams overlap and are barely distinguishable from each other in the Middle Ages, a phenomenon we can recognize in the treatment of this theme beginning with the fourth- or fifth-century Macrobius, via St Augustine and onward: see Steven F. Kruger, *Dreaming in the Middle Ages* (Cambridge, 1993). **3** Thomas Aquinas, *Summa Theologica*, III, Q 54, Art. 1 Ad. 2. **4** *ST*, III, Q. 57, Art. 6. **5** *ST*, I, Q. 51, Art. 2. See also Addis and Arnold's *Catholic dictionary* (1951) where visions are defined in a thomistic fashion as follows: 'In the ecclesiastical sense a vision is the supernatural appearing of the Deity, or angels, or saints, or even of the devils and the damned. It is not a mere subjective imagination of these, but their objective reality', p. 823.

participate in the affairs of the living. This can occur in several ways; either by the special grace of God, such as in miraculous events involving saints, or occasioned by good or evil angels, i.e. demons.[6] For St Thomas the point is to demonstrate that visions or revelations can take place *after* biblical revelation, and that the visions can be physical observations of bodies in time and space. That is, that they have an objective existence independent of who is observing.

But what did the visionary of the Middle Ages see? In other words, how do the visions appear to the visionary, and in the visionary's accounts? And, not least, how are we to understand this thing that the visionary sees? Carolly Erickson has formulated it in the following way: 'Visions erased the shear line between the known and the unknowable, the discoverable and the revealed. They interlocked the simultaneous realities; they made visible the unseen; they clarified the hidden shape of truth.'[7] The following is a discussion of the connection between visions, images and cognition with memory as a central element.

In order to illustrate this I will begin with the Flemish thirteenth-century mystic Hadewijch's descriptions of her visions, which have also been treated in Rob Faesen's essay in this volume.[8] As an extension of this I will also take a closer look at other mystics, both from this period and from later, and their visions.

THE VISIONS OF THE VISIONARY

When we read Hadewijch's description of her visions, it is first of all interesting to note that their point of departure is the liturgical celebration – that is to say common church activities institutionalized by the Church and accessible to all believers. We find the same 'common element' in the description of what she sees in her visions as well.

In the introductory section of the seventh vision she explains that she sees an eagle flying from the altar towards her, and thereafter she sees Christ as a little child on the altar.[9] In the next phase of the vision Christ reveals himself to her in his divinity, and offers her both a host and a chalice. She describes how the host is taken out of the ciborium and the chalice from the altar. In the eighth vision she describes an allegorical mountain with five alternate paths to climb it, and how she is guided by a man who may be a concrete individual, but who is also an allegory or a symbol of compassionate human nature. The significance of these elements is discussed by Faesen, but what we will take notice of in this context is her description of the visionary act, what she *sees*. All of the elements of the vision are familiar figures and

---

6 *ST*, I, Q. 89, Art. 8. Thomas discusses this further in connection with divination in *ST*, II–II, Q. 95, Art. 95 and in a discussion on prophesies in *ST*, II–II, Q. 174, Art. 5. In 'Supplement' Q. 69, Art. 3 some of the same questions are treated as in bk I, Q. 89, art. 8. **7** Carolly Erickson, *The medieval vision: essays in history and perception* (New York, 1978), p. 28. **8** As Rob Faesen points out in his essay, we know nothing about Hadewijch aside from her written texts.

symbols; what we recognize as conventional iconography from the visual universe of the Middle Ages, such as we find in church decorations and illuminations in books and manuscripts, as well as in other literature regarding mystical visions and theological tracts. Hadewijch is far from unique in this respect, and we will take a closer look at one of her contemporaries, Gertrude of Helfta, and the community she was a part of.

The Helfta monastery in Eisleben in Germany was a centre for mysticism in the second half of the thirteenth century. Three female mystics lived there at the same time: Mechthild of Magdeburg (1208/10–81/2), Mechthild of Hackeborn (1241/2–99) and perhaps the most famous of them all, Gertrude (the Great) of Helfta (1256–1301/2). These three nuns have left behind four texts written between the 1260s and the 1290s.[10] Gertrude's major work *The herald of divine love* contains descriptions of many of her visions. When we look at Gertrude's descriptions we find much of the same content as in Hadewijch, though there are perhaps even more explicit references to specific physical images.

In one of Gertrude's visions she describes how she saw Christ and the Holy Virgin sitting by his side. On this occasion she could also see the Virgin's immaculate womb (*Apparuit quoque immaculatus uterus Virgines*) as transparent as the purest crystal (*purissimae crystalli*). Through this clear crystal she could see the Virgin's inner organs, which were penetrated and filled with divine grace, radiating the way gold swathed in multi-coloured silk shines when seen through crystal (*velut aurum diversi coloris serico convolutum elucere solet per crystallum*). Gertrude saw the little flourishing child (*puerulus ille floridus*), God's only begotten Son, rejoicing by his virgin mother's heart.[11] This is a description that resembles a visitation group – with a reliquary – from the Dominican convent of St Katharinental, where a crystal is placed on the abdomens of the Virgin Mary and Elisabeth, who are both with child.[12] We cannot establish a direct connection between Gertrude of Helfta and this visitation group, which was presumably made after her death, but as Jeffrey Hamburger points out, 'the immediate and obvious conclusion to be drawn from an example such as this is that Gertrude's vision draws on her experience of a representation of *Maria gravida*'.[13]

Several of Gertrude's visions also reveal how physical images could contribute to an

9 See Faesen, this volume, pp 39–40. See also Hadewijch: *The complete works*, pp 280–4. **10** For a discussion of these three mystics and the Helfta community, see Caroline Walker Bynum, *Jesus as mother* (Los Angeles, CA, 1982), pp 170–262. In the Helfta monastery Cistercian monastic rules were followed, but they were not part of the order. By the end of the thirteenth century all of their priests and confessors were Dominicans. **11** See Gertrude of Helfta, *Le Héraut* (1968–86), bk IV, ch. 3, art. 4, pp 50–2. See also Jeffrey Hamburger, *The visual and the visionary* (New York, 1998), p. 118. **12** The Visitation Group from *c.*1305 is today housed in the Metropolitan Museum of Art in New York. For a discussion of this sculpture composed of multiple figures, see Hans Belting, *Likeness and presence: a history of the image before the era of art* (Chicago, 1994), pp 414–15, ill. no. 249, and Hamburger, *The visual and the visionary*, p. 118, fig. 2.2, p. 117: see the *Metropolitan Museum of Art's* webpage: www.metmuseum.org/collections/search-the-collections/464596?img=4. **13** Hamburger, *The visual and the visionary*, p. 118. There are several examples of this type of images, both in painting and in sculpture, showing the pregnant Mary – most often as a visitation motif with Elisabeth like the 'Katharinental' example.

interaction with the seeking soul, both as a basis for meditation and in order to come alive as part of the visionary experience. Meditation, in this context, has to do with practical, moral thought and reflection, as Jean Leclercq describes it: 'It implies thinking of a thing with the intent to do it; in other words, to prepare oneself for it, to prefigure it in the mind, to desire it, in a way, to do it in advance – briefly, to practice it'.[14] Gertrude describes how she got a particular individual to pray the following prayer for her in front of a crucifix (*ante imaginem crucifixi*): 'By your wounded heart, most loving Lord, pierce her heart with the arrow of your love, so that it may become unable to hold anything earthly, but may be held fast solely by the power of your divinity'. In the following, during the subsequent celebration of the mass, Gertrude describes how she was suffused with divine longing and cried out: 'Lord, I confess that I am not worthy (Matt. 8:8) through any merits of my own to receive the least of your gifts, but according to the merits and desires of all here present, I implore you of your goodness to transfix my heart with the arrow of your love!'[15] According to her own account, she immediately felt that these words brought her close to the divine heart of Christ:

> as much by the interior signs of infused grace as by certain signs which now appeared on the picture of your crucifixion (*per evidentis signi in imagine crucifixionis tuae demonstrationem*). After I had received the life-giving sacrament, on returning to my place, it seemed to me as if, on the right side of the Crucified *painted in the book* [my emphasis] (*videbator mihi quasi de dextro latere crucifixi depicti in folio*), that is to say, on the wound in the side, a ray of sunlight with a sharp point like an arrow came forth and spread itself out for a moment and then drew back. Then it spread out again. It continued like this for a while and affected me gently and deeply.[16]

This implies that the crucifix Gertrude is looking at is in a manuscript or book, i.e. an illuminated manuscript, presumably a prayer book. This would also be in keeping with her remarks about how she retreated to her regular place for prayer and meditation. From this we can clearly see how images play an important role in Gertrude's visions. Here the representation of the crucifix is the subject of meditation

14 Jean Leclercq OSB, *The love of learning and the desire for God: a study of monastic culture* (New York, 2003 (1961)), p. 16. This practice had its origins in a monastic tradition – but which eventually became a 'common' intellectual practice.   **15** 'Lord, I confess …' from Matthew 8:8 resembles the 'Domine, non sum dignus' prayer that is recited prior to communion.   **16** Gertrude of Helfta, *The herald of divine love*, bk II, ch. 5, art.1 and 2. Ref. Gertrude of Helfta in *Le Héraut, Tome II* (1968), pp 248–9. For more on this subject, see also Hamburger, *The visual and the visionary*, pp 126ff. Here quoted from Gertrude of Helfta: *The herald of divine love* (1993), p. 102. As an example of what type of manuscript illumination Gertrude may have used, Hamburger points to the illuminations in the so-called *Rothschild Canticles* from the end of the thirteenth century (Yale University Beinecke Rare Book and Manuscript Library MS 404, fos 18v–19): Hamburger, *The visual and the visionary*, p. 127.

and prayer, both as *instrumenta pietatis* and not least as *an integral part of the visionary experience itself.* The crucifix is both a preparative instrumental stimulus for the vision and the subject of the vision. The Eucharistic communion leads to a mystical union. To partake of the living sacrament, the host, in turn imparts life to the image of Christ. Many of the visions, both Gertrude's and those of other visionaries of the Middle Ages, take place during preparations for, or during the celebration of the Eucharist itself, which we have also seen in Hadewijch. In Gertrude's case it is moreover interesting that the vision can arise out of another person's intercession, so to speak. Both Gertrude and the other member of the Helfta community wrote or composed prayers for different individuals and purposes. This too clearly reveals how the visionary experience is associated with, and has its origin in, common devotional practices.

Mechthild of Magdeburg (1207/10–82/97), one of the other visionaries in the Helfta monastery, claims that the mass, with the sacrifice of the Eucharist, is a lower stage of communication – or of the senses – with Christ. By eating his body and drinking his blood one achieves a 'lower' form of unity with the deity, but it is of the same character and can merge into a 'more elevated' and more perfect *unio mystica*.[17] This differs, however, from Hadewijch's understanding in which the sacramental union is not a 'lower' form but a total union where God was in her: 'as if we were one without difference'.[18] St Catherine of Siena (1347–80) expresses a similar thought in her *Dialogo della Divina Providenza*, ch. 2: 'in communion the soul seems more sweetly bound to God and better knows his truth. For then the soul is in God and God is in the soul, just as the fish is in the sea and the sea in the fish.'[19] Richard Kieckhefer points to this connection between the Eucharist and a mystical experience:

> Some of the mystics, such as Meister Eckhart, tended to conflate the experience of mystical union with that of communion: partaking of the Eucharist was a way of joining one's soul with God in a way analogous to that of mystical absorption, and Eckhart was willing to use standard mystical language in referring to the Eucharist.[20]

It is precisely the Eucharist that is both the point of departure and the subject of Hadewijch's seventh vision.[21]

The Eucharist was the only repetitive and readily available form of union with God. It was a theologically guaranteed objective union regardless of whether or not one had a mystical experience. That is precisely why this was also a very frequent framework, or context, for mystical experience. The theological objectivity of a union with God

---

17 See Mechthild von Magdeburg, *Das fliessende Licht der Gottheit* (1995), book 2, chs 19 and 22. For more on the subject, see also Caroline Walker Bynum, *Jesus as mother*, pp 238, 258.   18 See Hadewijch's seventh vision: Hadewijch, *The complete works*, p. 281.   19 Here quoted from Catherine of Siena, *The Dialogue* (1980), p. 27. 20 Richard Kieckhefer, *Unquiet souls* (1984), s. 171.   21 See Faesen, this volume.

also gives credibility and authority to the visions. Gertrude's strong focus on the Eucharist and the teaching regarding the Real Presence are related to an emphasis on the significance and importance of physical images in the liturgical and devotional life.[22] The pious believer was expected to be able 'to see' the afflicted and crucified Christ in the consecrated and exalted host. Here too there was an interaction between physical sight and visions, which complemented each other. The many accounts of miracles involving bleeding hosts, such as the miracle in Bolsena in 1263, or the bread that was transformed into a little child or the 'Man of Sorrows', as in the Mass of St Gregory, underscored this visionary interaction.[23] This is what Hadewijch explains she sees in her vision. We can, in a sense, talk about a form of sacramental cult of vision during the Middle Ages. But this was dependent on a beholder who was capable of seeing the miracle and the invisible existence behind the ritual's visible appearance. The sacrament is both *res et signum*, it is at the same time a sign and what the sign represents. This is at the core understanding of the Real Presence, the concrete physical presence of the divinity in the world, which makes a direct communion – or union – with the divinity possible.[24]

God communicated through the image by giving life to dead matter. Here we see a parallel to that which occurs during the celebration of the Eucharist, where the dead matter of the sacramental objects – the bread and the wine – are miraculously brought to life and become life-giving via the transubstantiation of the Eucharistic elements of communion. This was a very central element of medieval religiosity: 'The liturgy lay at the heart of medieval religion, and the Mass lay at the heart of the liturgy', as Eamon Duffy formulates it.[25] In the celebration of the Eucharist, God and humans communicate directly with one another via the visible signs. During mass, Christ's sacrifice on Calvary was re-presented and made effective. Through the sacrament of communion, the believer became physically united with the sacrificial body, i.e. with Christ's suffering, resurrection and glory. The sacrament was the visible physical sign of the sacred body, which was also 'physically' present via its image.

VISIONS IN IMAGES – IMAGES IN VISIONS

What we notice about all of these visions are their explicit references to images or links between images and vision.[26] This is a connection that is found on many levels. An

22 For a discussion of the meaning of Eucharistic devotion in the Helfta monastery in particular, and more generally during the thirteenth and fourteenth centuries, see Bynum, *Jesus as mother*, esp. ch. 5. 23 See, for instance, the examples in Berndt Hamm's essay, pl. 7, and pls 5, 6. 24 On the understanding and reception of the Eucharist in the late medieval period, see Miri Rubin, *Corpus Christi: the Eucharist in late medieval culture* (Cambridge, 1991). See also Eamon Duffy, *The stripping of the altars* (London, 1992), pp 95–107. 25 Duffy, *The stripping of the altars*, p. 91. 26 Jeffrey Hamburger discusses a number of examples of book illuminations and other images that resemble or are very close to the descriptions given by many of the late medieval visionaries, among others many of the illuminations in the Rothschild *Canticles* from around 1300. See, for example, fos 18v–19r, which have parallels to Gertrude's vision, in which she is pierced by the arrow of Christ's love: see www.brbl-dl.library.yale.edu/vufind/Record/3432521. Hamburger, *The visual and the visionary*, pp 128–9 (fig. 2.9).

essential characteristic that is evident to us is *identification* via images. The visionary recognizes the persons she or he sees in the visions via, or with the help of, the physical images she has seen before. This aspect of recognition in the images is a central and common feature of a majority of the visions of the Middle Ages.

The most famous examples of this connection between various forms of images and visions can be found in St Francis of Assisi, to whom Christ spoke in a vision via the crucifix in the church of San Damiano in 1206, and his stigmatization on Monte Alverno, where Christ revealed himself to Francis as the six-winged seraph – a well-known medieval meditative and mnemonic figure.[27] St Thomas Aquinas also had visions in which Christ revealed himself and spoke to him through a crucifix as he knelt in front of the altar during devotions and meditation.[28] St Catherine of Siena provides another example of how physical images and visions merge together. A number of her visions are explicitly linked to meditation and prayer conducted in front of images, and she also mentions several times that what she sees in her visions are reminiscent of the way she has seen Christ or saints 'painted in the church'.[29]

Does this mean that visionaries actually only see (or saw) images and things that they had seen before and that reappeared in their memory – in such a way that neither the mystic herself nor anyone else recognized it as such? In order to shed light on this question, we can refer to the interesting explanation Christ gives to Gertrude in her vision, where he states that he makes use of visible things in order to express, or explain, that which is unfathomable to the human senses. In Gertrude, one might say, the theological doctrine of images receives visionary sanction directly from Christ.[30] A theory of '*visibilia per invisibilia*' is laid out here, which we find expressed by several of the Church Fathers as well as by pseudo-Dionysius (sixth century), St John of Damascus (*c.*657–*c.*749) and St Thomas Aquinas.[31] We can find parallel viewpoints expressed by her contemporary Meister Eckhart (*c.*1260–1329), who emphasizes incarnation as God's redemptive descent to Earth. According to Eckhart, the birth of the

---

27 Thomas of Celano's *The Second Life*, bk 1, ch. 6, and *The First Life*, bk 2, ch. 3: see Marion A. Habig, *St Francis of Assisi: writings and early biographies. English omnibus of the sources for the Life of St Francis* (Chicago, 1973), pp 370–1 and 308–11 respectively. See also St Bonavenure's *Major Life of St Francis*, chs 2 and 8, in Habig, *St Francis of Assisi* (1973), pp 640 and 729–32 respectively. The six-winged seraph is a biblical figure mentioned in Isaiah 6:2 and Ezekiel 1 and 10. We find it used in a number of contexts as a mnemonic and meditative figure, for example in Alain de Lille's *De sex aliis Cherubim* from the end of the twelfth century and in St Bonaventure in his *Itinerarium Mentis in Deum*: see Carruthers and Ziolkowski, *The medieval craft of memory* (2002), pp 83–102 and St Bonaventure, *Mystical Opuscula* (1960), pp 1–58 respectively. Hadewijch also had a similar vision in which she saw the Divinity in or via the six-winged seraph: see her thirteenth vision. Hadewijch, *The complete works*, p. 297. **28** Bernhard Gui, *Legenda S. Thomae*, chs 23 and 24: see Bernhard Gui, *The life of Saint Thomas Aquinas* (London, 1959), pp 42–3 and 43–4 respectively.   **29** See, for example, the first vita; *I miracoli della Beata Katarina* from around 1374. Published in Robert Fawtier, *Sainte Catherine de Sienne. Essai de critique des Sources. Sources Hagiographique* (Paris, 1922). See, for example, pp 218 and 222. See also Raymond of Capua, *Legenda Maior*, English ed.: *The Life of Catherine of Siena (Legenda Maior)* (Dublin, 1980).   **30** *The herald of divine love*, bk III, ch. 43. See Gertrude of Helfta: *The herald of divine love* (1993), p. 212. Bk IV, ch. 12 is of particular interest. See *Le Héraut, Tome IV* (1978), p. 334. Bynum, *Jesus as mother*, p. 200.   **31** See, for example, pseudo-Dionysius: *The celestial hierarchy*, chs 1, 3, *The ecclesiastical hierarchy*, chs 1, 5; St John of Damascus, *Divine images*, chs 1, 8 and *ST* I, Q. 1, Art. 9.

Saviour in Bethlehem gains *tropological* significance for the individual, such as allowing God to be reborn in his or her soul. It is interesting to note that, for Eckhart, spiritual experience does not necessarily imply extraordinary occurrences, but can be arrived at via ordinary sensing and experiencing of creation, even in ecclesiastical or theological texts, sacraments, rituals and practices.[32] The images make it possible to recognize and understand what one sees. This has to do with cognition via recognition and memory. The truth of the visions is verified by their similarities to commonly known images and motifs. We shall approach this by taking a look at another mystic of the late Middle Ages, Julian of Norwich who, in concentrated form, reveals to us some of the common and fundamental conditions for a kind of *visual cognition*, where the visions formed an integral part of an overall experience of cognition.

JULIAN OF NORWICH

Julian of Norwich lived as a hermit at the church of St Julian in Conisford, Norwich. We know very little about her life, but she was most likely born around 1342, and died some time after 1416. Julian of Norwich wrote down or dictated her visions or *showings* (*shewings*), as she calls them, in two versions. The short version, which is most likely the oldest, was probably written not long after she experienced the visions. The long version, which is a result of her own reflections on the visions and the spiritual elucidation of their content and meaning, was completed in writing in 1393, some twenty years later.[33]

Julian of Norwich had her visions, sixteen in all, during an illness when she was around 30 years old. Both she and those around her thought that she was dying, and a priest was therefore summoned. She viewed the illness, and its miraculous cure, as sent by God in order to prepare her for what was to come.[34] She had received all of the Church's last rites, including confession and communion, observances that could also be considered part of the contemplative preparations.[35] The priest held a crucifix in front of her as she lay there and recited:

---

32 See, for example, Olivier Davies, 'Late medieval mystics' in G.R. Evans (ed.), *The medieval theologians* (London, 2001), pp 221–31, pp 225–7 in particular. See also Bernard McGinn, 'Meister Eckhart: an introduction' in Paul Szarmach (ed.), *An introduction to the medieval mystics of Europe* (Albany, NY, 1984), pp 237–57. See also Richard Kieckhefer, *Unquiet souls*, pp 151 and 171.   **33** Regarding Julian of Norwich's life and the origins of the texts, see Edmund Colledge and James Walsh, 'Introduction' in Julian of Norwich: *Showings* (1978), esp. 17–23. See also Ritamary Bradley, 'Julian of Norwich: writer and mystic' in Paul Szarmach (ed.), *An introduction to the medieval mystics of Europe* (Albany, NY, 1984), pp 195–216.   **34** See ch. 2 in the short version, and ch. 3 in the long version, see *Showings* (1978), pp 127 and 179 respectively.   **35** In the devout individual's contemplative search and preparations for a visionary experience, we often find descriptions and presentations of these cleansing rituals as a precondition for the possibility of beholding God. It is not surprising of course when the visionary experience transcends the temporal dimension and approaches the next world, inhabited only by those who have been saved, those who are dead and live in the presence of God. The contemplative vision is the goal of man in a redeemed state ('For now we see through a glass darkly, but then face to face', 1 Cor 13:12). Regarding an understanding of contemplation and the possibility of such an experience during this life in the Middle Ages, see McGinn, *The growth of mysticism*, pp 50 ff.

Daughter, I have brought you the image of your saviour. Look at it and take comfort from it, in reverence of him who died for you and me. … I agreed to fix my eyes on the face of the crucifix if I could, …. After this my sight began to fail, and it was all dark around me in the room, dark as night, except that there was ordinary light trained upon the image of the cross, I never knew how.[36]

Her visions begin with the contemplation of a crucifix, which we find many examples of. It is this crucifix that is at the core of her sixteen *shewings*. The crucifix comes alive in these visions, so to speak: 'And at this, suddenly I saw the red blood trickling down from under the crown, all hot, flowing freely and copiously, a living stream'.[37] All of the *visions* or revelations she has occur consecutively, where one follows the other in the course of a rather short time lapse. The whole experience occurs during the day and it is still daylight when the revelations cease.[38] By mentioning this aspect of time, which is clearly important, Julian of Norwich emphasizes that she was lifted out of a worldly progression of time. In other words, she existed in another time dimension, i.e. in visionary time, or *aevum*. This is a time dimension that exists in between eternity and human time.

The category of time called *aevum* is important because here one had a time dimension that connected the two forms of existence, the temporal and the eternal. A time dimension of this kind was essential in order to explain and understand how communication with the Deity could *take place*. For *aevum* was, in a certain sense, also a *place* where this encounter could *take place*.[39] In other words, *aevum* represented the bridge between time and eternity, and was interpreted as the category of time that in a certain sense participated both in eternity and in human time, or historic time (*tempus nostrum*). This was the time of angels (*tempus angelorum*), that is, the time dimension inhabited by the angels: a different and more perfect time that had to exist for more perfect heavenly creatures.[40] One way of illustrating the visionary experience in medieval images was to have the visionary see through a window, or door, 'into' the divinely revealed truths. *Aevum* was a time conduit that existed between eternity in the realm of God – which represented non-time – and time. It formed a kind of opening between them – a kind of door, or window – into the sacred realm.[41] It is a time

---

36 *Showings* (1978), p. 128. 'Short version', ch. 1. It is also described in the 'Long version', ch. 3. **37** *Showings* (1978), p. 129. 'Short version', ch. 2. This vision resembles the many late medieval 'bleeding' Crucifixes and depictions of the 'Man of Sorrows'. **38** See, for example, 'Short version', ch. 21: 'And I lay still until night …', *Showings* (1978), p. 163. **39** See Barbara Nolan, *The Gothic visionary perspective* (Princeton, NJ, 1977), p. 146. **40** St Thomas of Aquinas treats this question in depth based on Aristotle's theory of the continuum, which is not only a spatial category but also a movement and temporal category. For this and a discussion regarding time dimension of angels in the work of Thomas of Aquinas, see Wolfgang Wieland, 'Kontinuum und Engelzeit bei Thomas von Aquino' in Ehrhard Scheibe and Georg Süssmann, *Einheit und Vielheit. Festschrift für Carl Friedrich v. Weizsäcker zum 60 geburtstag* (Göttingen, 1973), pp 77–90. **41** We can find examples of this in a number of illuminations depicting the Revelation of St John the Divine from the end of the thirteenth century. In Revelation 4:1 we read: 'After this I looked, and, behold, *a door was opened in heaven* …': see Suzanne Lewis, *Reading images* (1995).

conduit that opens during the celebration of the Eucharist as well. Communion is celebrated together with the angels and, there and then, communication and communion with God exists and is possible. Here again we see how the visionary mystic experience and the Eucharist are connected.

Most of the visions that Julian of Norwich describes seem to refer to well-known iconographic motifs such as the 'Man of Sorrows' and the 'Throne of Mercy'. Other motifs we find described by her are 'Christ in Majesty' and 'The Coronation of the Virgin'. At least it is possible to recognize elements of these in the descriptions she gives. It is therefore interesting that in her introduction to the short version she also explicitly refers to images as sources for the true knowledge of faith. She states that she prayed for three gifts from God. The first was 'to have a recollection of Christ's Passion ... so that I might have seen with my own eyes our Lord's Passion which he suffered for me, so that I might have suffered with him as others did who loved him, ...' In other words, what she prays for is a *recollection* or a *renewed viewing* of the Passion of Christ 'as Holy Church shows and teaches, and as paintings of the Crucifixion represent, which are made by God's grace, according to Holy Church's teaching, to resemble Christ's Passion, so far as human understanding can attain'.[42] Here she sets forth a whole theology of images and draws a direct connection between *memory*, *cognition* and the *act of seeing*.

In the introduction to the long version she specifies that it was a question of a physical vision: 'Therefore I desired a bodily sight, in which I might have more knowledge of our saviour's bodily pains'.[43] What she prays for is to see a 'memory image', and such a memory must have a 'prototype', which are the images that she has seen in churches. The 'higher' shall be recognized via that which is 'lower', between which there is a close relationship. But it is also worth mentioning that this 'remembered experience' has an actuality for Julian. It not only refers to something in the past, but is also a reenactment of the past. It is a 're-lived experience', where the purpose is a vicarious experiencing and imitation of the Passion of Christ. It is a form of *anamnesis*, as in the celebration of the Eucharist. The memory shall elicit a reenactment that will 'move' Julian closer to God. The memory is not only a passive reflection on/of past events, but also a dynamic re-enactment here and now. Memory is converted into real action for the one who remembers. We shall take a closer look at this.

THE DYNAMIC CHARACTER OF VISIONS

The visions marked the end of Julian's illness. They thus represented both a 'cure' and a rebirth to new life, a life that from this point and up to around 1393 was devoted to

---

42 *Showings* (1978), p. 125. 'Short version', ch. 1.   43 *Showings* (1978), p. 178. 'Long version', ch. 2. This is a striking similarity to Hadewijch's longing for the same kind of knowledge of Christs: '... all great sufferings', as described in the seventh vision. Hadewijch, *The complete works*, p. 280.

reflection, meditation and interpreting the content and significance of the visions. That is why the final text is far more elaborate and reflective. This gradual understanding was necessary, as she says, due to 'our blindness and ignorance', not because God wishes to hide something from us. It is the cognitive ability of human beings that is lacking. Therefore the sinner's greatest defect is his or her blindness, claims Julian, and it is this blindness that causes one to be a sinner, for the sinner does not see that God is love.[44] Julian emphasizes that the road to knowledge of God can be both long and tedious. The gradual cognition, or revelation, is not something that occurs merely on the individual level, it has a general character. This dynamic understanding of tradition, both on the universal 'historical' level and the individual level, is clearly expressed by Julian in her conclusion of the long version of *shewings*. From the very moment she had the visions, her greatest wish was to find out what God had intended with them. This prayer was answered only after nearly fifteen years, via gradual spiritual reflection and enlightenment.[45]

In other words, Julian of Norwich emphasizes that the visions were not an occurrence, now concluded, but rather the beginning of a process that is part of a greater context. The visions are necessary in order to pave the way for our understanding of the original revelation in the Bible: 'because he wants it better known than it is'.[46] She is always careful to make it clear that what she writes is in keeping with the teachings of the Church, and one of the purposes of her visions is to emphasize that the Church is holy because the Holy Spirit dwells in it. At the same time, this means that the revelation that has been given is not conclusively understood. This is an important point, which has to do with the fundamental understanding of meaning and interpretation during the Middle Ages. It was universally understood that meaning was manifold and complex, and that truth was not easily or unambiguously perceivable by the human intellect. Awareness was at all times directed at this ambiguity of meaning, and was put into practice via the *quadriga* or the fourfold method of interpretation.

St Thomas Aquinas treats this polysemous aspect in his first question in *Summa Theologica*, where he discusses what theology – *sacra doctrina* – is all about. Here he lists the four basic methods of reading or interpreting the Bible: historic or literal, allegorical or typological, tropological or moral, and anagogical or spiritual.[47] This recognizes the fact that the biblical texts could be understood on many levels and that they had to be interpreted. This is an understanding that has a long tradition and dates

---

44 *Showings* (1978), p. 159. 'Short version', ch. 19.   **45** *Showings* (1978), p. 342. 'Long version', ch. 86.
46 *Showings* (1978), p. 342.   **47** *S.T.* I, Q. 1, Art. 10. See also Harry Caplan, 'The four senses of scriptural interpretation and the mediaeval theory of preaching', *Speculum*, 4 (1929), 286. There is extensive literature on the interpretation and understanding of the Bible in the Middle Ages. Two central and classical texts are: Beryl Smalley, *The study of the Bible in the Middle Ages* (Notre Dame, 1978 (1951)), and particularly Henri de Lubac, *Medieval exegesis: the four senses of Scripture (Exégèse médiévale: les quatre sens de l'écriture)* (Grand Rapids, MI, 1998 (1959–64)). See also Jan Schumacher, 'Breaking the bread of Scripture. On the medieval interpretation of the Bible', *Collegium Medievale*, 6:2 (Oslo, 1993), 107–32; Henning Laugerud, 'Polysemi og den dynamiske tradisjon', *Passepartout. Skrifter for kunsthistorie*, 25 (Aarhus, 2005), 94–103.

all the way back to the evangelists. We find examples of this in Luke's account of Jesus preaching in the synagogue in Nazareth or on the road to Emmaus, where he also lays out the Old Testament texts as references to himself. These are passages that are referred to repeatedly in exegetical texts from the Middle Ages.[48] This polysemic method of reading the Bible was already established in the early days of the Church and became a major concern for the theologians of ancient Christianity. In his *De doctrina christiana*, St Augustine (354–430) develops a hermeneutical theory based on the understanding that the biblical texts have manifold meanings and must be understood on different levels.[49] This is related among other things to his view that language is imperfect as a result of Original Sin. For St Augustine, language is not transparent but veiled, and although Holy Scripture is divinely inspired, it is after all a text written in human languages, and humans, with all their defects and failings, will have to interpret it. In other words, it is not a 'perfect' presentation of the truth about God, but rather a guide to show us in what direction to look.

We can find a similar view of it expressed by his contemporary St Jerome (*c.*342–420) as the fundamental condition for translating the Bible into Latin. In his fallen state man is forced to interpret because God is beyond all mutable things, and because not only man himself, but also the most important medium of experience – language – is mutable and mortal. St Augustine emphasizes that it is possible to deduce things from the Bible that the author of a particular text did not understand or see. Or the author may have understood, but the interpretation of the text had not drawn the entire significance out to its final conclusion.[50]

For the reader of the Christian Bible in the Middle Ages, the Old Testament was 'reconstructed' in the texts of the New Testament. The older text is only meaningful in light of the newer text. The New Testament provides a key for interpreting the Old Testament.[51] The dialectical expansion from one level of significance to another appears to be built into the Bible's structure and creates an awareness of itself in the reader, an awareness that grows and develops with time.[52] This does not only apply to the reading of a written text.

An image of Christ on a church wall or in a prayer book could form a basis for a set of associations for medieval women and men, and have so many connotations that it virtually came to life. Images could thus represent the beginning of a number of new related images in the beholder's inner gaze. 'There is no "one-to-one" relationship between symbols and their referents such as we are used to in iconographic interpre-

---

48 Luke 4:16–30 and Luke 24:13–35. Schumacher, 'Breaking the bread of Scripture', p. 114. Another example with clear parallels to later exegetic practices can be found in the Acts of the Apostles, where the apostle Philip helps an Ethiopian to understand an Old Testament text and the various levels of significance contained in the preaching of the gospel of Christ. Acts 8:26–40. **49** St Augustine: *De doctrina Christiana*, ed. and trans. R.P.H. Green (Oxford, 1995), esp. bk III. **50** See, for example, St Augustine's *Confessions*, bk 12, chs XVIII, XXXI. See also Schumacher, 'Breaking the bread of Scripture', pp 109–11 and Brenda Deen Schildgen, 'Rhetoric and the Body of Christ' in B.D. Schildgen (ed.), *The rhetoric canon* (Detroit, IL, 1997), pp 151–73. **51** Schumacher, 'Breaking the bread of Scripture', p. 113. **52** Northrop Frye, *The great code* (San Diego, CA, 1983), p. 225.

tation', writes Michael Camille. 'Images likewise do not signify one thing but many.'[53] Julian of Norwich and the other visionaries lived in a cultural context where one was familiar with the idea that to read a text in the Bible, for instance, or view a picture, triggered creative processes. To meditate over a passage in the Bible was a way of reading in which the text created new images. It is a dynamic understanding of tradition that is expressed here; a way of thinking about understanding that describes a kind of cognitive movement. The manifold interpretations – the polyphonic character of the 'text' – create life, as St Paul writes in 2 Corinthians 3:6: 'for the letter killeth, but the Spirit giveth life'.

These levels of meaning are not separated from each other but are related: 'What is implied is a single process growing in subtlety and comprehensiveness, not different senses, but different intensities or wider contexts of a continuous sense, unfolding like a plant out of a seed'.[54] This has to do with a form of ethical reading, where the various levels are understood in a consecutive and continuous act of interpretation. The manifold ways of interpreting thus also become a useful and perhaps necessary system for remembering in order to give the reader a tool for concluding the entire reading process: '*Littera* and *allegoria* (grammar and typological history) are the work of *lectio* and are essentially informative about a text; *tropology* and *anagogy* are the activities of digestive meditation and constitute the ethical activity of making one's reading one's own'.[55]

At the same time we must remember that in a Christian theological context this does not imply that one is discovering new things in the Bible, but understanding the same eternal truth in a better and more correct manner. Yet a better understanding can also be said to be something new. A 'new' truth is not necessarily something fundamentally new, but merely a question of seeing the same thing from a different perspective. A perspective of this kind implies a framework that the interpretation can operate within. Here the manifold perspective – the polysemic one – leads to tradition understood as a dynamic entity. This medieval polysemic perspective is a manner of thinking and meditating in which ambiguity is institutionalized and set into practice, and is not a problem to be solved. In this way of thinking the various levels of meaning do not exclude one another, but are mutually complementary and even presuppose one another. 'The truth' thus becomes a mutable entity, something that develops over time, in which the framework for interpretations forms part of the same dynamic tradition. The visions and the visionary were central agents in this tradition, as it was understood during the Middle Ages. It is not only the visions themselves that must be interpreted and elucidated with a continuous expansion of their significance, as we see, for example, in the writings of Julian of Norwich; they are themselves a part of the gradual revelation and the interpretative process – also of biblical revelation. The

---

53 Michael Camille, 'Him whom you have ardently desired you may see' in Meredith Parsons Lillich (ed.), *Studies in Cistercian art and architecture*, 3 (Kalamazoo, MI, 1987), pp 137–60 at p. 144.   **54** Frye, *The great code*, p. 221.   **55** Carruthers, *The book of memory*, p. 165.

mystical experience was itself rooted in this understanding of the Bible: 'The tropo-logical level comprises a key to what is often vaguely termed medieval "mysticism", in the sense that the core of mysticism consists of the stories and metaphors of Scripture being translated into an inner drama of the soul.'[56]

Herein lies the basis for the awareness we can find in the Middle Ages of an inter-pretive ambiguity, and the *quadriga* was an existential hermeneutics that was not limited to biblical interpretations. Symbolic thinking, which is also connected to memory, iconography and topologies always has what we can call a *fourth* level of interpretation: *the anagogical*. This is the purpose of every interpretive method or process of understanding; to rise to a higher understanding of God. A possibility that is accessible to all. It is therefore important to remember that the *quadriga*, along with the medieval 'symbolic way of thinking' has an existential perspective. It is not an isolated or instrumental key or system for interpretation.

VISIONS – IMAGES – MEMORY

Julian's observations regarding the theology of images explain how physical images can be related to the mental or inner images that the visionary sees. The images are created by the mercy of God and by resembling and representing the sufferings of Jesus Christ on the cross. The image reflects or represents the original image. She also expresses an interesting interpretation of the connection between vision and cognition. Julian prays for the opportunity to see the Passion of Christ in order to understand the teachings of the Church better. The visible, 'to see', thus leads to cognition that occurs on many levels, and she divides her 'visions' into the following three categories or modalities: 'physical vision', 'words (or conceptions) formed in the mind' and 'spiritual vision'.[57] Julian of Norwich operates here with three categories of visual cognition, which are based on St Augustine's theory of the three types of human vision: physical vision (*visio corporealis*), spiritual or 'inner' vision (*visio spiritualis*), and finally, intellectual vision (*visio intellectualis*).[58]

We can see that there is no clear distinction between images and visions, that it is, rather, a question of different visual experiences on a kind of mutual sliding scale. Neither for Hadewijch or Gertrude of Helfta, nor indeed for Julian of Norwich did the physical images which they had set up as prototypes or models for their visions appear without their being aware of it, as a form of unconscious psychological response.[59] They were all built on 'a common stock of images, rooted in Scripture and

---

56 Schumacher, 'Breaking the bread of Scripture', p. 125.   **57** *Showings* (1978), s. 167. 'Short version', ch. 23. It is the spiritual vision, the deeper meaning of the revelations, which she elucidates in the long version of the description of her visions.   **58** St Augustine in *De Genesi ad litteram*, ch. 12, 7: see Henning Laugerud, 'Visuality and devotion in the Middle Ages' in Henning Laugerud and Laura Katrine Skinnebach (eds), *Intruments of devotion* (Aarhus, 2007), pp 173–88.   **59** These are obviously not persons with psychological disorders. In that case it would have meant that all of Europe was struck by an epidemic of insanity, both in western and eastern Christianity, as Richard Kieckhefer has pointed out. Richard Kieckhefer, *Unquiet souls*, p. 2.

the liturgy, assimilated to experience through prolonged meditation and recitation and available to artists and mystics alike'.[60] The eagle that Hadewijch sees in the beginning of the seventh vision is a well-known symbol that incorporates a number of references and representations, and has a multitude of potential meanings. It was a commonly known figure, not only as a metaphor or inner image, but also from various types of church decorations.[61] It was also well known as a mnemotechnical symbol. This has to do with what we can call the *cognitive environments* of the visions. Time and space, vision and memory are all cognitive categories. They are essentially a set of symbols, motifs and figurations used to think and structure thought with, all of which are related to memory as a cognitive pivotal point. It is in memory – and in the cognitive operations involved in memory – that images and visions are woven together as the visible signs with which God communicates with human beings. Medieval symbolism served an important and complex purpose that becomes clear when viewed from this mnemological perspective.

St Thomas discusses memory in his treatment of the virtues where he lists memory as one of the seven parts of prudence (*prudentia*).[62] This reflects the importance and the moral significance of the memorial art commonly held by medieval thinkers. Hugh of St Victor (*c.*1096–1142) states in the preface to his *Chronicon* from 1130 that ignorance and forgetfulness are the same – the one leading to the other.[63] Memory related to knowledge of the World as well as the Self, but more importantly, it related to the knowledge of God and Ultimate Reality. As St Augustine formulates it: 'If I find thee without memory, then I shall have no memory of thee; and how could I find thee at all, if I do not remember thee?'[64] This memory was both of the past, the present and the future; 'to remember the eternal joys of Paradise and the pains of Hell', as Boncompagno da Signa (*c.*1170–1240) states in his *Rhetorica novissima* from around 1235.[65] In medieval reflections on, and understanding of, memory we can clearly detect multi-spatial and multi-temporal perspectives, but also its foundation for knowledge. For both St Augustine and Boncompagno the knowledge of the future was based on memory; the future was, in a sense, something to be recognized.

Memory was part of man's mental capacities and was rooted both in sense perception and in abstraction. Memory was not a passive act of 'mechanical' registration; it interpreted reality – as it was understood during the Middle Ages. It was at the same time creative and 'conserving' – memory was something to be stored and

---

60 Hamburger, *The visual and the visionary*, p. 119.   **61** The eagle might symbolize many things; for example, John the Evangelist or divine inspiration, and was thus a motif commonly used on the pulpit or lectern used for reading the gospel. It might also symbolize Christ, but also the sense of sight, to mention some of the meanings that could be inferred or attributed to it. For a more thorough discussion of this topic, both more general and more specific, see Kristin B. Aavitsland, *Imagining the human condition in medieval Rome* (Burlington, 2012), esp. pp 141–64.   **62** *ST*, II–II, p. 49. The theological virtues are: Faith, Hope and Charity, the cardinal virtues are: Prudence (or Wisdom), Justice, Fortitude (or Courage) and Temperance (or Moderation).   **63** Grover A. Zinn Jr, 'Hugh of Saint Victor and the art of memory', *Viator*, 5 (1974), 211–34 at 219.   **64** St Augustine: *Confessions*, 10, ch. XVII, see St Augustine: *Confessions* (2002), p. 187.   **65** Boncompagno da Signa, *Rhetorica novissima*, in A. Gaudentio (ed.), *Bibliotheca Iuridica Medii Aevi*, 2 (Bologna, 1892), p. 275.

reactivated. This medieval memory was centred on symbols and symbolic figurations, and it was memory that caused the symbols, the images, to 'speak'.

Thus there is a sliding transition between the outer corporeal pictures, sense impressions of different kinds and the inner mental images. This is not merely a function of the memory techniques, but has also to do with memory as the place where the outer and inner images meet in connection with knowledge. Memory, then, is a kind of inner marking; the thing to be remembered shall be 'impressed' into/onto your mind and body. What you take in through your senses shall be meditated on and imprinted on your mind, just as the stigmata of Christ were 'imprinted' on/to the bodies of St Francis and Hadewijch.

Internalizing information or knowledge had to do with creating and storing inner or mental images, which connect visuality and thinking. These 'memory images' were understood as physical mental pictures that were vital for human understanding. This was already evident in the classical understanding of memory.[66]

There was more than one sort of *ars memoria* known during the Middle Ages, as Mary Carruthers has emphasized, and this art of memory made use of the classical tradition to its own ends and with its own inventions and combinations. It was an 'invention' of its own, developed from meditational practices to fit the needs of monastic prayer and for the memorizing of theological truths, and later developed and more commonly used in all kinds of contexts concerning knowledge and understanding. It was a technique of meditative invention with a deliberately crafted cognitive and inventive use for the 'images' gathered from material stored in memory, 'images' seen inwardly with the mind's eye, in a technique that emphasized 'recollection'.[67] The mnemonic places and symbols are cognitive schemata rather than objects. That is, they are pragmatic. They may entail likenesses of things but are not 'real' or 'identical' with the things that are to be symbolized or remembered. They are heuristic tools used to reach towards things, not the things themselves. 'Within mnemonic space, however, such symbols become cues or heuristic devices which access memory.'[68] This 'mnemonic space' could be a church interior, a manuscript page or the mind itself.

This reveals medieval mnemotechnics as a dynamic way of thinking, as mentioned in the discussion on the *quadriga* above: it was 'the matrix of a reminiscing cogitation, shuffling and collating "things" stored in a random-access memory scheme, or set of schemes – a memory architecture and library built up during one's lifetime with the express intention that it be used inventively'.[69] *Ars memoria* was a craft that gave a

---

66 Cicero says, for example, that the impressions that stand out most clearly in our minds are those that are received via the senses and that of all the human senses; the sense of sight is the keenest. Consequently, the thing to be remembered will be held most easily in the mind by creating an image of it. Cicero, *De oratore*, bk II, 87, 357. Marcus Tullius Cicero, *De oratore*, I (London, 1979 [1942]), p. 469. **67** Mary Carruthers, 'Boncompagno da Signa at the cutting-edge of rhetoric', *Journal of Medieval Latin*, 6 (Turnhout, 1996), 44–64, esp. 45. **68** Jill Bennett, 'Stigmata and sense memory', *Art History*, 24:1 (2001), 1–16 at 4. **69** Mary Carruthers, *The craft of thought* (Cambridge, 1999), p. 4.

person the means and wherewithal to invent his material, both beforehand and on the spot. It was a compositional art, as Carruthers has pointed out: 'The arts of memory are among the arts of thinking, especially involved with fostering the qualities we now revere as "imagination" and "creativity"'.[70] Closely linked to the medieval understanding of a dynamic tradition and polysemous meaning.

Images of all kinds, symbols and allegories are 'effective' for many reasons where memory is concerned. One of them is their aptitude for rhetorical concentration, of being able to compress a large amount of content into one expression: an expression that is syntagmatic in the sense that its references are a selection of several elements that belong together or are joined together. In the Middle Ages, pictures, paintings in churches, manuscript illuminations etc. were, for the most part, what we would define as symbolic. They are, in a sense, 'image signs' that imply more than they show in an actual visual sense through their aptitude for this rhetorical concentration. Images also have a simultaneous emotional and persuasive appeal. The emotional appeal (*pathos*) is connected to and strengthens the persuasive appeal (*logos*) among other things by making it easier to remember, to take in the message. As Gerhart Ladner formulates it,

> symbols are understood to form a bridge between the experience of the senses and that which lies or reaches beyond. In this understanding symbols are referred ultimately to the coexistence of similarity and dissimilarity between the creatures and God, which the Middle Ages conceived as the analogy of being.[71]

The understanding of memory in the Middle Ages is related to a way of thinking in which visuality and knowledge are tightly interwoven, and images, symbols and figurations are central. Not in the sense that the pictorial schemes necessarily must be seen as based on a particular memory system or specific texts on memory: 'but rather that certain ideas about the relationship of memory to imagery inform both the 'arts' of memory and the production and use of devotional imagery'.[72]

This is not a question of reaching towards knowledge or spiritual enlightenment through iconographical interpretation, but of exploiting the heuristical dimension of the image to stimulate memory: 'This in turn produces a "deeper" knowledge through identification or, more precisely, through the devotee's ability to "become" the image, to imitate Christ'.[73] What one 'sees' makes an impression. Sight was embodied: 'To perceive or sense … is to be materially altered'. The example of St Francis' stigmata on Monte Alverno shows how his flesh became: 'moulded into the image of the crucified Christ'.[74] St Bonaventure emphasizes this very clearly in his biography of St Francis,

70 Ibid., p. 9.   **71** Gerhart B. Ladner, 'Medieval and modern understanding of symbolism', *Speculum*, 54:2 (1979), 223–56 at 225.   **72** Jill Bennett, 'Stigmata and sense memory', p. 2.   **73** Ibid., p. 8.   **74** Suzannah Biernoff, 'Carnal relations: embodied sight in Merleau-Ponty, Roger Bacon and St Francis', *Journal of Visual Culture*, 4:1 (London, 2005), 42.

the *Legenda maior*, describing this incident. His flesh had become 'wax' in the hands of God: 'God is the divine sculptor, fashioning the image of Christ out of flesh; but he is also the Word, writing his creation into existence'. The marks of the crucifixion have been 'written' on the flesh of St Francis. 'To gaze, like Francis, at a crucifix, or to meditate on the Passion, would have been to enter into this fabric of associations and expectations.'[75] From this vantage point, viewing is not just a matter of interpretation or cognition, but a transformative process in which the viewer is affected directly and physically through a sensory encounter with an 'object': 'In effect, one becomes the image through an encounter with it'.[76] These images stored in the memory inevitably relate to the person who holds them in his or her mind. They were seen as physiological affections, and thus a part of the person, and therefore ethical; clearly demonstrated by the visionaries, and their yearning for – and response to their visions.[77]

The medieval mnemonic systems were primarily heuristic in nature, which mean that they were concerned with retrieval as opposed to a hermeneutic – or iconographic – scheme, which is primarily meant to be interpreted.[78] This heuristic character and basis explains why the arts of memory in medieval times were dynamic and creative. The collective ideas, motives, figures, topics etc. were meant to be personalized with this heuristic aim. 'Reminiscences are not quotations, elements of phrases borrowed from another. They are the words of the person using them; they belong to him', as Jean Leclercq formulates it.[79] It was an aid for creativity, and for individuation and internalization of knowledge and insights. But we are not speaking of dichotomies or clearly separate distinctions here. If the two can be separated, we are probably talking about two ways of understanding in one and the same operation. Interpretation has in itself a mnemonic aspect, as noted earlier. It is a way of recovering stored information, and at the same time of dynamically activating the interpreter's own personal and cultural memory. The image is productive rather than being merely representational. The mode of viewing in the Middle Ages was characterized by an understanding of interactivity, which in many ways is demonstrated in the visionary experience.[80]

This opens up to some broad vistas of understanding, where the 'image' is charged with a physical re-collective force, which alters the beholder or believer and brings him or her into a state of internalizing and experiencing the truth through the embodiment of memories. The symbols mean, refer, affect and connect via a dissimilar similarity to knowledge in an embodied sense, and all this through memory. The 'memory image' was a bodily experience and memory a sense memory, and this sensuality was seen as

75 Biernoff, 'Carnal relations', p. 43. See Marion A. Habig, *St Francis of Assisi* (Chicago, 1973), pp 729–36. 76 Jill Bennett, 'Stigmata and sense memory', p. 6. 77 Carruthers, *The book of memory*, p. 49. 78 Ibid., pp 19–21. 79 Leclercq, *The love of learning*, p. 75. 80 For a more detailed discussion of the sensorial aspect of memory, see Henning Laugerud, 'Memory: the sensory materiality of belief and understanding' in Laugerud et al. (eds), *The saturated sensorium*.

crucial for exploiting the heuristic dimension of the 'image' to stimulate memory. The symbol should produce affects and effects; a kind of bodily alteration of the devotee. The 'memory image' generated a realization of the truth in Christ in the mind and body of the devotee, making it possible to inhabit the scene(s) or place(s) (*loci*) of the Crucifixion for instance, and experience that which transcends any referential description. In this way the 'memory image' becomes rhetorical evidence, *evidentia*, to be witnessed with one's own eyes, *autopsia*. This is why the image becomes productive rather than descriptive, and all this is part of the visionary experience and its reception.

Here we can see how visions, 'memory images' and other pictures relate to one another, with memory as a cognitive pivotal point. All these different images are mutually related to one another on many levels, and through memory one is able to recognize and know God as he reveals himself in the mystic visionary's experience. This is also a visual vocabulary, which can be communicated and recognized by others because *the images* are accessible for everyone – not only the visionary. The same is also true of the contemplative striving that became a more common religious ideal attainable for all – particularly in the late Middle Ages. In this respect, Barbara Nolan points to the interesting fact that all of the 'spiritual pilgrims' in medieval visionary literature are often described as unreflective, apathetic persons, who had no particular spiritual concerns. They are not particularly philosophical or holy; in other words they represent Everyman. The point of this is, of course, to emphasize that the message is aimed at all and sundry. The purpose is to provide the common individual with a model to emulate for spiritual counsel and comfort. It is meant to underscore the fact that salvation is accessible to everyone and that God can become an active force in the lives of all human beings. This had relevance for devotional practices and the devotional life; it was something that could be emulated and experienced by anyone at any time, here and now. In this way, visions are woven into medieval spiritual practices, not only for the visionary but strictly speaking also for every devout Christian.

CONCLUSION

The visionary experience, the mystic's vision, has to do with seeing what is normally hidden from our gaze. '*Vidi arcana Dei*', says Catherine of Siena: 'I have seen the secret things of God'.[81] The mystical revelation is a visualization of the invisible, which begins in the temporal and physical sphere, but which points *beyond* human existence. If God is to reveal Himself, He must do it in a way that the human intellect can acknowledge. In order to be visible, He must be recognizable. The manner in which God appears in physical reproductions is the manner in which He also appears in visions. The content and message of visions would also have to be communicable to

---

81 See Raymond of Capua, *The Life* (1980), pt II, ch. VI, §185, p. 179.

others; i.e. to all and sundry. In other words, they had to be communicated via familiar motifs and figures in order to be accessible. At the same time, the message to be communicated was an elaboration on and explanation of something that was – at least partially – already known.

Here we are at the core of the mystery of Christianity, *the Incarnation* – where God descends to earth and becomes visible – and its purpose, which is the salvation of mankind. The plan of salvation is the objective. To see Christ/God is to be redeemed and it is the gaze that redeems. Both the inner and outer gaze – not to mention that it is a *visio* that is accessible to all. The visionary's *visio*, when it comes down to it, is nothing more than a sign that shows what the physical image – what everyone can see – signifies. It is an image of an image in an endless chain of signs, which all lead to God so that mankind can be restored to the grace of God and be redeemed.

Memoria was at the core of this, what we might call a kind of 'cultural system' or cognitive environment that was the fundamental matrix of thinking. The 'system', this cognitive environment, itself represents meaning. This is a way of thinking that is consistent with an understanding of embodiment, which is at the core of Christian thinking. I am, of course, referring to the Incarnation, Communion and the Resurrection of the body. The various parts of the 'cognitive environment' relate symbolically. The thing that is to be remembered and internalized also provides some of the means and structures for this remembering; it is a 'system' where everything is interlaced.

The visionary experience was thus something that could be made permanently accessible *through* images. Just as the first-person narrators in the visionary literature conveyed their experiences and recognition of a moral and virtuous life for the sake of the redemption of their own souls and as a model for their readers, the images likewise convey insights and experiences as a model for their public. The beholder, listener or reader would, with the help of grace, reconsider his temporal life and acknowledge his place in the story of salvation (*sacra historia*) on the basis of his own experience of images or writings made heartfelt through memory. In this context, the individual beholder's life is woven into the story of salvation. *Sacra historia* and personal history would merge together and in this state of a kind of 'visionary' vision, where the truths of faith were revealed in the temporal sphere, the individual place in the story of salvation would be revealed. Through a 'revelation' of this kind, the gradual cognition of God's will would be acknowledged through the signs he revealed to mankind. 'Alone they would not find heaven or the spiritual acuity proper to souls near the end of the Last Age. Only through the power of vision and the authoritative guide provided for their edification can they realize the allegorical sense of their quest and envision spiritual peace'.[82]

Translated by Francesca M. Nichols.

---

82 Nolan, *The gothic visionary perspective*, p. 140.

4 Christ the wounded lover and affective piety in late medieval Ireland and beyond

SALVADOR RYAN

Many of the essays in this volume deal with the role of the senses in late medieval devotional life – seeing, hearing, touching, tasting and even smelling the objects of that devotion in a variety of surroundings to which the devotee was drawn through the exercise of the religious imagination, often with the aid of contemporary works of meditation. This language of the senses was especially evident, of course, in mystical works such as those of Mechtild of Hackeborn (1241–c.98), Gertrude of Helfta (1256–1302), Angela of Foligno (c.1249–1309), Birgitta of Sweden (1303–73) and Julian of Norwich (1342–c.1416). On one occasion, recounting the experience of her soul having been taken to Christ's breast to experience the heat of his love, Gertrude spoke of being 'revived by the aromatic odours of life-enhancing perfumes; intoxicated by sweet savours interiorly tasted', proceeding to whet the appetite of anyone intent on approaching 'this paradise' by adding 'Oh what will he not see, hear, smell, taste, feel!'[1] The arresting power of religious imagery was also a significant element in exciting the senses to devotion. The first visit of a pilgrim to a cathedral like Chartres, with its spectacular rose windows, must have been akin to entering beyond the earthly vale into a heavenly realm. In the words of Abbot Suger, the patron of the abbey of St Denis, displays such as these 'ravished and refreshed [the] soul by their beauty'.[2] Likewise (for those who could afford them), the first time one's eye fell on a lavishly illustrated Book of Hours. Even for those who did not have the means to travel far from their native village or town, or to purchase expensive illustrated works of devotion, many local churches afforded an opportunity to step into a strikingly visual religious world of more meagre stained glass offerings and, frequently, of colourful wall paintings.

Survival rates of these elements of the medieval devotional past vary across Europe. Unfortunately, Ireland has fared particularly poorly in this regard on a number of levels. Only a few fragments of shattered stained glass images from medieval Ireland survive and very little in the way of medieval wall painting.[3] Neither do we know to what extent the writings of the female mystics mentioned above circulated in Ireland and we can only grasp at the few hints that we do get to speculate on what has not

---

1 Gertrude of Helfta, *The herald of divine love*, ed. and trans. Margaret Winkworth (New York, 1993), bk II, chs 7, 8. **2** *De Administratione*, xiii, in *Abbot Suger on the abbey church of St Denis and its art treasures*, ed. and trans. E. Panofsky and G. Panofsky-Soergel (Princeton, NJ, 1979). **3** See especially Josephine Moran, 'The shattered image' and Karena Morton, 'Aspects of image and meaning in Irish medieval wall paintings' in Rachel Moss, Colmán Ó Clabaigh and Salvador Ryan (eds), *Art and devotion in late medieval Ireland* (Dublin, 2006).

survived. And yet, despite the paucity of late medieval Irish devotional texts and artefacts – which pales when compared with those found in England, for instance – there is, nevertheless, some evidence to suggest that the richness of the late medieval mystical tradition did exert an influence on the Irish religious imagination. And among the places where one can find traces of this is a somewhat unlikely source: the religious verse of a hereditary caste of professional poets who were, in the main, laymen, and whose oeuvre has long been considered by scholars to be rigidly stylized, articulating a largely immutable world view and, in Eleanor Knott's words, 'a flat table-land stretching from the thirteenth to the seventeenth century'.[4]

The present essay examines the extent to which many of the mystical themes explored in other contributions to this volume can be found in the religious works of Irish bardic poets, with particular emphasis on expressions of 'blood piety' and the use of highly sensualized imagery of carnal love which was often associated with mystical devotion to Christ's passion. When the evidence is sifted through, there is a case to be made that the influence of mystical thought on the late medieval Irish devotional world was greater than has previously been acknowledged.

AFFECTIVE PIETY

Affective devotion, characterized by mental and emotional involvement with the various life situations of Christ, attentiveness to the limitations of his humanity, sympathy with his physical pain, and sorrow for the sins of humanity, which were understood to be deeply and causatively entwined with his experience of passion and death on a cross, became an important feature of Irish devotional life in the fourteenth and fifteenth centuries. The mystical theology of Anselm of Canterbury and Bernard of Clairvaux followed, in turn, by the flowering and circulation of devotional works by members of the new mendicant orders (in particular, the Franciscans) were important elements in the growth of this devotional approach. Typifying this trend is an Anglo-Irish poem entitled 'Christ on the Cross' that appears in a fourteenth-century manuscript, British Library Harley 913 (*c.*1330), containing a number of religious poems, one of which is ascribed to a certain 'Friar Michael of Kildare'. This poem, written in the original in a form of Middle English that can claim to be among the earliest written examples of 'Hiberno-English', invites its hearers to

> Look at his nails, in hand and also in foot, and how the streams of his precious blood flow. Begin at his head and look all the way to his toes. You will find in his body only excruciating suffering and affliction.[5]

---

4 See especially Salvador Ryan, 'A slighted source', *Cambrian Medieval Celtic Studies*, 48 (winter 2004), 75–99 at 76. This view of Eleanor Knott and others has been largely revised in more recent years.   **5** Angela Lucas, *Anglo-Irish poems of the Middle Ages* (Dublin, 1995), pp 122–4 at p. 123.

This was the sort of poem in which, in Angela Lucas' words, 'we are made to feel the pain and see the blood'.[6] The manuscript, which contains English, Latin and Norman French verse, is heavily influenced by Franciscan themes and some of its material, such as poems on the Ten Commandments, the Seven Deadly Sins and the need for repentance, may well have been used as an aid to preaching.[7] The link between visualizing Christ's abject suffering on the cross and the aim of eliciting genuine contrition from the sinner is effectively communicated in the same poem in the invitation which runs 'Look at your Lord, man, where he hangs on the cross, and weep, if you can, tears entirely of blood'.[8] The reference to tears of blood here firmly underlines the ideal that was being held before the listener: bloody tears were a very striking indication of depth of sorrow. From about the thirteenth century, the Virgin Mary was depicted as weeping bloody tears of grief on the death of her son, one of the earliest examples being found in a thirteenth-century Latin versified life of Mary, a devotional work known in short as the *Vita Rhythmica*.[9] Here then, the sinner was expected to imitate the sorrowful Virgin in her response to the passion, even if she herself had no sin to bemoan. Another Anglo-Irish poem, entitled 'Fall and Passion', also found in the Harley 913 manuscript, has Mary weep bloody tears: 'when she saw him die on the cross she had no more than four bitter tears of blood to shed'.[10] By the fifteenth century, Mary's tears of blood had become a fairly common feature in native Irish bardic religious poetry. As the Franciscan order expanded into Gaelic Irish areas of the country, and especially with the rise of the Observant reform movement, it increasingly attracted members of the native Irish into its ranks – and many of these were drawn from members of the native literary elites, including the hereditary bardic families. Figures such as the late-fourteenth-century Tadhg Camchosach Ó Dálaigh and the fifteenth-century Observant friar, Philip Bocht Ó hUiginn, widely regarded as the 'best versifier of devotion' in his day, are two notable examples of this.[11] This close connection between the late medieval Irish mendicants (particularly the Franciscans) and the native learned class would be particularly significant for the spread of religious ideas and new forms of devotion, including the increasingly affective approach to meditating on Christ's life and, more pointedly, his death. This relationship has recently been traced in some depth by Edel Bhreathnach.[12]

---

6 Ibid., p. 195.   7 Colmán N. Ó Clabaigh, *The Franciscans in Ireland, 1400–1534* (Dublin, 2002), p. 140.
8 Lucas, *Anglo-Irish poems of the Middle Ages*, p. 123.   9 *Vita Beate Virginis Marie et Salvatoris Rhythmica*, ed. Adolf Vögtlin, *BLVS*, 180 (Tübingen, 1880). See especially Andrew Breeze, 'The Virgin's tears of blood', *Celtica*, 20 (1988), 110–22; for the wider tradition behind this motif, see Vernam Hull, 'Celtic tears of blood', *Zeitschrift für celtische Philologie*, 25 (1952), 226–36.   10 Ibid., 111.   11 Ó Clabaigh, *The Franciscans in Ireland*, p. 141. For the wider development of mendicant orders in late medieval Ireland, see Colmán Ó Clabaigh, *The friars in Ireland, 1224–1540* (Dublin, 2012).   12 Edel Bhreathnach, 'The mendicant orders and vernacular Irish learning in the late medieval period', *Irish Historical Studies*, 37:147 (May 2011), 357–75. See also Salvador Ryan, 'The devotional landscape of medieval Irish cultural Catholicism *inter hibernicos et inter anglicos*' in Oliver Rafferty (ed.), *Irish Catholic identities* (Manchester, 2013), pp 62–76.

MEDIEVAL RELIGIOUS TEXTS IN IRISH LIBRARY CATALOGUES

Before we examine in a little detail some examples of affective piety that emerged in Gaelic Irish religious texts of the fifteenth and sixteenth centuries, it is worth turning to what little we can glean from Irish library lists of the late medieval period. Given the paucity of surviving records, we are fortunate that a codex from the Franciscan library at Youghal in Co. Cork is extant, which documents holdings from the period 1490–1523. From this catalogue, one can make the reasonable assumption that other Irish Franciscan friaries of comparable size must have held broadly similar collections. We will confine ourselves to mention of some notable spiritual and devotional works of the age. Among the volumes found at Youghal were the following: the *Legenda Aurea* (Golden Legend), whose hagiographical accounts were hugely influential; a book of devotion containing 'many litanies of the saints and Richard the hermit in one volume' (this most likely refers to the English mystical writer Richard Rolle/Richard of Hampole, *c.*1290–1349); the sermons of the Blessed Abbot Bernard (of Clairvaux) in one volume (which most likely included his famous sermons on the Song of Songs); the *De Contemptu Mundi* of Lothar of Segni (later Pope Innocent III); the *Imitatio Christi* of Thomas à Kempis; the *Soliloquium* of Bonaventure (addressed to a person considering religious life and outlining the four mental exercises to be undergone in order to arrive at contemplation of God); a copy of the ubiquitous devotional work, *Meditationes vitae Christi*, here recorded as a life of Christ by St Bonaventure (this ascription was common at the time; however the work was most probably by the thirteenth-century Franciscan, Johannes de Caulibus); the Life of Christ by the German Carthusian, Ludolph of Saxony (*c.*1295–1377); and a collection of fifteenth-century sermons by a Dutch preacher, Paul Wan.[13] The other substantial late medieval library catalogue that survives is that of the Fitzgeralds, earls of Kildare, residing at Maynooth. This dates from the early sixteenth century and has recently been examined by Aisling Byrne.[14] Given the resources of the Fitzgeralds (and their standing as successive lord deputies of King Henry VII and King Henry VIII in Ireland), it is likely to have been an exceptionally impressive collection in its own day. It has some titles in common with the Franciscan library at Youghal (such as the *Dialogues* of Gregory the Great) and possesses what seems to be a French version of the *Legenda Aurea* and what Byrne has suggested is an Irish translation of the *Meditationes vitae Christi*. There is also an Irish translation of the *Liber de Passione Christi* attributed to Bernard of Clairvaux, a text that appears in a number of other devotional collections of the period.[15] The manner in which works found in an ecclesiastical library (such as that of the friars at Youghal) could find themselves turning up in the devotional

---

13 For the full catalogue, see Ó Clabaigh, *The Franciscans in Ireland*, pp 158–80.   **14** Aisling Byrne, 'The earls of Kildare and their books at the end of the Middle Ages', *The Library*, 7th ser., 14:2 (June 2013), 129–53. **15** See, for example, a table of some common devotional treatises which appear in Gaelic Irish manuscripts of the fifteenth through seventeenth centuries: Salvador Ryan, 'Wily women of God in Breifne's devotional collections' in Brendan Scott (ed.), *Culture and society in early modern Breifne/Cavan* (Dublin, 2009), pp 31–47.

collections of a secular lord can be seen in the example of the *Breviloquium* of Bonaventure. This short work of theological doctrine (compiled before 1257) is found in the Youghal catalogue, but it is also listed as appearing in part in a late fifteenth-century Irish manuscript, Bodleian Library MS B513 associated with the Mac Parrthaláin family of Breifne.[16] Interestingly, the section of the *Breviloquium* that appears in this devotional miscellany is specifically that concerning Christ's passion.

Although we do not possess any further surviving library catalogues from late medieval Ireland, we are, on occasion, afforded tantalizing glimpses of what must have been a much more vibrant intellectual and devotional culture than we have sometimes imagined to be the case; for instance, the evidence of a Lambeth Palace Library manuscript, MS 357, dating from the fifteenth century and originating in Duleek, Co. Meath, where there was located an Irish cell of Llanthony priory of the Canons Regular of St Augustine in Wales.[17] This includes Richard Rolle's *Super novem lectiones mortuorum* (his nine lessons on the Office of the Dead), the *De Laude Caritatis* of Hugh of St Victor (*c.*1096–1141), a work entitled *Meditaciones b. Bernardi de lamentacione b.v. marie et passione filii sui* (*Liber de passione Christi?*) and a prophecy attributed to Hildegard of Bingen. The popularity in Ireland of the mystical writer and hermit, Richard Rolle, is further attested in wills made by John Collyn, dean of Waterford in the late 1460s and 1470s, which allude to his possessing a copy of Rolle's commentary on the psalter.[18] We will also have cause to mention the early thirteenth-century Middle English 'Rule' for Anchorites, known as the *Ancrene Wisse*, in the course of our discussion. At this point, it is hardly surprising that this work may also have been known in Ireland. A late thirteenth- to early fourteenth-century manuscript from the Victorine abbey of St Thomas outside Dublin (Trinity College Dublin MS 97) contains a text known as 'The Dublin Rule', which is aimed at male anchorites and draws at least part of its inspiration from *Ancrene Wisse*.[19] Now that we have surveyed some of the evidence for the circulation of popular mystical and devotional texts in late medieval Ireland, we can turn to how affective piety (and particularly that associated with the love of Christ for souls and the response that was expected in return) manifested itself in some of the religious texts of late medieval Gaelic Ireland.

---

16 Brian Ó Cuív, *Catalogue of manuscripts in the Bodleian Library at Oxford and Oxford College Libraries* (Dublin, 2001), i, p. 256.   **17** See especially Kirsty Bennett, 'The book collections of Llanthony Priory from foundation until dissolution (*c.*1100–1538)', 2 vols (PhD, University of Kent, 2006). The link to the Lambeth Palace Library archives is as follows: http://archives.lambethpalacelibrary.org.uk/CalmView/Record.aspx?src=CalmView. Catalog&id=MSS%2f357 (accessed 29 Oct. 2014). I am grateful to Colmán Ó Clabaigh OSB for drawing my attention to this manuscript.   **18** See Niall Byrne, *The Register of St Saviour's Chantry of Waterford* (Dublin, 2013), pp 13, 54. Once again, I am grateful to Colmán Ó Clabaigh OSB for this reference.   **19** Colmán Ó Clabaigh, 'Anchorites in medieval Ireland' in Liz Herbert McAvoy (ed.), *Anchoritic traditions of medieval Europe* (Woodbridge, 2010), p. 169.

IRISH EXAMPLES OF AFFECTIVE PIETY AND COURTLY LOVE

In a tract on the Sacrament of Penance, *Scáthán Shacramuinte na hAithridhe* ('The Mirror of the Sacrament of Penance'), which was published in 1618, Aodh Mac Aingil,[20] an Irish Franciscan friar based at the Irish College of St Anthony in Louvain in the early seventeenth century, chose to employ the following language when speaking of the disposition of penitents:

> Therefore, the soul that accepted Christ as a lover in baptism, should spurn the adultery of the devil, i.e. sins, and to foster hatred for them, not only because of the punishment that comes to the soul (from sin), i.e. Hell for all eternity, but, principally, because of the love of God, its lover.[21]

Although Mac Aingil was writing at a much later date than the medieval authors we have been discussing, he was nevertheless using a language that would have been very familiar to most of them. In referring to Christ as lover or spouse, and the Devil as an adulterer, Mac Aingil was drawing on imagery that had a long tradition in both Jewish and Christian writing. In the prophetic literature of the Old Testament, especially Isaiah, Hosea and Ezekiel, God is often represented as spouse, the love that unites him to Israel being compared to the nuptial love of a married couple. In Hosea, for instance, we find similar imagery to that used by Mac Aingil in his tract on Penance. The suffering of Hosea on account of his spouse's betrayal serves to illuminate Israel's unfaithfulness to her God and, by extension, the love that God continues to show Israel in spite of this:

> Therefore I will now allure her and bring her into the wilderness, and speak tenderly to her … On that day, says the Lord, you will call me 'My husband' and no longer will you call me 'My Baal' ['my Master'].[22]

However, this tender image is absent only a few verses earlier when God threatens his spouse, Israel, vowing to put an end to her whoring and even stating that he will make her like a wilderness, turn her into a parched land and block her way (to her lover) with thorns.[23]

This literary tension between the anger of the rejected spouse and his loving mercy would also appear in depictions of the relationship between the crucified Christ and sinners in the later Middle Ages. In a well-known article, first published in 1962, Rosemary Woolf argued that the image of the warrior Christ riding into battle (and

20 For the life of Mac Aingil, see Mícheál Mac Craith, 'Mac Cathmhaoil (Mac Aingil), Aodh (MacCaghwell, Hugh; Cavellus, Hugo)', *Dictionary of Irish biography online* dib.cambridge.org/quicksearch.do;jsessionid= AF9EF5AA6111D8132BA475DDD23ADA9B (accessed 19 Sept. 2014) **21** Aodh Mac Aingil, *Scáthán Shacramuinte na hAithridhe*, ed. Cainneach Ó Maonaigh (Baile Átha Cliath [Dublin], 1952), p. 9. My translation. **22** Hos 2: 14–16. New revised standard version. **23** Hos 2:2–3; 2:6.

warring variously against the devil and mankind's sinfulness), a common means of speaking about the crucifixion and death of Christ, underwent a transformation in the age of the *amour courtois*. The primary motivation behind Christ's passion also shifts and his foray is now spurred by an intense love for his people – albeit unrequited – which extends to him allowing his own weapons to turn against him. These weapons of crucifixion (the *arma Christi*), which he carries, are no longer primarily directed at an enemy but, rather, point towards himself, as the emphasis on Christ's physical suffering increases and he is increasingly fashioned, quite literally, as the Image of Pity of late medieval art.[24] For instance, Christ's knightly shield (which was conceived of as his human body, covering his divinity), is depicted as being pierced through in death for his lover. In the thirteenth-century manual for anchoresses, the *Ancrene Wisse*, the piercing of Christ's body armour is regarded as the key to releasing his love:

> His beloved should see by it how he bought her love, letting his shield be pierced, his side opened to show her his heart, to show her how openly, how deeply he loved her, and to draw out her heart.[25]

The image of Christ as chivalric knight is also prominent in the writings of Julian of Norwich, although perhaps not given the attention it deserves, as argued by Maria Prozesky.[26] Berndt Hamm has observed elsewhere in this volume how the incarnated God allows himself to be wounded for the sake of sinners, remarking how his inner love for humanity is manifested through the outer opening of his body (the side-wound).[27] The wooing Christ of the *Ancrene Wisse* sets out his stall in order to win the anchoresses' fervour: he points out that he is the fairest, richest and highest-born of their would-be suitors, and that he is courteous and generous. To illustrate the latter (and to relate it more closely to his passion) he states that 'one says of a generous man that his hands are pierced – as mine are'.[28] In response, the anchoresses were encouraged to 'reach out for him with as much love as you sometimes have for some man'.[29] Hamm has illustrated, by means of the fifteenth-century image of a Benedictine 'Nonnenmalerei' from Eichstätt, how the soul of this nun was conceived of as intimately united with her wooing bridegroom in his open-heart wound.[30]

The development of the idea of Christ the lover of the soul in the later Middle Ages owed much to the convergence of a number of influences from the twelfth and

---

24 Rosemary Woolf, 'The theme of Christ the lover-knight in medieval English literature' in Heather O'Donoghue (ed.), *Art and doctrine: essays on medieval literature* (London, 1986), pp 99–118.   25 *Anchoritic spirituality: Ancrene Wisse and associated works*, ed. and trans. Anne Savage and Nicholas Watson (Mahwah, NJ, 1991), p. 192; Bernard McGinn, *The flowering of mysticism: men and women in the new mysticism, 1200–1350* (New York, 1998), p. 189.   26 Maria Prozesky, 'Imitatio in Julian of Norwich: Christ the knight, fruitio and the pleasures of courtesy', *Parergon*, 30:1 (2013), 141–58.   27 Hamm, this volume, p. 16.   28 *Anchoritic spirituality*, pp 193–4; Denis Renevey, '1215–1349: texts' in *The Cambridge companion to medieval English mysticism*, ed. Samuel Fanous and Vincent Gillespie (Cambridge, 2011), p. 94.   29 *Anchoritic spirituality*, p. 197.   30 Hamm, this volume, p. 18.

thirteenth centuries onwards. One of the most powerful of these was a renewed interest in the sensual imagery of the Song of Songs, exemplified best, perhaps, by Bernard of Clairvaux's eighty-six sermons on this biblical book alone, to say nothing of the works of his successors. As noted by Brian Patrick McGuire, this led to a situation in which 'the very monks who had denied to themselves the pleasures of physical love were thus bombarded by its images'.[31] Imagery from the Song of Songs would also fuse with borrowings from medieval romance in examples such as the mystical poetry of thirteenth-century friars. Alessandro Vettori remarks that,

> In keeping with biblical and theological models, erotic love was regarded as the most fitting metonym for divine expressions of love toward human beings, and it was frequently adopted as a metaphor in poetry. In Franciscan poets of the thirteenth century, the secular doctrine of courtly love and love formulations in the tradition of the Christian Church Fathers come together and amalgamate.[32]

This imagery was not confined, however, to Franciscan poets on the Continent, nor indeed to medieval English anchoritic texts or to English religious lyrics that praised Christ the wooing Lover-Knight. An affective piety, which adopted quite a carnal approach to passion devotion, can also be found in late medieval Irish sources.

THE LOVE-WOUNDS OF CHRIST

Attuned to the devotional trends of the age, the professional poets of Gaelic Ireland who, for the most part, were laymen, devoted a large portion of their art to exploring the theme of Christ's passion and death, and in particular the cult of Christ's five wounds. Pre-eminent among these wounds was the side- or heart-wound; this was conceived of as the door to the well of Christ's love. In the Middle English allegory of the 'Charter of Christ', which was adopted by Irish bardic poets such as Tadhg Óg Ó hUiginn and Philip Bocht Ó hUiginn in the fifteenth century, the crucified Christ is depicted as writing a charter of peace between God and humanity – his skin forming the parchment and the lance the pen with which it was written. Tellingly, Christ's breast wound is conceived of as the inkwell into which the pen is dipped and his blood the ink.[33] The sixteenth-century Irish poet Tuileagna Mac Torna Ó Maolchonaire calls the Charter of Christ a 'testament of love' in a poem written in anticipation of a pilgrimage to the site of St Patrick's Purgatory (Lough Derg).[34] That Ó Maolchonaire

31 Brian Patrick McGuire, '*c.*1080–1215: culture and history' in *The Cambridge companion to medieval English mysticism*, p. 40.   **32** Alessandro Vettori, *Poets of divine love* (New York, 2004), p. 112.   **33** For a very short introduction to this allegory, see Salvador Ryan, 'Signed in blood' in Salvador Ryan and Brendan Leahy (eds), *Treasures of Irish Christianity*, 2 (Dublin, 2013), pp 85–7. Also Andrew Breeze, 'The Charter of Christ in medieval English, Welsh and Irish', *Celtica*, 19 (1987), 111–20. For a recent comprehensive treatment of the Charter in the context of Christ's 'love-deed', see Cristina Maria Cervone, *Poetics of the Incarnation* (Philadelphia, 2012), pp 86–105.

chooses to call Christ's charter (which is his crucified body) a document of love recalls
the conceit, found in the so-called English 'Long Charter' text, of the 'loue dede'
('love-deed'), encompassing both the act of Christ's sacrifice on the cross for love and
the charter document of Christ's crucified body which formally attests to what Christ
bequeaths to humanity: namely, the gift of the land of heaven.[35]

In medieval contemplative literature, the heart-wound was often regarded as the
location in which the Christian was expected to reach the pinnacle of spiritual ascent
– the state of *unitio* or union with God. It is hardly surprising that this wound was
frequently conceived of in sexual terms. In the words of Denise L. Despres, 'the
eroticism of the wound, which is linked to parturition, nursing and penetration, is
inescapable'.[36] According to some Gaelic Irish bardic poets, it is only when Christ
receives the heart-wound on the cross that his love and mercy are released. The
sixteenth-century bardic poet Muirchertach Ó Cobhthaigh expresses it in this way in
the poem *Dlighidh liaigh leigheas a charad* ('A leech should cure his friend'):

> When his body's veins tortured him
> And broke open the door of his heart for his folk
> They had almost lost the game (of salvation)
> And no other man came to save them.[37]

Ó Cobhthaigh follows in the tradition of poets such as the fifteenth-century Tadhg
Óg Ó hUiginn who describes in graphic terms Christ's sufferings on the cross in the
poem *Slán ar n-a mharbhadh mac Dé* ('Alive again after death is God's Son'):

> A burning affliction was the depth of his wounds, the bursting of his breast, the
> splitting of his feet's white skin and his hand's reddened palms.

> And as yet I have said nothing of his wounding by the thorny crown which
> compressed his head and by which the covering of his veins was burst.[38]

Yet there may be something more to these bardic verses than mere physical
suffering. A thirteenth-century mystical text, *The seven manners of loving* by the
Cistercian, Beatrice of Nazareth (1200–68), which is a good example of what has been
termed *minnemystik* or 'courtly mysticism', causes us to pause for thought. According
to Beatrice, the fourth manner of love involves 'great pleasure' and 'great sorrow' – the

---

34 Shane Leslie, *Saint Patrick's Purgatory* (London, 1932), pp 167–72.   35 See especially Cervone's discussion of
this in *Poetics of the Incarnation*, pp 86–94.   36 Denise L. Despres, 'Ecstasy, intimacy and Middle English
contemplative culture' in *A companion to British literature*, 1, ed. Robert de Maria Jr, Heesok Chang and
Samantha Zacher (Chichester, 2014), p. 239.   37 Lambert McKenna (ed.), 'Christ our Saviour', *Studies*, 38
(1949), 187, stanza 28.   38 Lambert McKenna (ed.), *Aithdioghluim Dána*, 2 vols (Dublin, 1939–40), poem 78,
stanzas 24–5.

experience of the *abyssus caritatis* or 'abyss of love'. The fifth, meanwhile, combines a heightened sense of passion and madness in which it seems that the soul is wounded again and again. Beatrice extends the traditional theme of the *vulnus amoris* ('wound of love') based on Song of Songs 2:4 in the following way:

> It seems to the soul that the veins are bursting, the blood spilling, the marrow withering, the bones softening, the heart burning, the throat parching, so that the face and all the members perceive the inner heat, and this is the madness of love. At this time she also feels an arrow piercing through her heart all the way to the throat and beyond to the brain, as if she would lose her mind.[39]

Here, though, the human soul experiences the physical symptoms of longing for Christ, which are almost a mirror image of the passion (*passio*) of Christ on the cross. As discussed in Rob Faesen's essay above, Hadewjich's Pentecost vision involved similar imagery:

> such madness and anxiousness beset my mind that it seemed to me that, if I did not content my Beloved, and if my Beloved did not fulfill my desire, I would go mad and going mad I would die. On that day my mind was beset so anxiously and painfully by desirous love that all my separate limbs threatened to break and all my separate veins were in travail.[40]

The part played by the arrow in Beatrice's text, however, is significant. In Irish bardic verse on Christ's passion, the Roman soldier Longinus was considered to have unlocked Christ's mercy on the cross by the act of piercing his side with a lance. In the poem *Deacair aighneas éarca ríogh* ('Terrible to hear the King's *éiric* claimed') by the sixteenth-century poet Diarmuid Ó Cobhthaigh, Christ enters on his power when his side is pierced, and thereby 'vast was the harvest of humanity saved when it beheld thy only Son's wounded breast'. Indeed, the poet continues, 'the man who pierced him, now a prince in rank, went unpunished into his house; never was (the infliction of) a wound so well rewarded'. In a later verse, Ó Cobhthaigh notes that 'the furnace of his breast was heated – surely this proved his love'.[41] In the case of Beatrice of Nazareth, the lance, which was understood to draw forth a torrent of love from Christ's heart, works in reverse; assuming the form of an arrow piercing the human heart, it causes the heart to lose itself in a madness of love. Yet in the case of Gertrude of Helfta, the imagery is more powerful still, as discussed in Henning Laugerud's essay in this volume. Gertrude asked a companion to pray before the crucifix that her (Gertrude's) heart might be transfixed by Christ's arrow of love and held fast by the power of his

---

39 McGinn, *The flowering of mysticism*, p. 172. This is McGinn's own rendering of the original, drawing on two separate translations. See note on p. 405. **40** Faesen, this volume, p. 37. **41** Lambert McKenna (ed.), *Aithdioghluim Dána*, poem 63, stanzas 7, 12 and 30.

divinity in order that her heart might henceforth be incapable of holding on to any earthly thing.[42] For the sixteenth-century Irish poet, Tadhg Óg Ó Dálaigh (d. 1520), the lance acted more as signpost than arrow. In the poem *Ní cluain ghabhála grás Dé* ('No appropriated field is God's grace'), he speaks of how Christ issues an invitation to humanity to enter into his heart, the point of the lance of Longinus showing the way:

> God wished not us to be kept out of his heart;
> The spear in his breast points the way in for us;
> No man was excluded from it,
> Though men have ever wished to keep a foe at a distance.[43]

The invitation to union with Christ on the cross is exemplified in the devotional work entitled *Stimulus Amoris* or 'The Prickynge of Love' attributed to the late-thirteenth-century Franciscan, James of Milan. This Latin work was translated into many languages including Irish (as *An bhroid ghrádha*) and enjoyed wide circulation. It is found in fragmentary form, for instance, in a late fifteenth-century Irish manuscript (British Library MS Additional 11809), written by the famous scribe Uilliam Mac an Leagha and discovered hidden in the walls of the ruined Hore Abbey at Cashel, Co. Tipperary, in the late eighteenth century. The manuscript also contains a number of other devotional texts that exemplify the affective piety of the age, such as Irish translations of the following texts: the *Meditationes vitae Christi* (which had been first translated to Irish as recently as 1461 by a choral canon of Killala in Co. Mayo), the thirteenth-century *Vita Rhythmica* life of the Virgin Mary, the Middle English 'Long Charter of Christ' text, and a fourteenth-century treatise, composed by a spiritual adviser to a nun, and which was entitled *Instructio pie Vivendi*.[44] These are just some of the Irish vernacular translations of Latin devotional texts that were commissioned in the fifteenth century. This mirrors similar developments elsewhere, captured in Michael Sargent's insightful remark that owing to the translating industry of the fourteenth and early fifteenth centuries from Latin to Middle English 'the fifteenth and early sixteenth centuries were the great age of thirteenth- and fourteenth-century spirituality'.[45]

Manuscript collections such as these support the argument that many of these texts appealed to a similar devotional market. In any case, in the twenty-third chapter of the *Stimulus Amoris*, the author speaks of how meditation on the Passion leads the soul

---

42 Laugurud, this volume, p. 53.   **43** *Aithdioghluim Dána*, poem 71, stanza 35.   **44** See *Catalogue of Irish manuscripts in the British Library [formerly British Museum]*, ed. Robin Flower, ii (repr. Dublin, 1992), pp 545–51. The original Latin text was composed at the House of Saint Victor in Paris, which belonged to the Augustinian Canons, an order that enjoyed great popularity in medieval Ireland. For the Irish translation (by Uilleam Mac an Leagha), see John McKechnie (ed.), *Instructio pie vivendi et superna meditandi* (Dublin, 1933 and 1946). **45** Quoted in Michelle Karnes, *Imagination, meditation and cognition in the Middle Ages* (Chicago, 2011), p. 226.

into the pierced side and thus into the heart of Jesus. Walter Hilton's less explicit rendering of James of Milan's Latin text reads 'Thou shalt then come to his heart and there thou mayst rest thee as in thy bedstead'.[46] The twenty-sixth chapter of *Stimulus Amoris* treats at length of the spiritual joys that follow after the quieting of the soul by spiritual 'inebriation'.[47] James of Milan presents the union of the soul and God in terms of a mystical joining of wounds. Having felt his way into his wounded spouse, the lover's soul becomes wounded with love (experiencing the *vulnus amoris*) and, thus wounded, he applies his wound to that of his lover (Christ), wound being joined to wound. Here, in a reversal of the Song of Songs tradition, Christ becomes the feminized lover. One commentator, Wolfgang Riehle, posits a play on the words *vulnus* and *vulva*, a claim that is substantiated by the strong connection between the two in medieval religious art.[48] Much of this imagery can be discomfiting for the modern reader who is perhaps not normally accustomed to a blending of the religious and the erotic. And yet, as Mary Carruthers reminds us in a recent work (in the context of a different example), the 'shock of the carnal/spirit duality' recalls 'the essential paradox of incarnation'.[49] This is what Hamm has called elsewhere in this volume 'the most intimate somatic-spiritual communication to people of all time'.[50] In the sixteenth-century Irish bardic poem *Mairg as aighne i n-aghaidh breithimh* ('I pity the man who argues his own case with a judge'), Diarmaid Ó Cobhthaigh speaks of God accompanying humanity in exploring the depths of Christ's side-wound in a manner that cannot but evoke the erotic imagery of some of the continental mystics:

> God explored with us the depths of Christ's breast,
> Sore for his Son that exploring!
> He led us into the centre of it;
> How proud we should be to be akin to such a guide![51]

James of Milan's idea of passion meditation as 'an entering into Christ's wounds and a journey towards his heart',[52] is echoed in an undated poem by Brian Caoch Ó Dálaigh who attests that 'the wound in his breast is the way to his heart'.[53] But the

---

46 Walter Hilton, *The Goad of Love* (ed. Clare Kirchberger, repr. Whitefish, MT, 1995), p. 143.   **47** The idea of 'spiritual intoxication' is also found in the *Instructio pie vivendi*, where it is described as follows: 'This is the true felicity of the soul, and the blessed soul which possesses the spiritual felicity wholly is the one which has endeavoured to turn frequently the mouth of the heart to drink from the precious vessel, i.e. the body of the Lord, which was pierced and often tormented so that the beloved disciple might drink all that he required from it and be filled with the temperate nourishment and spiritual intoxication which contains the bliss of the soul fully … as the drunkard weeps, be you afflicted by tears of devotion … as the drunkard sings, rejoice you in the melody of your heart particularly … as the drunkard laughs, fill yourself with the heavenly joy … as the drunkard speaks extravagantly, be you filled incessantly with the heavenly glory'. Máirín Ní Dhonnchadha (ed.), 'Mary, Eve and the Church, *c*.600–1800' in Máirín Ní Dhonnchadha et al. (eds), *The Field Day anthology of Irish writing*, 4 (New York, 2002), pp 141–2.   **48** Wolfgang Riehle, *The Middle English mystics*, trans. Bernard Standring (London, 1981), p. 46.   **49** Mary Carruthers, *The experience of beauty in the Middle Ages* (Oxford, 2013), p. 4. **50** Hamm, this volume, p. 15.   **51** Lambert McKenna (ed.), *Aithdioghluim Dána*, poem 66, stanza 36. **52** Karnes, *Imagination*, p. 155.   **53** Lambert McKenna (ed.), 'Our salvation', *Studies*, 38:3 (1949), 468.

breast-wound of Christ was also conceived of as a place of refuge for humanity (as early as Gregory the Great in the sixth century, and later adopted by Bernard of Clairvaux and Bonaventure the 'clefts in the rock' referenced in the *Song of Songs* 2:14 were associated with Christ's wounds).[54] Ó Cobhthaigh identifies Christ's breast-wound as 'the only ship-haven for Eve's race … wherein he sheltered us … the wealth of that harbour, his heart, should induce Eve's race to return to it'. He also reminds Christ how he steered a 'ship of rescue … for thy children into the haven of thy bleeding heart'.[55]

LOVE, SUFFERING AND DEATH

Most fundamentally, however, the opening up of Christ's breast-wound was understood as a sign of Christ's love. The sixteenth-century Irish poet, Fearghal Ó Cionga, in the poem *Mairg as urra re héacht ríogh* ('Tis a grave thing to be responsible for [ordering] a King's exploit), remarked: 'He might easily have saved himself from the spear in his breast; he let his side be pierced; never have we experienced such love!'[56] The spear itself was sometimes spoken of in terms of a measuring rod of that love (only to be surpassed), as in the example of the unattributed bardic poem *Leigheas an bheatha bás Dé*:

> Deep as the spear was plunged in thy breast,
> Deeper still, deeper than those gory points in the heart,
> Went thy excessive love for me;
> 'tis not hard for me, therefore [to be saved].[57]

That 'excessive love' of Christ also became associated with the cause of his death in the minds of some Irish poets. For instance, another unattributed poem entitled *Íocadh Críost cumaoin a mháthar* ('May Christ requite his mother's service') recalled how 'the heat of his love [was] so inflamed that it killed him, the third of the three branches'.[58] Meanwhile, in the poem *Mairg nach taithigh go teagh ríogh* ('Woe to all who frequent not the Lord's house'), Ó Cobhthaigh speaks of 'the Son who died in a transport of love'[59] and in another poem, *Díon cloinne i n-éag a n-athar* ('The death of their Father caused his children's salvation'), he depicts Christ (here spoken of as 'father') dying of love on the cross:

> The death of their Father, Lord and Judge of the world,
> Caused his children's salvation;

---

54 Karnes, *Imagination*, p. 156.   55 Lambert McKenna (ed.), *Aithdioghluim Dána*, poem 66, stanzas 10, 23.   56 Ibid., poem 59, stanza 38.   57 Ibid., poem 95, stanza 6.   58 Lambert McKenna (ed.), 'To the Blessed Virgin', *Irish Monthly*, 58 (1930), 467, stanza 12.   59 McKenna (ed.), *Aithdioghluim Dána*, poem 67, stanza 27.

Their father died as he could not keep (within his heart)
His love for his race.[60]

In the religious verse (*laude*) of the thirteenth-century Italian Franciscan poet Jacapone da Todi (d. *c.*1306), we find a close correlation between love and death in the relationship between Christ and the soul. The bridegroom promises his unfaithful bride that he is willing to die for her if only she will return to him. In order to achieve union with Christ, the bride leaves everything behind, including her clothes, and she ascends the cross with Christ. The following exchange occurs between bride and bridegroom in Jacapone's *lauda* number 42:

> Soul, since you have come to me,
> Gladly will I answer you. Come,
> See, this is my bed – the cross.
> Here, we will be one. Come to me
> And I will quench your thirst.
>
> O my love, naked will I scale that cross,
> To suffer and to die with you.
> Lord, clasped close in your embrace,
> In joy will I suffer and die.[61]

In the mystical literature of the Middle Ages, much of which was directed at a female religious audience, special emphasis was placed on achieving *imitatio Christi* by mounting the cross and becoming one with Christ in his passion. Caroline Walker Bynum explains:

> Women's efforts to imitate this Christ involved becoming the crucified, not just patterning themselves after or expanding their compassion toward, but fusing with, the body on the cross. Both in fact and in imagery the imitatio, the fusion, was achieved in two ways: through asceticism and through eroticism.[62]

The response of the bride to Christ's love was essentially that: to be crucified with him through poverty, shame and suffering until death: that was to be the life of the anchoress. This is clearly seen in a thirteenth-century English anchoress's prayer called *The Wooing of Our Lord*:

> My body will hang with your body, nailed on the cross, fastened, transfixed within four walls. And I will hang with you and nevermore come from my cross

60 Ibid., poem 64, stanza 1.   61 Jacapone da Todi, *The Lauds*, trans. Serge Hughes and Elizabeth Hughes (New York, 1982), pp 145–6; Vettori, *Poets of divine love*, p. 135.   62 Caroline Walker Bynum, *Fragmentation and redemption* (New York, 1992), p. 131.

until I die – for then I shall leap from the cross into rest, from grief into joy and eternal happiness. Ah Jesus, so sweet it is to hang with you.[63]

And yet this impulse, reminiscent of St Paul's assertion in Galatians 2:19 that he has been crucified with Christ and that he no longer lives, but Christ lives in him, was not confined to anchorites. In the anonymous bardic poem *Dursan do mhartra, a Mheic Dé* ('Cruel thy suffering O Son of God'), the poet requests that he share in Christ's passion. This included being beaten by the hammers that struck Christ, being assailed by the thorn-spikes that gnawed at his flesh and being pierced by seven shafts of sorrow as Mary was (here he is perhaps influenced by what were sometimes referred to as the *arma Virginis*, the seven swords that pierced Mary's heart). His final request, however, runs: 'May I mount the cross for thy sake and suffer death for thy death; may my blood be shed in thine; may I be wounded in thy wounding'.[64]

BIRTH AND RE-BIRTH

There is yet another aspect of the side-wound of Christ that is worth exploring briefly, namely its being understood as the birth canal of the Church. Patristic writers such as Tertullian, Augustine and Isidore of Seville were fond of drawing parallels between the Genesis depiction of Eve being born from the side of Adam and the 'New Eve' (the Church) emerging from the side of Christ on the Cross. The blood and water flowing from the side of Christ were often understood to symbolize Baptism and Eucharist, but also, in some moralized bibles of the thirteenth century, they were linked to the Sacrament of Penance. In the poem *Mairg nach doirteann a dhéara* ('Woe to him who sheds not tears'), the early seventeenth-century Irish poet, Fearghal Óg Mac an Bhaird, makes what could be argued is a tenuous connection between the image of Christ as 'Mother' on the Cross (an image that was not uncommon in the Middle Ages)[65] and sincere contrition:

> As his heart was drained of water for our love
> Our tears shed in spite of (?) the world's charm
> – great proof of love –
> Suffice to cleanse our souls.[66]

Here the water flowing from Christ's side (which might be likened to the rupture of membranes before a woman gives birth) stimulates the shedding of another kind of water – the tears of the contrite sinner. Here a direct link was made between the

63 'The Wooing of Our Lord' in *Anchoritic spirituality*, ed. Anne Savage and Nicholas Watson, p. 256; McGinn, *The flowering of mysticism*, p. 190.   64 McKenna (ed.), *Aithdioghluim Dána*, poem 92, stanzas 7, 18.   65 See especially the classic study by Bynum, *Jesus as Mother*.   66 Lambert McKenna (ed.), 'Sorrow for sin', *Irish Monthly*, 56 (1928), 438, stanza 19.

passion of Christ and the response of the soul in repentance and contrition, a movement that was a favourite of medieval Franciscan preachers. The association that I have made between the water flowing from Christ's side and a birthing mother's 'breaking of the waters', curious though it may sound to modern ears, would not have been at all unusual for a medieval monk. Indeed, as Bynum reminds us, in the twelfth to fifteenth centuries it was common in Cistercian and Carthusian writings to imagine Christ as a heavily pregnant woman and the renewed human race to which he was about to give birth on the Cross, huddled into his heart. One thirteenth-century female Carthusian wrote as follows:

> For when the hour of your delivery came you were placed on the hard board of the cross … and your nerves and all your veins were broken. And truly it is no surprise that your veins burst when in one day you gave birth to the whole world.[67]

And yet, in a remarkable passage from James of Milan's *Stimulus Amoris*, quoted by Michelle Karnes, the meditant who has entered the wounds of Christ (approaching them as shelter wherein he is fed with delightful food and intoxicated with Christ's drink) becomes fearful of being 'birthed' forth into the world. Here is how he ruminates on the prospect:

> But I fear greatly lest the time for birth arrive, and I be expelled from these delights that I enjoy. But certainly, even if he births me, he will have to give me milk from his breasts as a mother, wash me with his hands, carry me with his arms, console me with his kisses, and hold me in his lap. I know what I will do. Even if he gives birth to me, I know his wounds are always open, and through them I will enter into his womb, and repeat this until I am joined to him inseparably.[68]

It is difficult not to spot echoes here (at least in part) of Isaiah 66:11–12. On the possibility of re-entering Christ's wounds, Susannah Biernoff comments that

> the sacrificial body empties itself out in an eternal flow of blood, but it is also a womb that can be re-entered. Jesus as mother gives birth through his side and re-envelops his children in the deep crevices of his flesh.[69]

In commenting on imagery found in Julian of Norwich (*c.*1342–*c.*1416), Bynum captures a similar concern when she remarks that 'To Julian, the blood poured out of

---

67 Bynum, *Jesus as mother*, p. 153.   **68** Karnes, *Imagination*, p. 157.   **69** Susannah Biernoff, *Sight and embodiment in the Middle Ages*, p. 161.

a mother God has overtones of uterine and birthing blood, although it is significant that Julian sees Christians as nestled into a God out of whom they shall never come'.[70]

The passion poetry of the bardic poets is full of references to the fecundity of Christ on the cross and, indeed, to the fruitfulness of the cross itself. Ó Cobhthaigh particularly enjoys playing with this image as in this instance from *Mairg as aighne i n-aghaidh breithimh*:

> Men are the blossoms of the fruitful, heavy laden tree,
> And so that tree is as a fruitful wood
> And bore all men as its blossoms on its top.[71]

In the poem *Deacair aighneas éarca ríogh*, Ó Cobhthaigh speaks of the flowing blood of Christ as sustaining the new life of the human race:

> The blood rain of Thy Son's wounds is the shower that made our seed grow. It was a blessing for the children for whom his side was pierced; the heavier the rain the brighter the sunshine after it![72]

For Ó Cobhthaigh, the preparation for this new life was made by the lance or spear that prepared the ground of Christ's flesh for humanity's growth, as shown in this stanza from *Fiú a bheatha bás tiarna* ('The Lord's death is as valuable as was his life'): 'With the spear that pierced his breast, he ploughed the field whence he reaped a rich harvest of humanity'.[73]

INFIDELITY AND CAPTURE

But for Gaelic Irish poets, too, there was also the need to flee to Christ's wounds for protection and shelter against the advancing storm (and thus to return to the site of one's birth). Yet not everyone chose to do so. In such cases, where individuals were not prepared to enter willingly into Christ's heart-wound, they would need to be gathered in some other way. In the poem *Daingean Connradh fa Chairt Ríogh* ('Strong is a Contract Drawn up on a Royal Document'), the poet Brian Caoch Ó Dálaigh speaks of a red net of breast-blood spread across the stream flowing from Christ's side-wound; and the sense is of this bloody net acting as a camouflage that hides the hunting Christ from an unsuspecting human race.[74] There is also a somewhat obscure reference by Muirchertach Ó Cobhthaigh in *Dlighidh liaigh leigheas a charad* that relates how 'Before he [Christ] had finished the "round game" it had left a mark on his right side; he arranged his folk over the board of his heart; a full board had never yet been won'.[75]

---

70 Bynum, *Wonderful blood*, p. 207.   71 McKenna (ed.), *Aithdioghluim Dána*, poem 66, stanza 34.   72 Ibid., poem 63, stanza 29.   73 Ibid., poem 65, stanza 30.   74 Lambert McKenna (ed.), 'Our Salvation', *Studies*, 38 (1949), 468, stanzas 9, 11.   75 Lambert McKenna (ed.), 'Christ our Saviour', *Studies*, 38 (1949), 187, stanza 12.

1 New Year's greeting with Christ child. Coloured single-sheet woodcut print. Probably from Ulm, around 1460–75.

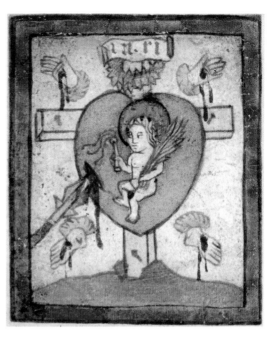

2 Infant Christ inside the heart. Coloured single-sheet woodcut print on paper, 7 x 5.5cm, Upper Germany, c.1470; copy: Albertina, Graphische Sammlung, Vienna, inv. no. 1925/317.

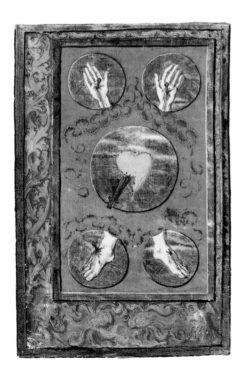

3 The five major wounds of Christ. Manuscript miniature from an edification treatise. Manuscript from Cologne, 1508.

4 A nun in the heart of the Crucified, with Christ as a bridegroom. Coloured ink-drawing on parchment, 8.4 x 7.4cm, from the end of the fifteenth century, Benedictine abbey of St Walburg in Eichstätt, inv. no. A3. With thanks to Prof. Jeffrey F. Hamburger, Harvard, for supplying this image.

5 'Vision des hl. Bernhard' (Vision of St Bernard). Coloured single-sheet print on paper 28.2 x 20.4cm, from southern Germany around 1450; work by Jörg Haspel zu Bibrach; copy: Albertina, Graphische Sammlung, Vienna, inv. no. 1930/133; Schreiber no. 1271.

6 'Eine Domenikanerin umarmt den Passionschristus' (A Dominican nun embraces the suffering Christ). Miniature on paper, glued to a prayer book, 14.8 x 11cm; second half of fifteenth century. Strasbourg: Bibliothèque du Grand Séminaire, MS 755, fo. 1.

7 (*opposite*) Master of the Velden high altar: epitaph of the Dominican nun Dorothea Schürstab with the Mass of St Gregory, painting on fir wood, 128 x 92cm, around 1475, formerly Saint Katharina's Convent, Nürnberg. Germanisches Nationalmuseum Nürnberg, Gm 521.

Griest fiestu hailiges antlit vnsers bxhalters · Jn dē
da schiner die gestalt des götlichen glanczes · Gedru
ket in ain schne wisses diechlin · Vñ gegebē veronice
czü ainem zaichen der liebe · Griest fiestu geezierd der
welte ain spiegel der hailigen · Den da begerend czü
schowen die hymelschē gaiste · Künige vns von allē
finde · Vnd sieg vns zü der selige geselschafft · Griest
fiestu vnser gloxi in disem herrten hintliessenden vnd
schwachem leben · Fier vns czü dem vatterland o du
selige figure · Zü sehend das wöneuglich antlit cristi
vnsers herren · Bis vns ain sichxere hilff ain siesse erkie
long trost vnd ain schirme · Das vns nit schade müg
die beschwoerong vnser fünde · Sonder das wir nies
send die ewige rü o amen
    So fil sind gegeben tag applas vnd karcn disem
gebet das ich sy bie nit künd wol begriffen

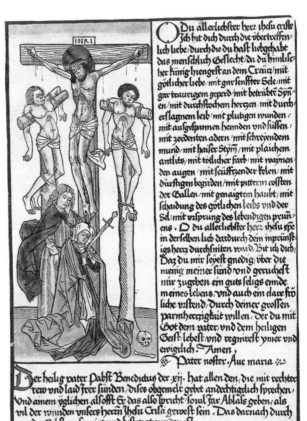

Odu allerliebster herr ihesu criste
Jch bit dich durch die obertreffen=
lich liebe · durch du hast liebgehabt
das menschlich Geslecht/da du hmlise=
her künig hiengest an dem Creü3/mit
götlicher liebe/mit gar sennffter Sele/mit
gar traurigem geperd/mit betrübt Syn=
en/mit durchstochnem hertzen/mit durch=
erslagnem leib/mit plutigen wunden/
mit ausgespannen hennden vnd hüssen/
mit zeederten adern/mit schreyendem
mund/mit haiser Stÿm/mit plaichem
antlite/mit tödlicher farb/mit verwaynen=
den augen/mit seüfftzender kelen/mit
dürstigen begirden/mit pitterm costen
der Gallen/mit genaigtem haubt/mit
schaidung des götlichen leibs vnd der
Sel/mit vrsprung des lebendigen prün=
ens · O du allerliebster herz ihesu xpe
in derselben lieb dardurch dein inprünst
igs hertz durchschniten ward/Bit ich dich/
Daz du mir seyest gnedig/vber die
menig meiner sünd vnd geruchest
mir zugeben ein guts seligs emde
meines lebens/vnd auch ein clare frö=
liche verstend/durch deiner grossen
parmhertzigkait willen/Der du mit
Got dem vater/vnd dem heiligen
Geist/lebest vnd regnirest ymer vnd
ewigklich · Amen
    ✠ Pater noster · Aue maria ❖

Der heilig vater Pabst Benedicus der xij · hat allen den/die mit rechter
rew vnd laid jrer sünden/dises obgemelt gebet andechtiglich sprechen/
Vnd ainem yglichen alsofft Er das also spricht/souil jar Ablass geben/als
vil der wunden vnsers herrn Jhesu Cristi gewest sein · Das darnach durch
annder Pabst confirmirt vnd bestaigt worden ist ❂

8 The face of Christ on the veil of Veronica,
coloured single-sheet woodcut on paper,
12.9 x 11.2cm, from Ulm around 1482;
printed by Konrad Dinckmut, copy:
Germanisches Nationalmuseum Nürnberg.

9 'Der Gekreuzigte zwischen den Schächern' (The
Crucified among the thieves). Single-sheet print on paper
with text printed in xylography, 35.2 x 25.3cm, southern
Germany, c.1480. Munich, Staatl. Graphische Sammlung,
inv. no. 118.124; Schreiber no. 964.

10 'Seitenwunde und wahre Länge Christi' (Side-wound and true length of Christ). Single-sheet print, *c.*1484–1500, 12 x 8.8cm, Munich, Staatl. Graphische Sammlung, inv. no. 63248; Schreiber no. 1795.

11 (*below*) The *Vera Icon* handed over from Christ to Veronica. The image is part of a Passion cycle painted on the outer wings of the altarpiece from Frørup Church in Denmark, *c.*1480. With permission from Jens Bruun.

12 (*next page*) Brussels, Koninklijke Bibliotheek, MS 2879–80 (= MS A), 49r. The text of *Vision 7* begins on line 13 of the left column (see the indications in the Middle Dutch text in Faesen's essay, this volume). This is the oldest manuscript of Hadewijch's works. It dates from the second quarter of the fourteenth century; its provenance is unknown, but it was in the possession of the Carthusians of Herne by the second half of the fourteenth century, and later belonged to the regular canons at Rooklooster in the Sonian Forest (near Brussels).

vecht na sine vroicheit · als ghe
raen van te m ghebruikene en in
kinne en in op ghenoemtheiden
te ghene die mi ghenoech na mi
ne wille sijn · Je gheleide di god
en melcke wed in die vrde welt
d du salt ghelmake alle voete
des du hier wed coms inte ghehe
len name mijns ghebrukens d
du in ghedoept vest in mine diep
heit · En te vri met dien weter
vraght inmileke in mi seluen

¶ O ene eingen daghe wi nu
broent inte dagheract en
men sant mettinne in te vke en
it was d en mijn lijse en mine
avon en alle mine lede scude
en benede van beghise en mi
was allt dicke heeft gheheost
soe vwoedeleke en soe vseleke
te moede rat mi vochte iene wa
re mine lief ghenoech en mij
lief en vuulde mine met dat
it skruende soude vwoede ende
al vwoerende skue · Doe was mi
van beghoerlek in soe vreleke
te moede en soe wee varmi al die
lede die it hadde sonderinghe wae
de breke en alle mine avon waeh
sonderinghe in arbeite · Die begi
red it toe m was die es onseggse
leke enegh reiene oghte iemens
die it kinne en rat selue rat ich
af leggse mochte ware ogehoel t
vde al die die te mi mene bekine

met beghite wike · en die voe in
me belime ne ware · Als mach
ick af seggsen · Je beghite mijns
lieues te volle te ghebrukene en
te belime en te ghelmakene in
allen vollo ghebroke sine melch
ghebrukeleke mett wile en te
mine d inte gheltane en stere te
wetene in omgheblelechede te
valne vat it hem wed rat ogehoele
hole ghenoech ware tuuer en enech
en t allen te vollen gherche ghe
noech te vozghene in ell vozhet
en d toe voidie va binne vat hi
mi met ste godheit in eneghou
gheeste ghenoech en al wae vat
hijs sond ontkliue · vantte gichte
woelic meest boue alle ghichten
die it te ghewoes vat it ghenoech
wae in allen grote vozhene · wat
vat es vat volcomeste ghenoech vo
te wallene god met gode te sine
want vats vozlse en pine ellente
en in ghe nuwe vnoye te sine en
vat al late comfe en gaen sonder
vnoyen en el ne ghene smake d
afte hebbene van suete mine
en hellen en vullen · als begh
vie vat mi god wae lse mete ge
noech te sine · Doe nu alds vie
seleke te moede was voe vtagie
vande outvad comfe gheuoghse
te mi ene aeie die groet was
en hi teize te mi wiltu vvoe
Doe gheveize d en it wi op

13 Epitaph for Konrad Zingel, commissioned in 1447, showing the Mass of St Gregory. Konrad
kneels with his two wives and children in the narrow section below the main motif.
With permission from St Egidien Kirche, Nürnberg.

14 *Johannesschüssel*, 1215–25 (platter: sixteenth century), limewood, Naumburg, cathedral treasury. Bildarchiv der Vereinigten Domstifter zu Merseburg und Naumburg und des Kollegiatstifts Zeitz.

15 *Johannesschüssel*, c.1500, limestone, Niddegen (today: Cologne, Schnütgen Museum). Photograph © Soetkin Vanhauwaert.

17 *Johannesschüssel*, c.1500, papier-mâché, Leuven: M – Museum. © M – Museum, Leuven, photograph Paul Laes.

16 *Johannesschüssel*, c.1500, silver and copper, gilded, St Katharinenthal, cloister (Zürich: Schweizerisches Landesmuseum). Photograph credit: J. Frings et al. (eds), *Krone und Schleier. Kunst aus mittelalterlichen Frauenklöstern* (Munich, 2005), pp 418–19.

18 Erhard Altdorfer, Retable of Saint
John with the veneration of a
Johannesschüssel by pilgrims, 1511.
Gutenstetten, parish church.
© Karl-Horst Ott.

19 Robert Campin (1378–1444), *Merode
triptych*, *c.*1420–5, New York, The
Cloisters, Metropolitan Museum of Art.

20 *The Holy Spirit descending over the apostles*, Maasland lectionary, second half of the twelfth century. New York, Pierpont Morgan Library, MS 883, fo. 62v.

21 *Annunciation ex aurem*, thirteenth century, Braunschweig/Magdeburg, Vienna, Österreichische Nationalbibliothek.

22 *Creation of Adam*, twelfth century, mosaic, Monreale Cathedral.

23 Filippo Lippi (1406–69), *Annunciation*, *c*.1440, New York, Frick Collection.

24 Gentile da Fabriano (*c*.1370–*c*.1427), *Annunciation*, *c*.1421–5, London, Thos. Agnew & Sons Ltd.

25 Unknown artist, *Enclosed garden with medallion with the mystical hunt for the unicorn (St Augustine, the Virgin and Child with St Anne, and St Elizabeth)*, c.1530, various media: wooden sculptures, textile, wax, oil on wood (medallion), 134 x 97.5 x 22.2cm, Mechelen (Malines), Gasthuiszusters.

26 Simone Martini (1284–1344), *Annunciation*, 1333, Florence, Uffizi.

27 (*above, left*) *Annunciaton as acheiropoietos*, thirteenth century, Florence, Santissima Annunziata.

28 (*above, right*) *Mandylion*, fourteenth century, Genoa, San Bartolommeo degli Armeni.

29 Iconoclast and Crucifixion (detail), Chludov psalter, eighth century, Moscow, Historical Museum, fo. 67.

30 *Marbre faux with Annunciation*, fifteenth century, Firenze, San Marco Monastery.

Der xxxj bruder der do starb, hieß leupolt
vnd was ein paternoster

31 An industry of devotional instruments for manual manipulation, mediation and meditation. Paternoster maker from *Hausbuch der Mendelschen Zwölfbrüderstiftung*, *c.*1425, Nürnberg, Stadtbibliothek, Amb. 317.2°, fo. 13r.

32–35 Still alive and sensorially present, still exuding, still instrumental to the pious perception and devotion of believers. Stills from the *Antenna Sud* television network transmission of the annual extraction of 'sacra manna' from St Nicholas' bones in his burial crypt in Bari on 9 May 2012 (www.antennasud.com).

In this instance, Christ's passion is part of a contest to win back humanity, without losing anyone. The placing 'over the board of his heart' of the people he wished to redeem might be imagined as designed for easy tipping of the whole number of humanity into its chambers of refuge.

Such clandestine manoeuvres by Christ might well be regarded as consisting of a capture of souls against their will just as a love-sick knight might carry off a young maiden. However, this approach was not necessarily regarded as unloving: after all, in the Book of Hosea, God was pleased to block the way of his beloved with thorns and to build a wall against her in order to retain her for himself (Hos 2:6). Poets such as the fifteenth-century Tadhg Óg Ó hUiginn in the poem *Ag so brágha dheit a Dhé* ('I surrender, O God, to thee') entreated Christ to preserve them from sin even if that meant restricting their freedom: 'Wind a net around me daily, let me and my body consort not; I have no chance to escape if my body and I be together'.[76] Likewise, the sixteenth-century poet Diarmuid Mac an Bhaird, in the poem *Fada a-tú i n-aghaidh mh'anma* ('Long have I been in disobedience and ruining my soul') explains how human infidelity grieves God greatly:

> If thou, my friend, wouldst serve heaven's king,
> Thy consorting with thy paramour –
> An act that wounds the heart of Mary's Son –
> Is far from being the way to serve him.[77]

In an unattributed bardic poem, *Dona an t-each-sa fhuair mh'anam* ('Sorry the steed my soul has got'), the treatment of the soul by the boorish body is presented as far more serious, with even a hint of sexual violence:

> Thou harlot, I am the soul,
> In a cell poor and lonely,
> Cursing thee, a drunken body;
> An assault has violently destroyed me.[78]

This theme is also present in the work of thirteenth-century Franciscan, Jacopone da Todi, who describes in lauda 27 a violent attack on the soul by three brutes – the world, the flesh and the devil – after which the soul is left with a rotten and infectious wound. The common association of sin with disease and the Sacrament of Penance as a healing remedy would not have been lost on Jacapone's medieval audience.[79] The message was clear: rejection of one's true lover, Christ, exposed the Christian to a real risk of endangering his or her soul.

76 Lambert McKenna (ed.), *Dán Dé* (Dublin, 1922), poem 9, stanza 12.   **77** McKenna (ed.), *Aithdioghluim Dána*, poem 56, stanza 22.   **78** Ibid., poem 91, stanza 9.   **79** Vettori, *Poets of divine* love, p. 117.

CONCLUSION

In conclusion, this essay has attempted to achieve a number of modest goals. The first was to set out the evidence that mystical writings and works of affective piety such as those associated with figures such as Hugh of St Victor, Bernard of Clairvaux, Bonaventure, Richard Rolle, Ludolph of Saxony, Johannes de Caulibus and Thomas à Kempis among others circulated in late medieval Ireland and were part of the spiritual and devotional bloodstream. The second goal was to show that the influence of texts such as these reached far beyond the walls of the local friary. The extensive connections between orders such as the Franciscans and the hereditary literary families of Gaelic Ireland, examined more fully elsewhere by scholars such as Edel Bhreathnach, were real and created a vibrant culture of textual transmission and translation, particularly in the fifteenth and sixteenth centuries. This was also the period in which a number of devotional miscellanies were commissioned by families of sufficient means, driving demand for the translation and circulation of popular European religious texts.[80] My third goal was to bring some of the significant imagery surrounding the figure of Christ, lover of the soul, drawn from well-known mystical writings from England and the Continent, into conversation with a body of Irish religious poetry in which both sets of interlocutors have been kept apart for far too long. Of course, on account of the meagre surviving sources that we are dealing with, it is not possible to draw anything like precise lines of influence. What can, perhaps, be argued is that the devotional poetry of the professional poets of Gaelic Ireland and various mystical texts from England and the Continent at certain points drew from a wider tradition of affective piety and can be said to have much more in common than perhaps previously acknowledged. And it was a tradition that endured into the seventeenth century. In many respects, then, it is not surprising that the Irish Franciscan, Aodh Mac Aingil, chose to use the motif of Christ as lover of the soul in his 1618 tract on penance, *Scáthán Shacramuinte na hAithridhe*. The Franciscans had a long tradition of employing love poetry in the service of devotion. Mac Aingil depicts Christ waiting outside the window for the return of the soul, stating that, as lover of the soul, he never takes his eyes off his love, by day or by night. The motif of Christ as Lover had a long tradition behind it. Like many of his Franciscan confrères before him, Mac Aingil believed in the power of the motivation of love to wean Christians away from sin and onto the road of repentance and true contrition. He considered Christ the constant wooer of the soul, perpetually coaxing it to turn back to its true lover in love and contrition:

---

80 I have treated of this more fully elsewhere: see Salvador Ryan, 'Windows on late medieval devotional practice: Máire Ní Mháille's "Book of piety" (1513) and the world behind the texts' in Rachel Moss, Colmán Ó Clabaigh and Salvador Ryan (eds), *Art and devotion in late medieval Ireland* (Dublin, 2006) and *idem*, '"Wily women of God" in Cavan's late medieval and early modern devotional collections' in Brendan Scott (ed.), *Culture and society in early modern Breifne/Cavan* (Dublin, 2009).

He [Christ] speaks with soft and gentle words to your soul in this way: Come to me, my love, my spouse, my dove; flee from that bird of prey, the devil; I am your rock of refuge; come beneath my wounds and you will find sheltered harbours there.[81]

---

81 Mac Aingil, *Scáthán*, p. 16. For the continuing role of bardic religious poetry in seventeenth-century catechesis on the Sacrament of Penance, see Salvador Ryan, 'Penance and the privateer: handling sin in the bardic religious verse of the Book of the O'Conor Don (1631)' in Tadhg Ó hAnnracháin and Robert Armstrong (eds), *Christianities in the early modern Celtic world* (Basingstoke, 2014), pp 124–34.

5 Transfiguration: change and comprehension in late medieval devotional perception

LAURA KATRINE SKINNEBACH

> Jesus took with him Peter and James and his brother John and led them up a high mountain, by themselves. And he was transfigured before them.[1]

In the biblical story of the Transfiguration of Christ recorded in the Gospel according to Matthew, the true nature of Christ is revealed to his three selected disciples. The text describes how the face of Christ shone like the sun, and his clothes became dazzling white, and how Moses and Elijah suddenly appeared with him. Their presence is so real that it makes Peter utter to Jesus 'Lord, it is good for us to be here; if you wish, I will make three dwellings here, one for you, one for Moses and one for Elijah'. But suddenly a bright cloud overshadows them, and a voice from the cloud says 'This is my Son, the Beloved; with him I am well pleased; listen to him!' On hearing this, the disciples fall to the ground in fear, but Jesus comforts them and when they look up, they see only him.

The story concerns an important Christian theme: the manifestation of God before man and how man may come to experience the presence of God. According to Thomas Aquinas (1225–74), the Transfiguration was a strategic change knowingly incorporated by Christ in order to make the disciples – and man in general – comprehend a specific truth, as he stated in *Summa Theologica*: 'Christ wished to be transfigured in order to show men his glory, and to arouse men to desire of it.'[2] The Transfiguration was, according to the medieval theologian, in the interest of God who *wished* to be known. Thus, from the biblical story of the Transfiguration we learn how the understanding of the truth of God is brought about by a change (*trans-* which can also mean 'across' or 'beyond') in appearance (*figura*) as Peter, James and John are brought to realize the glory of God as a result of a sudden metamorphosis in the appearance of Jesus accompanied by the voice of God.[3] Comprehension is related to a change of figure and mode of perception as it is indeed the form and outline of Christ that changes as his body assumes clarity in the presence of the disciples 'as when the air is lit up by the sun', revealing the nature of God in a physically perceivable manner.[4] Through transfiguration, the nature of God becomes visible, audible and

---

1 Matthew 17:1–2.   **2** 'Christus transfigurari volut ut gloriam suam hominibus ostenderet, et ad eam desiderandum homines provocaret…' 3 ST q. 45 art. 3 answer. Latin text from R. Busa SJ, *Sancti Thomae Aquinatis opera omnia*, 7 vols (Stuttgart, 1979). English translation in *The Summa Theologica of St Thomas Aquinas* ed. and trans. Fathers of the English Dominican Province (1920).   **3** *Transfiguratus* is the Latin vulgate translation of the Greek word *metamorphosis*.   **4** 3 ST Q 45 art.1 rep. obj. 2. See also ST Q 45 art. 2 answer.

tangible. God can be sensed. The story describes how the disciples come to understand the nature of Jesus as the son of God as a result of a change in the appearance of Jesus that leads to a shift in mode of perception in the disciples.

This same shift in appearance and mode of perception, transfiguration, is a theme frequently found in late medieval visual culture and it delineates a constitutional condition for the practice of devotion. The prospect of a sensory encounter with God enhanced man's desire for God in spite of the paradoxical nature of the matter. How may God, who is ultimately spiritual and incomprehensible, be comprehended and encountered by man who is bound to a physical and material body? Beholding God face to face was an experience reserved for the future state of salvation whereas in this life we see only in 'a mirror dimly'.[5] Nevertheless, it was agreed by early medieval theologians and re-stated in the later Middle Ages that the Incarnation had legitimized sensory experience as a way of knowing God.[6] At the same time, matter was God's creation and he acted through and in it, through the Eucharistic bread and wine as well as through images, objects and natural elements.[7] Mystical writings, hagiography and images are bursting with examples of holy men and women experiencing a glimpse of presence and in some specific cases these experiences – as will be argued below – have transfigurational elements in them. One of the most important examples is the devotion to the *Vera Icon*, the true image of Christ transferred to a piece of cloth, a translation of the facial features of the God-Man condensed in an image that represents presence but yet also absence.[8]

In devotional guides and prayer books, a similar interest in perceivable revelation can be detected as a structural element. The incorporation of different modes of perception – through the use of objects, movement, words, gestures and locations – aimed at *transfiguration* of body, mind and surroundings. In this essay, I wish to investigate these devotional transfigurations in further detail. By analysing different examples of devotional practice taken from a combination of mystical texts, prayer books and images, primarily from Denmark and Germany, this essay seeks to inquire into these diverse transformations, focusing in particular on how the disclosure of God is facilitated and supported by the devotional process itself, intensified, as it were, by *practices of transfiguration*. It investigates the structure and design of devotional practice and, in particular, how it attempts to lead towards experiences of God by using the transfiguration – change in physical appearance – as backdrop. These changes could be applied to different objects, images or the body of the practitioner. The complex ideas about the ways in which God could be encountered were paralleled by equally complex systems of actions, strategically mobilized in the practice of devotion, requiring in particular the integration of the sense and perception.

---

5 1 Cor 13:12.   **6** K.B. Aavitsland, 'Incarnation: paradoxes of perception and mediation in medieval liturgical art' in Henning Laugerud et al., *The saturated sensorium*; C.M. Woolgar, *The senses in late medieval England*, p. 17.   **7** Bynum, *Christian materiality*, p. 35.   **8** Hamburger, *The visual and the visionary*, pp 332–3.

TRANSFIGURATION AND THE SENSORIUM

The senses and the formation of a devout *sensorium* – understood as the combination of inner and outer senses, programmed to perceive the holy – played a fundamental role in late medieval devotion.[9] Materiality and material objects such as devotional books or primers, portable or stationary images, single leaf prints with a combination of illustration and prayer, letters of indulgence containing devotional guidance, pilgrimage badges, rosaries, birth girdles and other small textual amulets, to mention just a selection, were assigned an important role in the performance of devotional practices where they were touched, kissed, beheld, kept in a purse or pocket, hung on the wall or from the belt or sewn into the clothes of the owner.[10] The body would simultaneously be preoccupied with a devotional pose or a sequence of poses alternating between kneeling, lying, lighting a candle, standing erect with arms crossed or stretched out. All this would *take place* at a specific private or collective location, either in church, in the open or in a private house, where different sensory impressions would impel the devotional experience.[11] The devotional event itself constituted an intricate amalgamation of material objects, bodily movements, mental exercises and a corradiation of perceptive impulses. The different elements were often combined in a sophisticated manner, and together they intended to produce different forms of praise and communication with God. Furthermore devotional practices were never isolated actions. They were influenced by the practitioner's memories of past experiences, the current and present situation, and anticipations of the future outcome.[12]

The practice of sensory perception, applied to the devotional process, served, in itself, to conform mind and body to *be* and to *behave* devoutly. It was believed that the senses were affected by sensory objects in the material world – the *sensibles* – as Aquinas stated: 'For this is what sensing is: to be affected in some way by a sense object'.[13] Aquinas argues that when we sense something, we are changed and affected (*immutatio*) by what we sense, so that the senses are formed according to the sensibles; 'in this way … sense, after it has been actualized by a sense object is like that object, whereas beforehand it was not like it'.[14] It was, then, important to guard the senses against negative and unproductive stimuli. An English writer stated around 1440 in a text called *Jacob's Well*:

> Keep your sight from lecherous lights and your ears from lecherous hearing and
> your mouth from lecherous speech and your nose from dishonest smelling and

---

9 Laura Katrine Skinnebach, 'Practices of perception' (PhD, University of Bergen, 2013), p. 213ff.   **10** See, for example, Bynum, *Christian materiality*; Erika Lauren Lindgren, *Sensual encounters*; Jeffrey Hamburger (ed.), *Crown and veil*; Don C. Skemer, *Binding words*; Richard Marks, *Image and devotion in late medieval England*; Susanna Biernoff, *Sight and embodiment in the Middle Ages*; Jeffrey Hamburger, *The visual and the visionary*; Hans Belting, *Likeness and presence*.   **11** Lindgren, *Sensual encounters*; Jonathan Z. Smith, *To take place: toward theory in ritual*.   **12** For a thorough invenstigation of the composition of devotional practice, see Skinnebach, 'Practices of perception'.   **13** Aquinas, *Commentary on de Anima*, II, 12, Pasnau, *Thomas Aquinas* (1999), p. 296. **14** Aquinas, *Commentary on de Anima*, II, 12. In Pasnau, *Thomas Aquinas*, p. 198 ff.

your limbs, hands and mouth and your other members from lecherous touching. These are the five wits and gates through which the enemies enter the heart.[15]

Protection of the bodily senses against the enemies of the heart was a common theme in medieval prayer books where the prayers frequently conclude with a petition, as in the anonymous Danish prayer book in which a prayer to Virgin Mary ends with the words 'help me to true peace in body and mind … and guard my five senses'.[16] The soul, it was argued, was affected by the acts of the senses. Devout movements and images, for example, which expressed pious content, could operate as catalysts that actuated the capacity of body and mind to conform to a devotional ideal.[17] These ideals were as many and varied as the different appropriations of faith that circulated in the period and the strategies employed for the purpose were multifarious and so was the combination of movements, objects, locations, words and perceptive engagements.[18] Ultimately, however, all shared a fundamental tendency to combine body and mind, so that both aspects collaborated in the devotion to God.[19] Devotional practice established mutuality between mind and body so that both could in*corpo*rate the devotional ideals.[20]

The senses were *instrumental* in the process, to use a term inspired by St Augustine, who claimed that an inanimate body does not sense anything, but through the bodily *instrumentum* the conscious soul is mixed with the outside world.[21] The outer instrumental senses absorbed the worldly *sensibles* and passed them on to the conscious and inner soul. This understanding sums up the medieval conception of perception, but in reality it was much more complex. Human perception was regarded as a complicated system of outer sensory and inner sensory faculties.

These inner faculties or 'inward wits' were the common sense, imagination, the cogitative faculty or phantasy, estimation and memory.[22] The outer senses were of

15 'Kepe þi syȝte fro leccherous syȝtes & þin eres from leccherous heryng and þi mowth fro leccherous speche and þi nose fro dishonest smellyng and þi lymes handys & mowth & þin oþere membrys fro leccherous towchyng. Þese ar þi v [five] wyttes & ȝatys [gates] through whiche þe feendys entryth into þe herte'. From Jacob's Well: Salisbury Cathedral MS 103, fo. 122. I quote from Woolgar, *The senses in late medieval England*, p. 12. 16 'hielp mek til san fredh bodhe til liif och iæl Hielp mek sancta maria til eet stadelight hoob · kerlighe troo · ydmygheet och raadh · at wernæ myne fæm synnæ · At fuldkomme the vii miskundelighe gerningher …'. This book is now in the Arnamagnaen Collection in Copenhagen as AM 418,12°, MDB II, no. 344. 17 Hans Henrik Lohfert Jørgensen, 'Sensorium' in Henning Laugerud et al., *The saturated sensorium*; Hans Henrik Lohfert Jørgensen, *I kroppens spejl* (Aarhus, 2004); Laura Katrine Skinnebach, *Practices of devotion*; Klaus Schreiner (ed.), *Frömmigkeit im Mittelalter* (2002). 18 Salvador Ryan, 'The most traversed bridge' in Kate Cooper and Jeremy Gregory (eds), *Elite and popular religion* (2006). 19 Bynum, *Holy feast and holy fast*; Bernard McGinn, *The harvest of mysticism in medieval Germany* (2006). 20 Skinnebach, 'Practices of perception' (2013). 21 '… et quamuis non sentiat corpus exanime, anima temen commixta corpori per instrumentum sentit corporeum et idem instrumentum sensus uocatur.' St Augustine, *De trinitate*, ed. and trans. E. Hill, *The work of St Augustine* (1993), V, XI i.2. Hill translates 'corpus exanime' into 'unconscious and lifeless body' but I have suggested the use of 'inanimate' because this term indicates more clearly how Augustine perceived the relation between body and soul. 22 For an overview of different theories on the inner senses, see Simon Kemp and Garth J.O. Fletcher, 'The medieval theory of the inner senses', *American Journal of Psychology*, 106:4 (winter 1993), 559–76; Stephen G. Nichols, Andreas Kablitz and Alison Calhoun (eds), *Rethinking the medieval senses*; Woolgar, *The senses in late*

course the five individual senses, but the words denoting them – taste, touch, smell, hearing and seeing – had many meanings that blurred the distinction between them. Taste, for example, could also mean to touch with the mouth. As we shall see in what follows, devotional practice expresses a similar spacious understanding of the senses and is often structured in ways that imitate the transfiguration and aids comprehension by incorporating shifts in mode of perception.

TRANSFIGURATION AND THE BODY

The *Vera Icon* mentioned above may be regarded as the visual prototype of bodily transfiguration. In the Middle Ages the *Vera Icon* was often connected to the legends about the woman called Veronica who, according to Christian tradition, wiped the face of Christ with a piece of cloth on his way to Calvary and as a result, an impression of the face of Christ was miraculously left on the cloth. Some medieval legends expanded on the miraculous powers of this *true image*, among others a Danish book called *Sjælens Trøst* (*Consolatio Animae*, 'The Consolation of the Soul') from the fifteenth century, in which it was related that Emperor Tiberius, who was deathly ill, had sent for Christ because he hoped to be cured by him.[23] At this point, Christ had already died and Tiberius was instead presented with the image on the cloth and cured. It was believed that this image, instituted by Christ himself, captured the true features of Jesus, transfigured before man as the son of God; the body of Christ transfigured as the image of the Redeemer.[24] The image was regarded as a portrait of Jesus and, thus, proof of the life and death of Christ and the legends about its miraculous powers illustrated that Christ was indeed present in spite of his absence. Thus it was the absence of Christ and the presence of the image that cured Emperor Tiberius of his deadly illness. The *Vera Icon* embodied at one and the same time the human features and Godly nature of Christ and transcended the dichotomy between absence and presence. Its miraculous production appropriated the veneration of sensory objects in general and images in particular, and it became immensely popular as a devotional focus in the later Middle Ages, depicted on single leaf prints and in altarpieces and even on the outside of church walls.[25] A late fifteenth-century altarpiece from Frørup church in southern Denmark features a painted version of the meeting between Veronica, whose name was often associated with the *Vera Icon*, and Christ on

---

medieval England; Michael Camille, *Gothic art, glorious visions*.   **23** The account of the legend in *Sjæla trøst* follows Jocobus Voragine and *Legenda Aurea* closely: Niels Nielsen, *Sjælens Trøst* (*Sjæla trøst*), 2 vols (Copenhagen, 1937–52), I, p. 29.   **24** During the Reformation, the *Vera Icon* and the story of the curing of Tiberius was used by the Roman Church as proof of the divine institution of images and served to legitimize the devotional use of visual objects: see, for example, the treatises by Hieronymus Emser 'That One Should not Remove Images of the Saints from the Churches nor Dishonour Them, and that They are not Forbidden in Scripture' and Johannes Eck 'On not Removing Images of Christ and the Saints' both ed. and trans. in Bryan D. Mangrum and Giuseppe Scavizzi, *A Reformation debate* (Toronto, 1998), pp 52, 101.   **25** Hamburger, *The visual and the visionary*, pp 317–88; Belting, *Likeness and presence*, pp 208–9.

the way to Golgotha (pl. 11). The image captures the very moment when Veronica, kneeling before the cross-bearing Christ, receives the miraculous image depicting the holy face. They are both touching the rims of the white piece of cloth, holding it out for the beholder to see, and this simultaneous touch and exchange of gaze marks the inauguration of the physical image as a potential passage though which Christ may be addressed.[26] Of significance here is the central position of the human sensorium; how the touch, the gaze and the bodily posture is instituted as a *new* way to experience the presence of Christ; the body of Christ transformed into a mediated and mediating *figura* that concurrently reveals his Godly nature.

Transformation of bodies into images was a recurring subject in medieval hagiography where the virtues and vices committed in the lives of saints and sinners were inscribed in their flesh and later transferred to the visual medium where their tortured bodies became the moral standards for medieval devotees.[27] Holiness and devoutness, so it was believed, were imprinted on the bodies and countenances of men and women.[28] There is a close relation between the transfiguration theme and the *imitatio* theme. According to Paul Binski, St Bonaventure (1221–74) implied in his *Life of St Francis* that the Transfiguration of Christ was the subtext to the 'greatest Franciscan theophany, the Stigmatization on Mount La Verna, not least in its emphasis on the esoteric nature of the events as a kind of *imitatio Christi*'.[29] Christ was transfigured in the flesh of St Francis, transforming his body into the *figure* of Christ for the inspiration of others. Transfiguration in this sense does, then, have a double meaning or effect; not only does it refer to a change in appearance of Christ but it also alludes to a change in appearance in the receiver of the perceptive impulses. The *figure* of the devout person *trans*forms according to the body of Christ, a *conformatio Christi*.

One specific example that illustrates the experience of such a transfiguration in detail comes from the writings of the Dominican monk Henry Suso (*c*.1300–66). In his *Life of the Servant*, an autobiographical book showing the trials, reflections and revelations he encountered on his life-long search for the truth of God, we meet numerous descriptions of incidents that take Suso to a new level of understanding. At one point he reports how one day he experienced an intense fire in his heart. His heart was burning with divine love and the torments were exceedingly strong. He retired to his cell and spoke in contemplation to the Lord: 'gentle God, if only I could think up a sign of love that would give testimony as an eternal symbol of love between you and me, one that no forgetting could erase'.[30] He then decided to engrave the name of Jesus Christ, the monogram IHS, deeply above his heart with a sharp object. Afterwards he went 'to the pulpit under the crucifix' and prayed the following prayer:

26 Barbara Baert, *Collected essays on 'Noli me tangere': the Woman with the Haemorrhage and the Head of John the Baptist*, esp. p. 63ff. **27** Frank O Büttner, *Imitatio Pietatis* (Berlin, 1983). **28** Jørgensen, 'Synets modernisering'; Bynum, *Holy feast and holy fast*; Biernoff, *Sight and embodiment*. **29** Paul Binski, 'The Northern Master at Assisi', *Proceedings of the British Academy*, 117 (2002), 87. **30** Frank Tobin, *Henry Suso* (New York, 1989), p. 70.

> My Lord and only Love of my heart, look at the intense desire of my heart. My
> Lord, I do not know how to press you into me further, nor can I. Alas, Lord, I
> beg you to finish this by pressing yourself further into the ground of my heart
> and so draw your holy name onto me that you never again leave my heart.[31]

Suso was well aware that he was only able to paint the letters on the skin of his body
– as an 'eternal symbol of love' – but the outward image and symbol was not sufficient
for him. He wished for Christ to finish the work and imprint his name even deeper
into his heart. The name would then, he hoped, be imprinted in a way that could
outlast even memory and the decay of human skin, an eternal symbol transcending
worldly time. One day after Matins, he sat down in a chair in his cell and shortly after
drifted off to sleep. It then seemed to him that clear light was flowing from his chest,
and when he looked down, he saw a golden sparkling cross with skilfully inlaid jewels
above his heart. He tried to cover it with some cloth but could not hide its beauty.
Gradually Suso came to an understanding of the meaning of the shimmering cross
above his chest. His deepest wish had been granted to him and the name of Christ that
Suso had carved onto his flesh as a bloody wound had, by the will of God, been turned
into an image of a cross in his heart. Christ was no longer merely present as letters
written *on* the body, but as a sparkling image of the passion contained *in* his body.
Suso now carried the ultimate symbol of the Passion in his heart.

What enlightens Suso in the pinnacle of this experience is the change of *figure* from
one image of Christ to another. His comprehension has been facilitated by a change
in figurative appearance when the letters on his skin, visible and haptic, are revealed
to him as the symbol of the Passion in the form of a cross within his body. Even
though he tries to hide the light, it is visible through the garment, permeating cloth,
flesh and mind. The letters IHS miraculously change and appear in different shape
and form, which leaves Suso in a state of enlightenment. He receives new understanding as a result of the change in appearance, a transfiguration both in the literal
sense of the word and as an allegory of the biblical event.

The letter-image above Suso's heart became a symbol of devotion to people around
him and his autobiography contains examples of how Suso's great devotion and faith
in the name of Christ inspired others. He treasured the letters above the heart because
of their direct linkage with the cross *in* his heart and tried to conceal it from the
curiosity of others. Word of his ingrained image did, however, start to circulate already
in his youth and one day a friend begged him to let him *see* it. Suso was, to begin with,
unwilling because he did not wish to agitate people around him, but was finally
persuaded by his friend's devoutness and opened his garment. His friend, however, was
not satisfied with just beholding: 'When he had seen it visibly present there on his
body right over his heart, he ran his hand over it and then his face, touching it with

---

31 Ibid.

his mouth. He wept from his heart with devotion, and the tears welled out and flowed over the servant's heart.'[32] Just as the letters had prompted a transfiguration of Christ before Suso, they now occasioned an almost ecstatic experience in his friend who touched it with his hands and mouth as if it was an image of the side-wound of Christ. As such, the letters IHS came to signify the Transfiguration of Christ, revealed to the devout practitioner through a change in appearance, a change that could be sensed. Like St Francis, and yet in a way very different from him, Henry Suso had been united with the image of God. And, in both cases, Christ has even left a lasting mark of their transfigurational experience.

The Transfiguration of Christ was, in the case of St Francis and Henry Suso, manifested in bodily form, impressed and submerged deeply into the flesh of the devout, their bodies – created in God's image and likeness – transformed into canvasses for the will of God, as *figurae* illustrating the presence – and absence – of God. The *Vera Icon*, images of and devotions to St Francis, and the reception of Suso's IHS mark on the chest by his followers, were all concerned with these bodily changes, which both legitimized their positions as holy 'images' and worked as focal points of devotions strategically structured for the purpose of producing experiences of God. The 'Veronica' offered an opportunity to experience the face of Christ, St Francis offered an opportunity to encounter a living *imago dei* and Suso, on a very local level at least, was revered for possessing an external as well as internal image of God. What these different examples of bodily transfiguration have in common is that they give weight and adhere to perception as a fundamental means for accessing the divine. The change in appearance leads to revelation and cognizance of Godly truths, and the experience of such changes – even if they were experienced second-hand, as in the case of Suso's friend – were linked to the practice of perception and ultimately incorporated into the practice of devotion.

TRANSFIGURATION AND OBJECTS

Bleeding Hosts, speaking and moving images and miracles performed by the bones of the saints were ways in which the true nature of Christ was revealed to startled believers and doubters.[33] The various visual renderings of the Mass of St Gregory, popular as it was in the northern part of Europe in the fifteenth century in particular, illustrate how objects were believed to be able to transform as a result of divine intervention and instil new understanding of the nature of God in the devout. The Host is disclosed as the flesh of Christ before Pope Gregory, convincing the bystanders of

---

32 Ibid., p. 168.   **33** Literature on these topics is vast, but see, for example, Peter Dinzelbacher, 'Religiöses Erleben vor bildener Kunst in autobiographische und biographische Zeugnisse des Hoch- und Spätmittelalters' in Søren Kaspersen (ed.), *Images of Kult and devotion*, pp 61–88; Bynum, *Wonderful blood*; Otto Gecser (ed.), *Promoting the saints*; Bynum, *Christian materiality*; Michael E. Goodich, *Miracle and wonders* (London, 2007); Robert C. Finucane, *Miracles and pilgrims* (London, 1995); Robert Bartlett, *Why can the dead do such great things?* (Princeton, NJ, 2013).

the reality of Transubstantiation. An epitaph from the Nürnberg area in Germany, commissioned by Konrad Zingel in 1447, integrates the Mass of St Gregory, the *arma Christi* and the 'Veronica' (pl. 13). This is not an uncommon juxtaposition of motifs, but this particular image accentuates the interconnection between Christ (the living flesh), the Host (the transubstantiated flesh) and the *Vera Icon* (the true representation of the human flesh of Christ); Christ rises from the altar/*sepulchre* and exactly below him on the *mensa* lies the host inscribed with an image of the Crucifixion on a paten covered by a white corporal, and from the mensa hangs the Veronica, constituting a vertical line linking different manifestations of the presence of Christ.[34] The body of Christ is linked with the bread *and* the true image, both 'placed' on a piece of white cloth, attributing to the image strong Eucharistic overtones; the presence of Christ in the host revealed during the mass resembles the (potential) presence communicated by the image of the true face.[35] Presence is contained *in and through* the material objects (bread and image) and revealed as a result of liturgical and devotional practice, perceived though touch, taste and vision accordingly

Zingel's epitaph exemplifies how different ways of perceiving Christ were regarded as productive in a devotional sense. Christ could be received through different senses and by combining different modes of perception that were fundamentally translatable. The image expresses a multi-sensory conception of perception. It is through our senses – and in particular by combining them – that we may come to comprehension of the truth of godly presence. A similar strategy can be found in devotional practice: a strategy that acknowledges the potential strength of figural transformations as a strategy for bringing about comprehension. Comprehension may be reached when the mode of perception is altered or transferred into a new medium. Else Holgersdatter's Book of Hours, from fifteenth-century Denmark, clearly exemplifies how the sensory experience could, in a very material sense, jump from one mode of perception to another. The rubric of one particular devotional practice explains that if someone had been overcome by any form of sadness or distress, he or she was encouraged to have an image of St Catherine of Alexandria made from wax and read fifty *aves* and *pater nosters* every day for twenty days in the honour of the saint. When these days had passed, the wax image was to be transformed into a candle and burned in the honour of St Catherine.[36] It is underlined that the candle was supposed to be made from the

---

34 Peter Strider, *Tafelmalerei in Nürnberg, 1350–1550* (1993). Esther Meier, *Die Gregorsmesse* (Köln, 2006); Caroline W. Bynum, 'Seeing and seeing beyond: the Mass of St Gregory in the fifteenth century' in Jeffrey Hamburger and Anne-Marie Bouché, *The mind's eye* (Princeton, NJ, 2006).   **35** Hamburger, *The visual and the visionary*, p. 333.   **36** 'Hwo ther ær stedh i noghen drøffuilsæ hellær i nogen nødh han skal ladæ giøræ iet billædæ aff vox æfftær sancta katerina billædæ konningens dottær aff alexandria och læsæ i xx daghæ samfeldh halff tridiæ sinnæ thyfuæ pater noster oc aue maria oc offræ them iomfrw sancta katerina For then gledælligh beboddælsæ som hennæ fader oc modhær finghæ før hun war født oc for then gled hun fæk ther hun ower wandh the halff tridiæ sinnæs xx mæstær meth then helligandz makt At hun villæ verduges til at bede for then menniske som æræ stedh i nødh heller nogen drøffwilsæ Fyrstæ thissæ xx daghæ æræ vdhæ tha skal man then samæ vox billædæ och giøræ ther iet lywss aff och brendæ thet i sancta katerina hieder oc bedæ gud om huadh bøn som man vil/ tha skal hun hanom vedæs vthen allæ thwiffwæl Amen': GkS 1613 4°, see also K.M. Nielsen, *Middelalderens Danske*

same image (then samæ vox billædæ och giøræ ther iet lywss aff). Perhaps the practitioner had to do the remaking herself, which would imply an explicitly tactile act, but it is more likely that it was possible to purchase a small, prefabricated wax image and later have it transformed into a candle. This would, however, presuppose a well-established system of production and exchange of wax in different shapes and according to size or weight.

This transformation *from* image and *into* candle constitutes an important change in practice; at the moment when the change is introduced, the practitioner is – according to the rubric – in a position to ask anything he or she wants, and then it will surely be granted. It is through the material transformation that the final plea is made possible. The physical and visible image is destroyed as if it is now supposed to be safely stored in the mind of the devotee. The sensory image has been transformed into a candle, physically lighting up the surroundings (and perhaps a material image of St Catherine) and metaphorically illuminating the mind of the devotee while she now addresses the saint with her wishes. The transformation of the wax is parallel to the transformation in the devotee; her sensory perception of the world has been turned into inner enlightenment. The 'body' of the wax, its outline and figure, is changed into the form of a candle whose light illuminates the clarity of the truth of St Catherine and imitates the transformation of the practitioner. Transfiguration – from image to candle, from darkness to insight – is an integrated part of the illumination.

A devotional practice from another Danish prayer book, from the beginning of the sixteenth century, was supposed to be performed against the plague. It involved a whole community that, together, performed a transformative practice:

The following masses are to be said against the plague

> The first is for St Anne, then one for St Sebastian, then one for St Anthony, then one for St Roch, then one for all Christian souls. These masses should be held with one candle each and let the entire house be measured (*maele*) around, and let all the people go there and have this thread spun and form a pretzel and hang it before the Virgin Mary. *Vita et spes nostra salue o maria sis nobiscum in omni via.*[37]

This particular prayer is the only one of its kind in the Danish medieval material.[38] It is composed of five votive masses followed by a cluster of actions. Votive masses were

---

Bønnebøger, 1–5 (1946–82), MDB 3, no. 854. Some examples (with reference to numbers in Nielsen) are 274, 284, 1121, 1134 and 1138. Here images and candles are mentioned explicitly.   **37** 'Tesse messer skal mand lade holle for pestilenzie. Item then første aff Sancta Anna, Item en aff Sancto sebasiano, Item en af Sancto anthonio, Iten en aff Samcto rocho, Item en aff alle cristen siell. Thesse messe skall hlles hwer meth eth lyws oc lade maele hwset om kringh oc lade alt folket gaa ther vdii oc lade saa snoo then tradh oc giør ther af en kringell oc hengen for iomfw maria. Vita et spes nostra salue o maria sis nobiscum in omni via': AM 784,4°, MDB IV, no. 1104. The text is often referred to as Visdoms spejl (Mirror of wisdom).   **38** There is one other example of the so-called Visdoms spejl (eth spegell fwld af fald wiished): AM 782,4° from 1523, but although the two manuscripts are very much alike, this praticular prayer is only featured in AM 784,4°. The two prayerbooks may, according to MDB,

traditionally held with a particular intention – in this case to cure an incidence of pestilence – which is also reflected in the inclusion of the two major plague-saints, St Sebastian and St Roch.[39] In combination with St Anne and a mass for all Christian souls, it secured full protection of the whole congregation involved, sick as well as healthy.

From the description it is difficult to get a clear idea of how the rest of the practice was supposed to be performed. First and foremost there is a certain ambiguity concerning the location of the practice: although it is clear that the masses would have taken place in the church, it is not clear whether the word 'house' refers to the church or a private house. Second, it is uncertain what material substance *that thread* is referring to or, for that matter, if it was in some way connected to the measuring of the 'house'. Furthermore one may wish to ask how many people it involved: the whole congregation or merely the members of one single household? And are we dealing with one or many people struck by the plague?

Concerning the location it is important to consider the context of the specific practice; the other texts of the prayer book. Although the description may seem to indicate that the practice takes place at the same location as the masses, which would be the church, it is, however, unusual to find the church referred to as a 'house' in the Danish material (except when mentioning the house of God, *gutz hus*). One would find the Danish word for church, *kirke, kirki* or *kirkæ*. It is likely, then, that the practice may have taken place in a private house. The rubric instructs the devout to go there, and in Danish the words *gaa ther vdii* specify that they are supposed to go *inside* the house.

The question concerning the thread is more puzzling. Inside the house the thread is being spun and then formed into the shape of a pretzel. The pretzel is then supposed to be hung before the Virgin Mary. If the last bit of information is taken into consideration, one can presume that we are dealing with an *ex voto*. These *ex-votos*, or votive gifts, were little figures, usually made of wax, used to express gratitude or devotion towards God, Christ, Mary or a saint who had provided help or a miraculous cure in a specific situation. The shape of the objects would usually carry a reference to the actual event itself; if someone had been cured from disease in the hand, the *ex-voto* would be given the shape of a hand or it could function as a mnemonic device, such as a crutch commemorating the illness that God had taken away. Numerous visual examples from the Middle Ages show these wax-objects – often hanging from the ceiling by the shrine or altar – shaped, for example, like ships, hands, feet, hearts, legs, livers, heads or wounds. *Ex votos* had a significant material quality as if part of the healed self was offered back to God.[40] Another significant and fundamental quality of

have been based on the same source: see Nielsen (1945), p. xxxv.   **39** On votive masses, see Ann E. Matter and Jeanne E. Krochalis, 'Manuscripts of the Liturgy', *The Liturgy of the medieval Church*, ed. Thomas J. Heffernan and E. Ann Matter (Kalamazoo, MI, 2005), pp 393–430, esp. pp 410–11.   **40** Bynum, *Christian materiality*, p. 112.

wax was its malleable and transitory materiality. *Ex votos* were usually transformed into candles after a while, burned and perished as smoke, as the wax-image of St Catherine mentioned above. The materiality itself expressed the perishable nature of man before the eternal God.

In the Danish example, the production of the pretzel and thus the transformation of the *thread* into a pretzel was the pivotal point of attention. The texts specifies that it is supposed to be *that* thread, thus referring to a specific thread. If the pretzel was supposed to be produced from wax, then perhaps the thread was made of wax too. If rolled very thinly, it might have been possible to form a thin thread that could be spun into a large figure. Another possible interpretation is that the thread simply referred to a thread of cloth used to measure the house and constitute the benchmark for the production of the pretzel. In any case, it is clear that there is a correlation between the circumference of the house and the pretzel.

The practice of measuring and counting was of great significance in the period. Devotions to the size of the true cross, nails and the body of Christ and to the five wounds and the total number of wounds applied to the body of Christ during the Passion were widespread practices that testify to the importance of shape, number and size.[41] *Shape* and, in particular, true form were inseparably related to matter but also to what it signified. Devotion to the shape and size of the Cross was, for example, not devotion to the thing itself, but to the *sign* of the presence of Christ. Because of the absence of the actual cross, a *similitude* of the cross was shaped and moulded by counting and measuring. The relic *in absentia* was contained in the numbers and figures, ready to be unfolded by the devout through the practice of maths and the production of an inner or outer visual representation. In the case of the Danish example, the practice of measuring could, then, be understood as a way in which the practitioner(s) could contain the true size of the house in a number. If understood in this way, the thread – whether it was made of wax or not – had a profound significance, binding the circumference of the house, the wax pretzel and the congregation together.

And this opens the question of the assembly of people. The practice explicitly invites 'all people to go there' (inside the house), suggesting a considerable number of people gathered in a shared attempt to fight pestilence. It is not clear whether the text is referring only to those affected by the illness, the owners of the particular house or perhaps the whole congregation. In any case, the practice shows similarities with other practices performed in order to dismiss or avert something evil, and the plague was indeed something often regarded as the doings of the devil, punishment for sins or

---

41 The Danish prayerbooks contain numerous examples of prayers to the five wounds and the number of wounds. The size of the cross the nails and the body of Christ are frequently found in English prayer rolls or *Bedes*: see Don C. Skemer, *Binding words*. St Bonaventure regards number, size, shape, rest and motion as the common sense objects: see St Bonaventure, *Itinerarium ad Mentis Deum*, Caput II, English translation in Ewert Cousins, *Bonaventure*, 2:3, p. 70.

even as a sign of Apocalypse.[42] Kramer and Sprenger reported in their famous manual, *The Malleus Maleficarum*, written in 1486, how St Bernard of Clairvaux once assembled a whole congregation, bidding them to hold lighted candles in their hand and collectively excommunicate the devil who had caused an innocent woman much malice.[43] The candles served to visualize and symbolize the boundaries of the devil's actions. In a similar fashion, the measuring of the house is a symbolic demarcation of the boundaries of the plague, bidding it to stay inside/outside. The involvement of many people serves to strengthen the symbolic act; all the assembled people rise and unite against the feared illness and they will all be covered by the protective force of the practice.

Although a closed interpretation of the Danish practice cannot be offered, the suggestions made above serve to shed new light on the devotional practice of transfiguration. What this practice seems to imply is first and foremost a collective protection against the plague. A group of people gathers *outside* the house, encircling it to guard it from attacks from the plague, and then moves to the *inside* where a pretzel – presumably made of wax – is produced. The movement from outside to inside is performed physically as well as mentally; inside the house the people prepare the final physical and material manifestation of the wish for protection, folded up and tied together in the significant form of the pretzel. This object, which has the form of the traditional Christian Lenten bread – visually imitating crossed arms – is then handed over to the Virgin, in whose arms the wellbeing of the congregation has now been placed. Everything is folded up and contained in the figure that signifies the communal wish for protection.

The wax and its transformative abilities receive a central position in the practice. It connects the house – where the pretzel is produced – with the church – where the pretzel is hung before the Virgin Mary. The pretzel-like figure 'contains' in its very materiality the measure of the house and the productive enterprise of the assembled people. It also holds in it the process of transformation from thread to pretzel. It is through actions and changes of the material substance that the wax is turned into an instrument of protection. The production of the pretzel-like figure carries an enormous amount of significance, contained in one simple figure; it now refers to the five saints, it signifies the size of the house and the collective effort of the congregation, and it signifies that the congregation trusts the Virgin – in collaboration with the saints – to protect *all*. The practice of perception is fundamental to this devotion: the sensory perception of the material change – visible, tactile and audible – as well as the

---

42 The plague as a result of the devil's doings is treated in *The Malleus Maleficarum of Heinrich Kramer and James Sprenger*, trans. Montague Summers (1928; 1971), for example, see pp 95, 99. For the plague as sign of Apocalypse and punishment of sins, see Laura A. Smoller, 'Of earthquakes, hail, frogs and geography: plague and the investigation of the Apocalypse in the later Middle Ages' in Caroline Walker Bynum and Paul Freedman (eds), *Last things: death and the Apocalypse in the Middle Ages* (Philadelphia, 1999), pp 156–87; Paul Binski, *Medieval death: ritual and representation* (London, 1996), pp 127–30.   **43** *The Malleus Maleficarum*, p. 166.

cognitive inner perception of the significance of the alteration of form. The wax transfigures into a protective device through the transformative process and the congregation is transformed *with* the performance of the practice – hopefully even healed. Inner and outer transformations perform a parallel and reciprocal progressive movement upwards towards a higher understanding of and faith in God.

CONCLUDING REMARKS

As exemplified above, late medieval devotion was often structured so that it strategically facilitated enlightenment. This was done by forming a setting in which sense perception could be made to shift into another perceptive mode. In the interaction of the senses a transfiguration takes place on the sensory level, mirroring the anticipated devotional progress on the spiritual level where God is now experienced with newly restored and configured senses. Through a combination of different devotional actions – perceptive actions, bodily movements, intended address and choice of setting – the mind and body of the pious practitioner went through a transformation that left him or her enlightened. But the mental and bodily transformation also altered the devotional process, establishing a reciprocal relation between practice and piety. Thus the devotional transfiguration happened on an individual level as well as on a practical level. Devotional practice was simply permeated by a sense of progress and transformation.

What the transfiguration-theme illustrates is that medieval devotees were well aware of the effect of combining different sensory modes of perception; by combining a variety of outer signs, the inner comprehension was affected. If Christ or Virgin Mary was seen, felt and heard, the illuminative effect turned out much stronger. The outer transformation – moving from one mode of perception to another – also affected the inner transformation. The mind was taken to a whole new level of comprehension through the figurative change. The incorporation of transfiguration in late medieval devotion served to transform and conform the senses into a devout sensorium, ready to sense the divine.

Dividing these types of changes is, of course, artificial and contrived since they are often all involved; it is often the case that a devotional practice involves a change in bodily position which then, in turn, results in a change of the inner disposition of that particular person which then again leads to a transformation of the outer appearance and a change in comprehension of Christ. Body, senses and objects are always involved in the practice of devotion where they are transformed and altered. As the considerations above indicate, the biblical Transfiguration had a parallel in the *practice* of devotion. It can be found in descriptions of devotional experiences where a similar understanding of *comprehension through change in appearance* is fundamental and it can also be found in instructions where the practice of devotional actions and the use of objects are fundamentally based on these ideals.

6 Don't judge a head by its cover: the materiality of the *Johannesschüssel* as reliquary[1]

SOETKIN VANHAUWAERT & GEORG GEML

A precious reliquary of the former convent of St Katharinenthal is preserved in the Schweizerisches Landesmuseum in Zürich (pl. 16). The platter on a sculpted foot carries a replica of the decapitated head of St John the Baptist, in which a relic cavity is hidden. According to a document (*c.*1589) describing the feast of Corpus Christi in the convent, this 'monstrance'[2] was carried around in the procession.[3] Shining with gold and silver,[4] this life-size goldsmith's work must have impressed all who beheld it.

Together with gemstones, these materials were (and still are) seen as the summit of the material hierarchy. Commentaries on relics and reliquaries by medieval authors like Thiofrid of Echternach (d. 1100) and Tridentine theologians like Carlo Borromeo (1538–84), up to the art-historical literature of the twentieth and twenty-first centuries, show that gold and silver were considered to be the most worthy materials for reliquaries containing precious bones of saints. As a consequence, precious materials dominated the exterior of the reliquary throughout the centuries and are considered an essential feature.

But not all *Johannesschüsseln* hosting relics were made of gold and silver. On the contrary, there is a significant number made of wood, without any precious metals or gemstones. This fact calls into question generally accepted notions about reliquaries: what was it that made the wooden *Johannesschüsseln* worthy of hosting relics? Did the materials used influence the perception of the reliquary and of the relic? Were these sculptures intended to contain a relic or did they become reliquaries at a later date? And finally, did the relic define the sculpture?

After an introduction to the *Johannesschüssel* itself and its complex relation with the relic cult, this essay will explore different views on the materiality of reliquaries in general. In a final part about the *Johannesschüssel* as reliquary, these views will be used in order to question some fixed ideas about reliquaries.

1 This essay was written in the context of a double research project under the direction of Barbara Baert supported by the Funding for Scientific Research Flanders and Leuven University. With special thanks to Paul Arblaster.   2 In the Wiener Heiligtumbuch from 1502 a similar *Johannesschüssel* on a foot is depicted and called 'monstrantz': Hella Arndt and Renate Kroos, 'Ikonographie der Johannesschüssel', p. 258.   3 Hanspeter Lanz, 'Johannesschüssel aus St Katharinenthal', pp 418–19; Barbara Baert, *Caput Joannis in Disco*, pp 88–9.   4 The *Johannesschüssel* is actually made in copper and silver and is partially gilded: see Lanz, 'Johannesschüssel aus St Katharinenthal', p. 418.

THE *JOHANNESSCHÜSSEL* AND THE LINK WITH THE RELIC CULT

The *Johannesschüssel* is a type of sculpture that emerged in the thirteenth century in the German-speaking area of Europe and was venerated widely (a veneration that continues in some places); it shows the severed head of St John the Baptist on a platter. Throughout the centuries, this motif has been interpreted differently by artists: the position of the head changes, the platters vary in form, many of the objects have different inscriptions on the rim and, most importantly here, a wide variety of materials was used, including stone, metals, terracotta, papier-mâché and, most often, wood.[5]

The *Johannesschüssel* is focal in the story of the passion of St John the Baptist, as narrated in the Gospels of Mark (6:14–29) and Matthew (14:1–12). John was imprisoned by Herod Antipas because he denounced the unlawful marriage of the already married tetrarch and his sister-in-law, Herodias. Herod was afraid of the popularity of the prophet and did not dare to execute him. But Herodias sought revenge for John's denunciations. Herod's birthday feast was a welcome opportunity: Herodias' daughter danced for the guests and Herod decided to grant her anything she wanted, up to half of his kingdom.[6] Incited by her mother Herodias, she asked for John's head. John the Baptist was decapitated and his head was brought on a dish.

The Bible does not mention the fate of the head after the banquet, but by the beginning of the thirteenth century, after many detours, the head relic of St John was situated at Constantinople.[7] Wallon de Sarton, a canon of St Martin's in Picquigny near Amiens, took the relic from the church of St George of Mangana during the Fourth Crusade and brought it back with him to Amiens. On 17 December 1206 it was carried through the streets of Amiens with all due solemnity and handed over to the bishop in the cathedral, where it is still preserved today.[8] But Notre Dame in Amiens was (and is) not the only church to claim the possession of this head relic. Numerous other skulls or skull parts attributed to John the Baptist can be found in Europe and the Near East, for example in San Silvestro in Capite in Rome, in San Marco in Venice, in the Topkapi Serail in Istanbul or in the Umayyad Mosque in Damascus. At the beginning of the sixteenth century, Martin Luther was aware of no fewer than twelve head relics in Western Europe.[9] The skull of Amiens was, however,

---

5 The motif of the head of St John the Baptist also appears in painting. For various examples and more information on the *Johannisschüssel* in both sculpture and painting, see Isabel Combs Stuebe, 'The "Johannisschüssel"'; Arndt and Kroos, 'Ikonographie der Johannesschüssel'; Baert, *Caput Joannis in Disco*. **6** The girl's name, Salome, is known through the writings of Flavius Josephus (*c.*37–post-100). Flavius Josephus, *The complete works* (1981), p. 382. **7** The fate of the head was discussed in many patristic writings. For an overview, see Baert, *Caput Joannis in Disco*, ch. 2: 'On relics'. **8** Charles du Fresne, *Traité historique* (1665); Auguste Breuil, 'Du culte de saint Jean Baptiste'; Charles Salmon, *Histoire du chef de saint Jean Baptiste*; Theodor Innitzer, *Johannes der Täufer* (1908), p. 402; Baert, *Caput Joannis in Disco*, pp 22–3. **9** Innitzer, *Johannes der Täufer*, pp 402–3; Louis Réau, *Iconographie de l'art chrétien* (1956), ii/i, pp 431–63; Combs Stuebe, 'The "Johannisschüssel"', 2; Arndt and Kroos, 'Ikonographie der Johannesschüssel', 245; Baert, *Caput Joannis in Disco*, pp 27–9.

the most famous. It was venerated as a cure for seizures, epilepsy, headaches and depression and other diseases connected with the head and throat, and attracted countless pilgrims.[10] It was promoted all over Europe in the form of lead pilgrim badges displaying the image of the relic.[11]

The engraving published by the historian Charles du Fresne, sieur du Cange, in 1665, shows the relic before the destruction wrought during the French Revolution (fig. 6.1).[12] The mummified skull is lying on a platter decorated with gemstones and pearls, the cavities of the eyes and nose filled with wax. Above its left eye, a small gap was noticed; around this small wound a legend was created, that was used as proof of the authenticity of the relic.[13] The origin lies in a short passage in St Jerome's *Epistula adversus Rufinum*, in which the Church Father tells how Herodias pierced the tongue of the severed head of John the Baptist with a needle, just as Fulvia did with Cicero.[14] In Amiens, this legend was transformed into Herodias taking revenge by cutting the head above the eyebrow with a knife, resulting in a popular motif in prints and mystery plays.[15] Today, it relates the *Johannesschüsseln* with a head wound to the skull of Amiens – or at least to the legend that was developed from it.

The *Johannesschüssel* does not have an obvious, demarcated function; it was used in several ways, and possibly one object served more than one purpose. *Johannesschüsseln* were carried in processions during the novenas of St John[16] and on other feast days, as was for example the *Johannesschüssel* of St Katharinenthal on the feast of Corpus Christi.[17] Sources suggest further that they have been used as props in religious drama.[18] The *Frankfurter Dirigierrolle* (first half of the fourteenth century), a play showing the passions of Jesus Christ and of John, tells us how a servant brought the head of John on stage right after his decapitation.[19]

Further, and maybe most importantly, the *Johannesschüssel* served as a devotional object. In the public sphere of the church, the *Johannesschüssel* was sometimes given a

10 Baert, *Caput Joannis in Disco*, p. 36.   11 Combs Stuebe, 'The "Johannisschüssel"', 8; Baert, *Caput Joannis in Disco*, pp 36–7.   12 Du Fresne, *Traité historique*. This engraving is also published in the *Acta Sanctorum*: Godfried Henschen and Daniel van Papenbroeck, *Acta Sanctorum: Junius* (1707), iv, col. 750; Arndt and Kroos, 'Ikonographie der Johannesschüssel', pp 246–8.   13 This was also mentioned in the description of the head relic in the *Acta Sanctorum*: 'Super oculum dextrum notatur foramen oblongum'. The text of the *Acta Sanctorum* refers to the wound as above the right eye, but is that the right eye for the beholder, or 'his' right eye? Anyway, the position of this wound, left or right, varies and is often discussed. The engraving (fig. 2) and the skull in Amiens seem to show a puncture above his left eye, and thus the right eye for the beholder. Henschen and van Papenbroeck, *Acta Sanctorum: Junius*, iv, col. 749. For a discussion on the symbolism of the position of the head wound, see Baert, *Caput Joannis in Disco*, pp 95–8.   14 Hieronymus, 'Apologia Adversos Libros Rufini', ed. Jacques-Paul Migne (1845), col. 488: 'Fecerunt haec et Fulvia in Ciceronem, et Herodias in Joannem: quia veritatem non poterant audire, et linguam veriloquam discriminali acu confoderunt.'   15 Arndt and Kroos, 'Ikonographie der Johannesschüssel', pp 301–7.   16 Gotbert Moro, 'Tafelngehen in Plessnitz', 75–85; Franz Mennemeyer, *Kult und Brauchtum*, pp 119–22; Charles Caspers, 'Het Sint Jansfeest', pp 121–35; Baert, *Caput Joannis in Disco*, pp 61–82.   17 For information and references, see the introduction, esp. note 3.   18 Oskar Thulin, *Johannes der Täufer* (1930); Combs Stuebe, 'The "Johannisschüssel"', 5; Arndt and Kroos, 'Ikonographie der Johannesschüssel', 302–6; Georg Geml, 'Frühe Johannesschüsseln' (MA, University of Vienna, 2009), pp 43–58.   19 Geml, 'Frühe Johannesschüsseln', p. 47.

6.1 Skull of John the Baptist in Amiens Cathedral (after an engraving in G. Henschen and D. van Papenbroeck, *Acta Sanctorum: Junius*, IV, Antwerp, 1707, cols 687–808 at col. 750).

spot on the altar, in order to enhance visibility and accessibility for parishioners and pilgrims, as is shown on the Gutenstetten altarpiece by Erhard Altdorfer (pl. 18). This was the case especially around the feast days of St John the Baptist. Also in the private sphere, the *Johannesschüssel* served a devotional function. Small alabaster plaques with the head of St John on a plate were popular domestic devotional objects from 1400 onwards, especially in England; various references to these are found in wills and lists of household goods.[20] The painted *Johannesschüssel* too seems to have functioned in a private context. For example, Cardinal Georges d'Amboise (1460–1510) ordered a painted *Johannesschüssel* by Andrea Solario in 1507, not only because of his special

20 Francis W. Cheetham, *English medieval alabasters*; Baert, *Caput Joannis in Disco*, pp 91–5.

devotion for John the Baptist but also hoping that his severe colic and fever attacks would be cured by this traditional image of healing power.[21]

In addition, in different ways, a significant number of *Johannesschüsseln* are connected to the cult of relics. First of all, they all impersonate the head relic of the saint. As mentioned above, some of them reflect the head relic of John the Baptist in Amiens in particular by means of the wound above the eyebrow. Sometimes it is painted on, as in the earliest known *Johannesschüssel* from Naumburg (1215–25; pl. 14),[22] sometimes carved, as in a stone example from Nideggen now in the Schnütgen Museum in Cologne (*c.*1500; pl. 15). Certain *Johannesschüsseln*, such as the one from Leuven (*c.*1500, pl. 17), were, like the relic in Amiens, venerated for a cure and thus functioned as a local ersatz relic.[23] Others host(ed) relics themselves, placed in the platter or in the sculpted head, either concealed at the back of the head or prominently to be seen at first sight. Sometimes the relic was placed in the section of the neck, as in a South German example (*c.*1500) now in Breda's Museum,[24] but more often it was positioned in an opening in the forehead, as in the head of John in the chapel of Grubbenvorst (sixteenth century; fig. 6.2),[25] or on the crown of the head, as in the head in Hemelveerdegem.[26]

In some of the *Johannesschüsseln*, the relics are not openly presented to the viewer, but hidden in the back of the head, as in an example from the Städtisches Museum in Göttingen (early thirteenth century),[27] one from the Germanisches Nationalmuseum in Nürnberg (fourteenth century)[28] or the one from Naumburg (pl. 14). In the latter, a small square recess was made in the crown of the head. As the metal ring on the rim of the platter suggests, the Naumburg *Johannesschüssel* either hung on the wall or was placed on an altar, as was usually done on the feast days of the Baptist – the nativity on 24 June and the decollation on 29 August. In both display positions, the recess was not visible – in the first case it was hidden behind the unconventional hair knot, in the second the neck was exposed and the relics were out of sight.[29]

Although the visibility of the relic(s) in these *Johannesschüsseln* may differ, there is one characteristic uniting all the sculptures named in this essay: they are not made of

21 Baert, *Caput Joannis in Disco*, pp 197–8; B. Baert, 'The head of St John the Baptist', pp 87–107, esp. p. 95. See also Barbara Baert, 'Saint-John's head on a plate'; Valentine Henderiks, *Albrecht Bouts*, pp 298–309. **22** Markus Hörsch, 'Johannesschüssel'. Gerhard Lutz suggested a new dating: see Gerhard Lutz, '*Schüssel mit dem Haupt Johannes des Täufers*', i, pp 689–91.   **23** Baert, *Caput Joannis in Disco*, pp 71–2. In the context of his discussion about the quotation of forms in the aesthetics of the cult image, Belting showed with the example of the icons of Luke that, in late Middle Ages, people believed that a copy could derive privileges from the original ("authentischen Urbild"): Hans Belting, *Bild und Kult*, pp 490–2.   **24** Baert, *Caput Joannis in Disco*, p. 55. **25** Peter Jan Margry, 'Grubbenvorst'; Baert, *Caput Joannis in Disco*, p. 55.   **26** The dating of this sculpture is problematic: see G. Van Bockstaele, *Hemelveerdegem* (1998), p. 118, figs 60–1.   **27** Arndt and Kroos, 'Ikonographie der Johannesschüssel', pp 275–6; Geml, 'Frühe Johannesschüsseln', p. 11.   **28** Arndt and Kroos, 'Ikonographie der Johannesschüssel', pp 283–4.   **29** The cavity was opened and emptied in 1686, as reported by Johann Carl Schoch in his description of Naumburg Cathedral. Relics of John the Baptist were found inside, but also of seven other saints: Walpurgis, Bartholomew, Nicholas, Margaret, Hedwig of Silesia, Gotthard and an unknown saint. Johann Carl Schoch, *Kurtze Nachricht von denen Merckwürdigkeiten* (1773), cols 60–1; see also Klaus Niehr, *Die mitteldeutsche Skulptur* (1992), p. 321; Hörsch, 'Johannesschüssel', p. 92.

6.2 John's head (with refilled relic cavity), fifteenth century, wood, Grubbenvorst, Presbytery of Our Lady of the Assumption. Photograph © Soetkin Vanhauwaert.

precious materials. Of course, precious *Johannesschüssel* reliquaries were produced too, for example the one from St Katharinenthal (third quarter of the fifteenth century) mentioned in the introduction (pl. 16),[30] or the *Johannesschüssel* carried by angels preserved in St Bavo's Cathedral in Ghent (1624) (fig. 6.3).[31] This only throws the question into sharper relief: what determined the choice of the materials? Why were some examples made in precious materials and others in simple wood or stone? And did the materiality of the reliquary change the perception of the reliquary and of the relics inside? Were these sculptures even seen as reliquaries? The *Johannesschüssel* as relic container raises a lot of questions, but before going into more detail on this, it is necessary to address some aspects of the materiality of reliquaries in general.

'BONES WITHOUT STONES WERE AT RISK OF NOT SEEMING SO PRECIOUS, AFTER ALL'[32]

As the relics of saints were believed to act as a point of contact between the faithful and God, they could not be held in whatever box came to hand. These important objects, often referred to as 'more precious than the most exquisite jewels and more purified than gold',[33] deserved important containers and as a result reliquaries were often precious objects. In her latest book, Cynthia Hahn formulates the function of a reliquary as follows:

> They are mentioned in the earliest texts concerning relics as a means of honoring and transporting the sacred substances of relics, but in addition, from the beginning, they have carried messages about the significance, authenticity and meaning of the relics they contain. Even if such messages are conveyed only by abstractions of the prestige of precious materials, reliquaries in their essence are mediations between relics and audiences.[34]

In this quotation, Hahn combines two important thoughts. First, she relates the reliquary to the significance, the authenticity and the meaning of the relic it carries. Second, she mentions the importance of the materiality of the container for its function as mediator. These two ideas appear indeed to be intertwined. As the reliquary is representing the relic, its materiality plays a huge role in the perception of the sacred remains by the faithful.

In the Middle Ages, relic and reliquary were often considered as one.[35] Therefore,

---

30 Arndt and Kroos, 'Ikonographie der Johannesschüssel', 258; Lanz, 'Johannesschüssel aus St Katharinenthal', pp 418–19; Geml, 'Frühe Johannesschüsseln', p. 26; Baert, *Caput Joannis in Disco*, pp 88–9.   **31** Elisabeth Dhanens, *Sint-Baafskathedraal Gent*, pp 240–1.   **32** Brigitte Buettner, 'From stones to bones', p. 57.   **33** This quotation is taken from the *Passion* of St Polycarp, written shortly after his martyrdom *c.*155. It is used, for example, in Anton Legner, *Reliquien in Kunst und Kult* (1995), p. 146; Bruno Reudenbach, 'Reliquiare als Heiligkeitsbeweis', p. 10; Scott B. Montgomery, *St Ursula*, p. 59; Buettner, 'From stones to bones', p. 43; Barbara Drake Boehm, '"A brilliant resurrection"', p. 149.   **34** Cynthia Hahn, *Strange beauty*, p. 9.   **35** Montgomery,

6.3 'Master with the Lion's Head', *Johannesschüssel*, 1625–6, silver, Ghent, St John's Church
(now known as St Bavo's Cathedral). © KIK-IRPA, Brussels.

reliquaries had to keep up with their precious content. The materials used for their
production had to be worthy; as a consequence, precious materials, such as gold, silver
and gems were very popular because of their earthly and spiritual value.[36] At the top
of the medieval material hierarchy, silver and gold were considered incorruptible, a
quality associated with the uncorrupted body and flesh of saints.[37] Gems, on the other
hand, were believed to contain powers themselves and thereby strengthened, even
complemented, those of the relic in the reliquary; they carried the *virtus* across to the
faithful.[38] In some contemporary texts, gems were considered to be representations of
the virtues of the saints and can thus be seen as the adornment preeminently suited to
the depository of their earthly remnants.[39] These precious materials gained additional
spiritual meaning, as they were associated with the heavenly Jerusalem and Paradise.

'Golden flesh, radiant bones' (2007). Thiofrid of Echternach found this unity indispensable: Hahn, *Strange
beauty*, p. 38.   **36** 'Seules ces matières sont jugées dignes de contenir leur précieux dépôt': Jean-Claude Schmitt,
'Les reliques et les images', p. 153. For a more general overview, see Thomas Raff, *Die Sprache der Materialien*.
37 Martina Bagnoli, 'The stuff of heaven', pp 138–9.   **38** Christel Meier, *Gemma Spiritualis* (1977); Gia
Toussaint, 'Heiliges Gebein und edler Stein', 46–9; Bagnoli, 'The stuff of heaven' (2011), pp 138–9; Hahn, *Strange
beauty*, pp 41–3.   **39** Bagnoli, 'The stuff of heaven', pp 138–9; Hahn, *Strange beauty*, p. 42.

The Book of Revelation relates how gems decorate the walls of the heavenly city and the streets are paved with pure gold, 'as if it were transparent glass' (Revelation 21:18–21).[40] These biblical associations with Heaven were confirmed in theological writings and so strengthened the idea of the precious reliquary as the heavenly body of the saint, radiating the heavenly light of God. As a consequence, the whole of container and contained, of reliquary and relic, were taken to represent both the heavenly presence (reliquary) and the earthly remnants (relic) of the saint.[41]

Still, this unity of the earthly and the heavenly body also contains a paradox, which could cause confusion for the believer.[42] The religiously worthless reliquary, made from gold and precious stones, nevertheless represented a great material value, which must have dazzled the beholder; in turn, the relic inside has no material value at all, but was priceless in the context of Christian faith. With this discrepancy in mind, a few medieval voices condemned the use of precious materials for reliquaries. Guibert of Nogent (1055–1124) argues in his *De sanctis et eorum pigneribus*: 'Why should anyone be granted the dignity of being enclosed in gold or silver, when the Son of God is buried in the lowliest rock?'[43] Then again Bernard of Clairvaux (1090–1153) complains in his letter to William of Saint-Thierry, known as the *Apologia ad Wilhelmum*, that pilgrims perceive a beautiful image of a saint as more holy if it is more coloured (that is, varied because of material riches) and writes bitterly that the beautiful container is more admired than the sanctity of its content is venerated.[44]

Still, precious containers were universally used and sometimes even considered necessary – as Hahn indicates – for the significance, the authenticity and the meaning of the relic.[45] Thiofrid of Echternach defends the use of gold for a reliquary. He even argues, as Hahn writes, that 'without the compensatory beauty of the reliquary, a relic could be repulsive'.[46] Nevertheless, he believes that reliquaries are more precious because of their content, and not because of their materials. The precious materials are meant to lead the beholder beyond the container to the even more precious relics inside. The faithful will see that, if they look with the eyes of their soul.[47]

However, instead of focusing on what the 'inner eyes' should see – that is, the grace

40 Schmitt, 'Les reliques et les images', p. 153; Bruno Reudenbach and Gia Toussaint, 'Wahrnehmung und Deutung von Heiligen', p. 38; Toussaint, 'Heiliges Gebein und edler Stein', pp 46–50; Erik Thunø, 'The golden altar', p. 73.   **41** Legner, *Reliquien in Kunst und Kult*, p. 242; Toussaint, 'Heiliges Gebein und edler Stein', p. 50; Thunø, 'The golden altar', p. 73. Another related duality that can be found in the unit relic–reliquary is the idea of body and soul: Hahn, *Strange beauty*, p. 24.   **42** Reudenbach, '"Gold ist Schlamm"', pp 8–9; Toussaint, 'Heiliges Gebein und edler Stein', p. 41.   **43** Guibertus de Novigentus, *Quo ordine sermo fieri debeat* (1993), pp 85–109, esp. p. 105, lines 621–3; Henri Platelle, 'Guibert de Nogent', pp 109–21; Thomas Head, 'Guibert of Nogent', p. 419; Hahn, *Strange beauty*, p. 16.   **44** Especially Apologia 28: see Conrad Rudolph, *The things of greater importance*, pp 10–11 and 278–83; Reudenbach, '"Gold ist Schlamm"', p. 7; Hahn, 'The spectacle of the charismatic body', p. 170; Bagnoli, 'The stuff of heaven', p. 138.   **45** Hahn, *Strange beauty*, p. 9.   **46** *Flores epytaphii sanctorum*, 2.3.79–92 in Thiofridus Epternacensis, *Goffridi Abbatis Vindocinensis* (1854), col. 347; Thiofrid of Echternach, *Thiofridi Abbatis Epternacensis* (1993), p. 39. See also Bagnoli, 'The stuff of heaven', p. 137; Hahn, *Strange beauty*, p. 23.   **47** *Flores epytaphii sanctorum* 2.2.70–80 and 2.3.93–100 in Thiofridus Epternacensis, *Goffridi Abbatis Vindocinensis*, cols 343, 347; Thiofrid of Echternach, *Thiofridi Abbatis Epternacensis*, pp 35–6, 39. See also Reudenbach, '"Gold ist Schlamm"', p. 9.

and glory of the saint in heaven – it seems as if, already in the Middle Ages, the precious nature of the material of the reliquary often overshadowed the holiness of the relic. This attitude reveals itself, for example, in inventories, in which the description of reliquaries is focused on the materials and their value, and not on their content.[48] Even clerics were aware that a relic's significance was often judged by its cover. In the chronicle of the monastery of Prüm (Germany), the story of the woman visiting the freshly arrived relics of Ss Daria and Chrysantus is told. She came to their tomb with lots of gifts, but when she saw that the relics 'did not shine with gold and silver' she left and took her offerings with her. The chronicle further describes how she was penalized for her contempt and lost all of her gifts and eventually died three days later as a punishment.[49]

In spite of stories such as these, present-day authors often assume that the materials of the reliquary somehow determine the value of the relic.

> As a result, the relic matter was ennobled by the precious materials at the outside and made vividly perceptible as heavenly and holy. Although theologically subordinate, the visually attractive and precious covering fulfils the visual authentication of the relics,

concludes Reudenbach.[50] However, as Bagnoli reminds us, this line of thought was also turned around:

> The use of precious materials was certainly part of the process of marketing relics: the opulent display of gold reliquaries studded with gems effectively proclaimed the relic's 'real' worth. This principle worked in both directions, and lack of a proper setting cast doubt on the authenticity of the relics.[51]

The perception of a relic could, by means of the reliquary and its materiality, easily shift: if worthy materials define the content of a reliquary, then a relic in a simple container could not have been very valuable, or could it?

Although most (known) reliquaries passed down through the ages are indeed made of precious materials, still some medieval reliquaries were made from other materials that were less costly. These less precious objects are too often overlooked, because they do not meet what is commonly expected of a reliquary. The *Johannesschüssel*, often

---

48 Reudenbach, '"Gold ist Schlamm"', pp 2–3. This phenomenon is mentioned by Dhanens, *De artistieke uitrusting*, p. 23.   **49** This story is told in the chronicle of the monastery of Prüm (Westeifel, Germany): Prüm monastery, *Historia translationis reliquiarum* (1852), cols 673–82, esp. 676. It is mentioned by Bagnoli, 'The stuff of heaven', p. 138 and Hahn, *Strange beauty*, p. 35.   **50** 'Im Ergebnis führt dies dazu, daß die Reliquienmaterie durch kostbare Materialien äußerlich nobilitiert und als himmlisch und heilig anschaulich erfahrbar wird. Obschon theologisch nachrangig, leistet die visuell attraktive und kostbare Verkleidung die anschauliche Authentifizierung der Reliquien': Reudenbach, '"Gold ist Schlamm"', p. 10.   **51** Bagnoli, 'The stuff of heaven', p. 138.

carrying relics although produced in wood or stone, is situated on the threshold between sculpture and relic, image and container, and is therefore the ideal starting point for a further reflection on the complex issue of the materiality of relic-containing sculptures.

THE BEAUTY IS IN THE EYE OF THE BEHOLDER

In a book about folk medicine (1891), Alfons de Cock writes about the cult of St John the Baptist in Kachtem (Belgium), where the saint is venerated for healing epilepsy and headaches. The church has two relics – one in a silver casket for the priests and one, as he describes, in the skull of a wooden head, 'representing the decapitated head of the saint' (fig. 6.4) that was offered to the people to venerate. Just like some of its golden fellows, this head of St John was carried in a procession during the novenas of St John on the occasion of his birthday in June. In 1888, according to de Cock, more than twenty thousand people came to visit the relics.[52] Although this reference is quite late, it nevertheless shows that this cult site was still popular at the end of the nineteenth century and its wooden reliquary perceived as a legitimate, significant representation of this saint and his relics.

These relics, however, are not just any relics. Just as the *Johannesschüsseln* of Naumburg, Breda, Niddegen and Grubbenvorst, the head of Kachtem carried a relic of St John the Baptist, who was very popular in the Middle Ages and later centuries.[53] He was the last prophet of the Old Covenant and the protomartyr of Christianity and took up a prominent position in the community of saints. An important aspect of his cult that illustrates this is the fact that, besides Christ and his mother, John the Baptist was the only person whose birth was marked by a feast day on the liturgical calendar.[54] He was truly a key figure in the Christian faith, having popular cult sites all over the Christian sphere, as in the twelve churches claiming his skull relic (as mentioned above). Given this popularity, it is hard to believe that St John's relics would have been put in a wooden container – a literal representation of his head relic – if this was perceived as less costly and therefore the relics as less valuable.

This negativity towards wooden containers can, however, be read between the lines of one of the major publications on reliquaries, Joseph Braun's *Die Reliquiare des christlichen Kultes und ihre Entwicklung* (1940). Being very thorough, Braun does not ignore the less costly containers and devotes parts of his chapter on materials not only to metals, crystal and glass, but also to stone, wood and fabric.[55] If you read carefully,

---

52 Alfons de Cock, *Volksgeneeskunde in Vlaanderen*, p. 102.   **53** The relic was taken out of the sculpture in 1956. The other mentioned *Johannesschüsseln* have also been emptied.   **54** See above. His birthday was celebrated on 24 June, his beheading on 29 Aug.   **55** Joseph Braun, *Die Reliquiare*, pp 83–144. Braun also briefly touches upon the existence of the *Johannesschüssel* in his chapter on head reliquaries. Although many wooden *Johannesschüsseln* contain relics, Braun only mentions one, along with fourteen others in more precious materials: ibid., pp 414–16, figs 479–81.

6.4 John's head, *c.*1625, walnut, Kachtem: St John's Church. Photograph © Soetkin Vanhauwaert.

it seems that Braun thinks that reliquaries made of wood are less preferable. In the introduction of the chapter, he refers to the writings of Carlo Borromeo and Vicar General Jacob Myller (1550–97) as lacking innovation. Although, remarkably, as Braun writes, they both *allow* the use of wood, and especially walnut, as a material for reliquaries. However, he proceeds to state that 'for outstanding, larger and more famous relics they suggest gold, silver and crystal as materials instead'.[56] This could lead to the assumption that wooden reliquaries were only to be used for less important

---

56 'Für hervorragendere, größere und berühmtere Reliquien aber empfehlen sie als solches Gold, Silber und Kristall': ibid., pp 83–4.

relics, because no owner of a significant relic would want to risk having it perceived as insignificant. Braun further acknowledges the fact that a lot of wooden reliquaries were made, because often too many relics were part of the treasury of a church or cloister and it was impossible to give them all a container in precious metals. That is why, according to Braun, 'they had to make do' ('sich zu begnügen') with wooden reliquaries.[57] Although his acknowledgment of their existence is quite important, this expression carries a strong sense of negativity. According to Braun, an owner of a relic would only have used a wooden reliquary if his funds were insufficient to give it one in precious materials, and it suggests the owner would not have been as happy with it.

Combined with the conception that precious materials are essential for transferring the spiritual merit of the relics to the beholder, this vision reduces wooden (and stone) relic containers to the status of being less than ideal. It further conflicts with the popular representation of the head relic of the Forerunner of Christ: would this really have been considered less preferable as a container, because of its cheaper materials? The same inconsistency appears with crucifixes. Anton Legner mentions various examples of simple, wooden sculptures of Christ on the cross that contain relics. The Imervard cross in Brunswick Cathedral (mid-twelfth century) held no fewer than thirty relics in a container that was hidden in the back of Christ's head.[58] This Romanesque cross is, however, made from oak. Likewise, the Gothic wooden crucifix in the Regensburg Schottenkirche contains relics placed in the same inaccessible, invisible spot, and in the Forstenrieder crucifix, a cavity for relics was made in the back of the wooden sculpture.[59] Legner writes about these sculpture reliquaries:

> The sanctum is neither visible in the stone of the altar nor in the head of the Crucified, but the vivid image of the Saviour on the Cross, surrounded by the aura of the numinousness, is the holiest and most worthy vessel to host the sanctum that therefore does not need to be visible to sanctify and take effect.[60]

According to Legner, these containers are thus proven worthy not because of their material qualities, but by means of the person they represent. The same reasoning is applied to sculptures of the Enthroned Virgin.[61] Could this also apply to the heads of St John the Baptist, the Forerunner of Christ? Some aspects of the history of the John's

---

57 Ibid., pp 133–4. **58** The relics were taken out of the crucifix in 1881 and placed in the altar of the Holy Mary. Anton Legner, *Reliquien in Kunst und Kult*, pp 235–6. **59** Johannes Taubert and Fritz Buchenrieder, 'Der Forstenrieder Kruzifixus', pp 81–102; Legner, *Reliquien in Kunst und Kult*, p. 238. **60** 'Das Heiltum im Altarstein wie im Haupt des Gekreuzigten ist nicht sichtbar, doch das mit der Aura des Numinosen ausgestattete plastische Bild des Heilands am Kreuz ist das heiligste und würdigste Gefäß für die Aufbewahrung erworbenen Heiltums, das der Sichtbarkeit nicht bedarf, um zu heiligen und zu wirken': Legner, *Reliquien in Kunst und Kult*, p. 236. **61** The examples of the Crucifix and the Enthroned Virgin are both complex, as (almost) no primary relics of both Christ and Mary are preserved. Nevertheless, these two sculpture types are often named in the context of the connection between relic and image: Taubert and Buchenrieder, 'Der Forstenrieder Kruzifixus', pp 81–102; Belting, *Bild und Kult*, pp 331–47; Legner, *Reliquien in Kunst und Kult*, pp 232–55.

Head of Kachtem suggest it does. A testimony of 1644 shows that this wooden head sculpture (fig. 6.2) was already perceived as 'de heijlighe relicquien van Sinte Jan' ('the holy relics of St John') before relics were added.[62] Maybe therefore it was considered worthy to contain relics later on.

This aspect opens up another question – the function of these objects. As noted in the first part of this essay, the sculpture of the *Johannesschüssel* served several functions, and their definition is often very complex. The original purpose of the sculpture in Kachtem is not known, but as a report from 1642 reveals, this sculpture did not originate as a reliquary; at the time of the report, the John's Head did not contain relics. Later on, however, relics were added.[63] The original function of the wooden head and platter of Naumburg is also not clear. According to Markus Hörsch, it was used as an *Andachtsbild* and functioned in the context of the altar (pl. 14). As already mentioned, this *Johannesschüssel* contained relics of several saints, among them a relic of St Hedwig. As she was canonized only in 1267, it is doubtful, but not impossible, that relics were in this sculpture from its origin. Possibly, her relics were added later to those already present in the head.[64] In contrast to the unclear Kachtem and Naumburg examples, the precious *Johannesschüssel* of St Bavo's Cathedral in Ghent (1624) was obviously intended as a reliquary (fig. 6.3). The inventories show that this is not the first *caput-in-disco* of the cathedral, but that this version replaced an older, also precious head reliquary of St John.[65]

As these three examples all contained relics, they are by definition reliquaries. But, the question must be asked: should we cling to this definition? Is every object containing a relic automatically a reliquary? Or should we add other criteria?

If we turn back to the quotation of Hahn, stating that 'reliquaries in their essence are mediations between relics and audiences',[66] it can be argued that the status of reliquary falls away when the relic is hidden, and the sculpture as a consequence does not function as a mediator, but stands on its own. A similar thought must have inspired Erich Meyer back in 1950, when he argued for a distinction between sculptures that contain relics as their primary function and sculptures that also happen to contain relics but primarily serve other purposes. In his opinion, only the former can be seen as reliquaries. He suggests that the latter are cult images, in which not the relic, but the sculpture is the object of veneration.[67] This would mean that of the *Johannesschüsseln* of Kachtem, Naumburg and Ghent, only the last can be called a reliquary with certainty: the head of Kachtem cannot be called a reliquary as it did not originate as one, and as the origin of the sculpture of Naumburg is not known, it is

---

62 Bisschoppelijk archief Brugge, Reeks B/F180. This *Johannesschüssel* and its history will be treated thoroughly by the author (Soetkin Vanhauwaert) in future studies.   **63** Rijksarchief Brugge, BB, nieuw kerkarchief 408. In a report from 1749 it is written that the wooden St John's head contains relics of St George: Rijksarchief Kortrijk, Archief van de Sint-Michielsparochie te Roeselare, n°. 1.   **64** Hörsch, 'Johannesschüssel', p. 91.   **65** Dhanens, *De artistieke uitrusting*, pp 87–9.   **66** Hahn, *Strange beauty*, p. 9.   **67** Erich Meyer, 'Reliquie und Reliquiar', p. 57.

not possible to determine whether it meets this definition. Many other works are in the same situation. Meyer himself already remarked that making the distinction between both 'categories' is often very hard. But is it necessary to differentiate reliquaries from (cult) images containing relics? Can one sculpture not be both? How can we determine how these objects functioned in their original context? And how can we know if people attached more importance to the relic or to the sculpture?[68]

One aspect that could be significant is the gradation of the visibility of the relic in the sculpture-container.[69] If the relic of a cult image is not seen as the object of veneration, but functions as a 'validator' within it, it should not have to be visible to the believer. A difference can be seen between, for example, the *Johannesschüssel* of Naumburg (pl. 14), in which the relics were hidden,[70] and the head in the chapel of Grubbenvorst (fig. 6.4), whose relic cavity took up most of the forehead and was thus very defining for the object. When looking at *Johannesschüssel* reliquaries in precious materials, we can see that the same models are used: the Ghent reliquary in silver and gold hides the relic from view (fig. 6.3), while the brass example from Eygelshoven (sixteenth century) displays its relic prominently in a big hole on its forehead (fig. 6.5). The difference is that the function of these *Johannesschüsseln* is given away by their materiality: because of their preciousness we assume they are reliquaries. Wooden sculptures that furthermore hide their relics do not reveal any recognizable aspect of a reliquary, which makes it impossible to know if these relics were known and thus could have added value to these objects. A sculpture was and is defined by the role of the relic it contains, but the perception and the status of the relic also changes through the meaning it has for the image and the role that it plays within it, visible or invisible.

These observations lead us to the complex interaction between relic and sculpture.[71]

---

68 One issue that makes the answer to these questions difficult is the change in function. If a sculpture did not originate as a reliquary, it does not necessarily mean it cannot have had that function as a primary position in the course of its existence. And what with reliquaries that were emptied? Another issue is the discrepancy between medieval and modern terms and categories and how they were and are interpreted. A related example is the term 'monstrance', that is exactly defined today, but was used for different kinds of objects in the Middle Ages. In the *Wiener Heiligtumbuch*, a *Johannesschüssel* is identified with the term 'monstrantz': *Wiener Heiligthumbuch* (1502, facsimile 1882), n.p. ("Der viert vmbgang"); this was also a common term for a reliquary at that time. This discrepancy is a fundamental topic when talking about medieval culture, but this question is too broad for the scope of this essay. Alicia Walker and Amanda Luyster's *Negotiating secular and sacred* (2009) touches upon a related aspect of this discussion.   **69** Of course the change in the importance of the visibility of the relic during the Middle Ages also has to be considered here. As Taubert already remarked, a discrepancy can be noticed when studying on the one hand the increasing interest for the visibility of the relic and on the other the hidden relics in sculptures: Taubert and Buchenrieder, 'Der Forstenrieder Kruzifixus', p. 102; Christoph L. Diedrichs, *Vom Glauben zum Sehen*.   **70** Was the congregation even aware that relics were part of these sculptures? And if they were not, how did the relics add value to these images?   **71** We are aware that this question touches on a wider issue of sculptures as recipients of relics; this certainly invites further research. Our essay teaches us that the *Johannesschüssel* can serve as an example in this area, due to its two-fold relation with the relic cult. As reliquary on the one hand and because of its connection with the skull relic in Amiens, this artefact proves to be on the threshold between both disciplines. This again shows the *Johannesschüssel* as an ambivalent and hybrid object. We hope to contribute further to this research in the course of the project *Caput Iohannis in disco*, under the direction of Barbara Baert (KU Leuven) supported by Funding for Scientific Research Flanders and Leuven University. Works questioning or discussing the relation between relic and sculpture include Taubert and Buchenrieder, 'Der

6.5 *Johannesschüssel*, sixteenth century (platter of a later date), brass, Eygelshoven, St John's Church. Photograph © Soetkin Vanhauwaert.

It is often thought that the sculpture houses the relic and represents the saint, while the relic gives the sculpture a reason for existence and protects it from accusations of idolatry.[72] 'In order to justify their base materiality and human origins relics were often buried deep inside [the images] or inserted around them.'[73] Although this reasoning is not generally accepted, the John's head of Kachtem can again serve as an exemplary case study to support this thesis. The *Ordinata* of the report of 1642 state that the parish must see to it that the head sculpture contains relics, if they want to use it for devotional purposes.[74] This wooden head of St John the Baptist was both cult object and 'reliquary', only because the Church would not legitimate the veneration of this sculpture without relics inserted.[75] The question that presents itself is: did the parishioners care about the materials of this sculpture? Would the parish have chosen a sculpture in other, more costly materials if they had known it would carry relics later on? It seems unlikely.

Forstenrieder Kruzifixus', pp 100–2; Belting, *Bild und Kult*, pp 331–47; Legner, *Reliquien in Kunst und Kult*, pp 232–55; Silke Tammen, 'Dorn und Schmerzensmann' (2011), pp 187–208; Bynum, *Christian materiality*, pp 105–21. **72** Meyer, 'Reliquie und Reliquiar im Mittelalter', p. 57; Legner, *Reliquien in Kunst und Kult*, pp 227–8; A.E. Fisher, 'Cross altar and crucifix' (2006), p. 48. **73** Bagnoli, 'The stuff of heaven', p. 142. Eye-catching in this quotation is again the reference to the material of the sculpture. Bagnoli hereby separates the sculptures with a 'base materiality' from the precious reliquaries, the meanings of the materials of which she has discussed previously. **74** RAB, BB. Nieuw kerkarchief, 408. **75** Because of this need for validation, the head sculpture of Kachtem can be found on the threshold between reliquary and cult image, and therefore this artefact can serve as a perfect example to instigate new research about the reciprocity between relics and images as a whole.

The *raison d'être* of a sculpture and the purpose of an inserted relic, visible or not, do affect the perception of these objects. These objectives of sculpture and relic may have influenced the materiality of the *Johannesschüssel*. The motif *in se* represents a relic, which makes it a hybrid object, hesitating between two options – reliquary and sculpture. On occasion, the *Johannesschüssel* is an actual reliquary, intended to preserve and display relics, and made of precious materials; sometimes it is just a wooden or stone sculpture, reminding the beholder of the actual relic, and serving as a devotional aid. However, now and then a mere sculpture was used as a container for relics, visible or invisible, known or unknown. If these low-priced heads of St John were not intended as reliquaries and were thus not manufactured as such, maybe there was no reason to use precious materials. Could the function of these wooden sculptures as cult image explain their difference from the relic containers in precious metals? For some, it probably can; for others it will not. As the sculpture itself represents the head (relic) of the Precursor, it seems as if it was always seen as something holy, as was the crucifix, no matter what materials were used. Apparently, both Forerunner and Saviour had no need for the additional meaning of gold and gems to be perceived as heavenly and therefore worthy to contain relics. Their devotional beauty is priceless regardless of their material.

CONCLUSION

Thiofrid of Echternach wrote: 'Who with fast faith touches the outside of the container whether in gold, silver, gems or fabric, bronze, marble or wood, he will be touched by that which is concealed inside'.[76] Although Thiofrid profoundly believed in the importance of the use of the most precious materials for the production of reliquaries, he still had faith in the power of more modest containers as well. In the end, the material of the reliquary did not matter, if you just believed in the efficacy of the container's contents. No matter what their function or purpose is today, we should look further than the glamorous exteriors of containers. It is not because non-precious reliquaries do not glitter that they are not worth our time and attention.

---

76 '*Si constantissimae manu fidei, exterior ejus attrectetur clausula, auri ac argenti bractea, seu cujuscunque pretii gemmula, sive quaelibet textilis vel productilis, aut fusilis aut marmorea vel lignea materia; ac si hoc tangatur, quod interius occultatur. Sic divinae majestatis potentia salutem in medio terrae operatur (Psal. LXXIII, 12).' Flores epytaphii sanctorum 2.3.18–22* in Thiofridus Epternacensis, *Goffridi Abbatis Vindocinensis*, col. 345; Thiofrid of Echternach, *Thiofridi Abbatis Epternacensis*, p. 37. Translation from Hahn, *Strange beauty*, p. 24.

7 The Annunciation and the senses: late medieval devotion and the pictorial gaze[1]

BARBARA BAERT

For most of us, there is only the unattended
Moment, the moment in and out of time,
The distraction fit, lost in a shaft of sunlight,
The wild thyme unseen, or the winter lightning
Or the waterfall, or music heard so deeply
That it is not heard at all, but you are the music
While the music lasts. These are only hints and guesses,
Hints followed by guesses; and the rest
Is prayer, observance, discipline, thought and action.
The hint half guessed, the gift half understood, is Incarnation.

T.S. Eliot, *The Four Quartets*

In this essay I revisit the Quattrocento iconography of the Annunciation from the standpoint of the senses. I argue that the devotional *Bildakt* and interchange between image and beholder in this period is unlocked by pictorial reflection – often reflexive as well – on the *sensorium*. This is particularly true of Tuscan interpretations of the theme from the Quattrocento by such artists as Filippo Lippi, among others. For this loosely constituted group of images we can show how performative interchange is built on new insights in optics, on certain convictions concerning the role of the ear (hearing), and even on intuitions regarding taste and smell. By viewing this *sensorium* as a complex *and* chiasmic osmosis (for example, seeing as hearing) that can be integrated into the iconography of the period, it is possible to establish a new, sensuous relationship between image and beholder. This relationship forms a fundamental agency in the complex phenomenon we call 'devotion'.[2] My essay aims to contribute to the devotional praxis by analysing the iconographical phenomenon of the Annunciation in terms of contemporary opinions about vision, incarnation, synaesthesia and the pulsating powers beneath the mystery of visible invisibility.

Since the early Christian origin of the theme, the iconography of the Annunciation has resonated with a particular energy concerning the legitimacy of the culture of the image as such. For is not the mystery of God-become-flesh precisely the emanation of an invisible Visage into the visibility of the Son? And is not this emanation analogous

1 With my gratitude to Henning Laugerud and Niels Schalley.   2 For this, see the doctoral dissertation by Laura Katrine Skinnebach, 'Practices of perception'.

to that other mystery: the possibility of expressing the divine artistically – tracing it in line and colour in the world of time and space? The Annunciation is therefore more than just the iconography of a biblical passage, for it thematizes and comments upon the beginning of the figurative process as something that flows forth from the principle of incarnation – the becoming flesh, and thus 'becoming image', of Christ himself. In short, the Annunciation is about the unnameable secret of the visual. Artists have perceived this secret to a greater or lesser degree and have brought this deepest of cores to the surface according to their various traditions. After all, the Annunciation touches on a startling paradox: incarnation, or the mystery of the image, that continues to escape us in its 'visible invisibility'.

THE ICONIC INTERSPACE

Luke 1:28–35 reads:

> And he came to her and said 'Greetings, favoured one! The Lord is with you.' But she was much perplexed by his words and pondered what sort of greeting this might be. The angel said to her 'Do not be afraid, Mary, for you have found favour with God. And now, you will conceive in your womb and bear a son, and you will name him Jesus. He will be great, and will be called the Son of the Most High, and the Lord God will give to him the throne of his ancestor David. He will reign over the house of Jacob forever, and of his kingdom there will be no end.' Mary said to the angel 'How can this be, since I am a virgin?' The angel said to her 'The Holy Spirit will come upon you, and the power of the Most High will overshadow you; therefore the child to be born will be holy; he will be called Son of God'.[3]

When a text is translated into an image, a third parameter escapes that I have elsewhere referred to as the iconic 'space between': the *interspace*.[4] It is known that from the moment a biblical passage falls into the hands of an artist, another dimension begins to operate that transforms the word into a sensual world where other laws concerning truth, reality and imagination hold sway. The transposition of Scripture into image ensures that the role of the senses also shifts. The image apparently limits itself to the visual; it knows no direct speech or auditory dimension. Reading a text is moreover a diachronic phenomenon. Looking at images is more complex: the eyes roam simultaneously across the surface and have a wilder way of connecting meanings.[5] Images are therefore capable of appending or compressing several textual moments at once. In short, the image has another relationship to internal and external

---

3 *The Harper Collins study bible, new revised standard version*, rev. ed. (2006).   **4** Barbara Baert, *Interspaces between word, gaze and touch* (Leuven, 2011).   **5** D.J. Van Den Berg, 'What is an image and what is image power', *Image & Narrative*, 8 (2004) (electronic journal).

time: it can divest itself of the mother text by having recourse to the language of symbols, which is only active visually.

Research into the layered meanings of images, known as 'iconology', is a constantly evolving process. Referring to the methodology developed by the renowned Erwin Panofsky (1892–1968), the connotations of the term have shifted subtly since the 1930s.[6] In its current form, iconology tends to be defined in the terms set out by W.J.T. Mitchell and others as

> the study of the visual medium by exploring the specificity of the medium and explaining the contents and the thematic traditions of images by confronting them with texts, material culture and the historical and anthropological backgrounds.[7]

What immediately sets this definition apart from its forerunners is its broad approach. Art history today, and in particular iconology, has embraced the study of the visual medium as such, a domain in which the study of so-called 'high' and 'low' art are on equal footing. Within this framework, cultural anthropology – briefly considered an essential sister discipline when the iconological method was being developed in the nineteenth century – has been rediscovered.[8] When Aby Warburg (1866–1929) unleashed his intuitive vision of image analysis in his project Mnemosyne – not coincidentally named for the mother of the Muses – he did not exclude non-Western art and even made comparative studies of the Italian Renaissance and the Pueblo Indians.[9]

The current English definition of iconology is framed by an analogous methodological revolution in German- and French-speaking regions. The *Bild-Anthropologie* of Hans Belting investigates prototypes and their mutations, and includes the body as medium.[10] According to the author, the relationship between body and image is archetypally rooted in the fear of death.[11] Georges Didi-Huberman, by contrast, connects art history to philosophy – not so much for the sake of a philosophy of art itself as for the sake of rethinking the image as such: *la pensée figurée*.[12] Didi-Huberman assumes that the image opens itself up to the viewer like a kind of portal into another realm of experience. For him the image is always an *image ouverte*. For

6 Erwin Panofsky, 'Zum Problem der Beschreibung und Inhalstdeutung von Werken der bildenden Kunst', *Logos. Internationale Zeitschrift für Philosophie der Kultur*, 21 (1932), 103–19. 7 Walter J.T. Mitchell, 'Interdisciplinarity and visual culture', *Art Bulletin*, 77:4 (1995), 540–4. 8 See also Barbara Baert, Ann-Sophie Lehmann and Jenke ven den Akkerveken (eds), *New perspectives in iconology* (Brussels, 2012). 9 Aby Warburg, *Einleitung Bilderatlas Mnemosyne*, ed. Martin Warnke and Claudia Brink (Berlin, 2000), pp 3–6. See also Eva Horn and Manfred Weinberg, 'Aby Warburg's "Ikonologie des Zwischenraums" im Horizont der Allegorie' in Eva Horn and Manfred Weinberg (eds), *Allegorie* (Wiesbaden, 1998), pp 233–47. 10 Hans Belting, *Bild-Anthropologie* (Munich, 2001). 11 On the impact of Belting's *Bild-Anthropologie*, see Sunil Manghani, Arthur Piper and Jon Simons (eds), *Images: a reader* (London, 2006), pp 292–314: 'Image Studies'. 12 Georges Didi-Huberman, *Ce que nous voyons, ce qui nous regarde* (Paris, 1992); Georges Didi-Huberman, *L'image ouverte* (Paris, 2007).

this reason one often speaks of Didi-Huberman's research as an *anthropologie visuelle*, and not as an anthropology of the image as developed by Hans Belting.[13] One of these openings, according to Belting, is launched by the Judaeo-Christian paradigm: the creation of man in God's image. This unity, however, this *ressemblance*, has been lost in the Fall: it became *défiguration* or *dissemblance*. The history of *la pensée figurée* is thus determined by an eternal quest for the restoration of this analogy. Art and iconography are characterized as an endless series of traces, phantoms of a lost covenant. The closest we come to this restoration is the moment of tumbling from one covenant into the other: the incarnation or *la promesse de retrouver l'image*. However, the incarnation is unimaginable: *l'image échappe*.

This essay seeks to transfer these new approaches to the Annunciation and its relationship to pictorial devotion. In the following section, 'Disguised symbolism revisited', I investigate the process by which the mother text is transformed into the visual medium as the embodiment of devotional space. Iconographical language makes use of other symbolic means that deepen or transcend narrative discourse. As far as the Annunciation is concerned, several striking layers of meaning are uncovered. From the section 'The opening toward the invisible' onwards, my search continues on the basis of the *sensorium*. Which senses play a role in iconography? And how do breath, speech, sight and hearing connect to one another at the level of the image, so that the image itself can likewise be called an 'incarnation'? In the last section of this essay, 'Iconogenesis or amorphous reception', the secret of the Annunciation culminates in the deepest traces of what artists try to achieve: the pathway that leads from the amorphous, the not-yet-represented, to the formed. Here, recent theories of *la pensée figurée* enter into the question, shedding new light on the Annunciation and the pictorial gaze of devotion.

DISGUISED SYMBOLISM REVISITED

The interpretive model known as 'disguised symbolism' involves peering through the symbolic surface. Developed by Panofsky with respect to the painting of the Flemish Primitives, the term refers to the ambivalence between painting that is true to life, on the one hand, and objects that are clearly recognizable as symbols on the other.[14] In the meantime, this position has been nuanced by approaching disguised symbolism through the anthropology of daily life.[15] The painted objects are not veiled symbols,

13 On these nuances, see Esther Cleven, 'Man and image: Hans Belting's anthropology of the image and the German Bildwissenschaften' in Barbara Baert et al. (eds), *New perspectives in iconology*, pp 143–60 and bibliography. Horst Bredekamp, *Theorie des Bildakts* (Berlin, 2010), wrote an *opus magnum* that comes close to the French *l'anthropologie visuelle* and *la pensée figure*. The author considers the image as *lebendig*; he develops the *handlungsstiftende Kraft von Bildern*. This particular power to 'live' comes close to the innocence of *l'image pulsante* in the essay by MarieJosé Mondzain, *L'image naturelle* (Paris, 1995), p. 11. 14 Erwin Panofsky, *Early Netherlandish painting* (Cambridge, MA, 1953), pp 142–3. 15 Jan Baptiste Bedaux, 'The reality of symbols', *Simiolus*, 16 (1986), 5–26; James H. Marrow, 'Symbol and meaning in northern European art of the late Middle

but instead owe their symbolic aura to the role they played in the daily life of fifteenth-century men and women. Exegetical symbols related to the virginity of Mary, for example, actively descended into the real environment of people living in the Middle Ages. It is thus the experience of the symbol and not the exegesis of the symbol that is represented in Flemish painting. In what follows, I use the notion of 'interior allegory' to develop this avenue further.

Nowhere do the gospels describe the appearance of the house or room in which the Annunciation is said to have taken place. Medieval authors sought nevertheless to fill this lacuna. For example: 'And he [Gabriel] came in the middle of the night behind closed doors to the worthy daughter of the heavenly father, the pure virgin Mary, who was there reading the holy prophecy of her father David' (Johannes Brugman, *c.*1400–73).[16] Yet artists too must have provided the Annunciation with suitable 'everyday' surroundings: this is the so-called paradigm of 'disguised symbolism' as we learned it from Panofsky. Indeed, from the fifteenth century onwards, when the artistic principle of *mimesis* reached a pinnacle of development, we also find luxurious contemporary spaces such as the one depicted in the Merode Triptych of Robert Campin (1378–1444) (pl. 19). The concealed symbol here is the candle on the table, which has not yet been snuffed.[17] The flame is a symbol of God, but there is already another form of God underway: the rays of light falling through the round window at the left bring with them a tiny Jesus on his way to Mary. The lily in the pitcher symbolizes Mary's virginity. The folds of her gown form a star: Mary as the star of stars. The two books probably stand for the Old and New Testament. Finally, there is the dynamism of looking inside and notionally entering the room, accompanied by the patrons.

A more recent interpretation of the Merode Triptych and its disguised symbolism, however, concentrates on contemporary sources in vernacular languages that can be grouped together under the rubric 'interior allegory'.[18] This type of allegory is based on a mental technique that accompanies the viewing of a painting as if stepping into the (pictorial) reality and spiritual experience of the interior.[19] These vernacular texts display an interesting affinity with the Annunciation. The faithful will project the lessons of the Annunciation onto his or her own room, will take its spare interior furnished only with bed, chair and candlestick as a spiritual point of departure: 'Near the bed is found peace and rest for the conscience; by the table penitence; by the chair a judgment of himself; and by the candlestick a confession of himself' (*De doctrina*

Ages and the early Renaissance', *Simiolus*, 16 (1986), 150–69.   **16** 'Ende hi [Gabriel] quam inder midder-nacht met beslotenre doeren totter weerdigher doechter des hemelschen vaders, der reynbe maget Maria, die daer lesende was die hoge weerdighe prophecie haers vaders davids': Petrus L.M. Grootens and Johannes Brugman, *Onuitgegeven sermoenen van Jan Brugman* (Tielt, 1948), p. 28.   **17** Bernhard Ridderbos, 'Objects and questions' in Bernhard Ridderbos, Anne van Buren and Henk van Veen (eds), *Early Netherlandish paintings: rediscovery, reception and research* (Amsterdam, 2005), pp 16–23.   **18** Reindert L. Falkenburg, 'The household of the soul: conformity in the "Mérode Triptych"' in Maryan A. Ainsworth (ed.), *Early Netherlandish painting at the cross-roads: a critical look at current methodologies* (New York, 2001), pp 2–17.   **19** Emanuel S. Klinkenberg, '"Wil diin herte bereeden gheliic eenen huze" de binnenhuisallegorie in de geestelijke letterkunde', *Queeste. Tijdschrift over middeleeuwse letterkunde*, 2:14 (2007), 126–53.

cordis, fifteenth century).[20] Some sermons and instructions even go into greater detail concerning the bed linens, the food on the table and the decoration of the space with flowers, as developed as early as Bernard of Clairvaux (1090–1153) regarding the Annunciation. To enter the room is to enter the mystical heart. Mary's room, where the angel enters – and by extension where we enter – is described as being decorated with pleasing flowers and herbs with a delicious perfume.[21] These descriptions are often intertextual references to the Song of Songs, in which the bride and bridegroom experience their love in a room. According to Reindert Falkenburg, the Merode Triptych is not only a typical medieval room in which the symbolic reality of the Annunciation is concealed, it also refers to the devotional instructions for entering a room, just as one would penetrate one's own soul. In this way the viewer is encouraged to feel, to touch, to smell and to hear what takes place in the space thus evoked in order to attain virtue.[22]

From the point of view of disguised symbolism, the Annunciation forms a mirror of reality, but from the perspective of interior allegory the faithful viewer will in turn serve as a mirror of this mirror. In the case of this meta-reflection, this doubling between viewer and pictorial world, the Annunciation becomes a moment that is 'consumed' by the gaze and the whole sensorium. If viewing means entering, a sort of endoscopy, then viewing also recalls the mystery of the Annunciation itself: the angel entering the room is like the Holy Spirit entering the Virgin.

This means that the pictorial setting invites us in an almost sensual and 'bodily' way to join and 'feel' the mystery of the event. In his *Ikonologie des Performativen*, Christoph Wulf initiated this specific aspect of the research:

> The production and perception of images is tied to use and context, that is, images are historically and culturally conditioned and differentiated. Images become performative when they, through use, manifest themselves as apparitions. They are tied to the actions and desires of the human body.[23]

To step into the room is to step into the process of Mary's conception: a conception that can only enable itself through the performative gaze of the beholder. It is our gaze, the sensuous empathy of smelling, touching and hearing *inside* the pictorial room that

---

20 Guido Hendrix (ed.), *Hugo de Santo Caro's traktaat 'De doctrina cordis'*, 2 (Leuven, 1995), p. 14: 'Biden bedde es te uerstane pays ende ruste van consciencien; bider tafele penitencie; biden zetel een vonnesse ziins sellefs; ende bi den candelare een bekennen van hem zeluen'.   **21** The sermon is known through a Dutch manuscript of the fifteenth century: *wi die floeren end die wanden mede vercieren sullen als mit welrukende bloemen*; Leiden University library, Ltk 2189, fo. 198v.   **22** When the house is cleaned (*gereynicht is van den voirleden sonden overmits die biechte ende veercyert is mit den gueden gewoenten der gesteliken levens*), then Christ can enter and teach us the virtues; Leiden University library, Ltk 2189, fo. 199.   **23** '*Die Erzeugung und Wahrnehmung von Bildern ist gebrauchs- und kontextgebunden, d.h. sie ist historisch und kulturell bedingt und differenziert. Wenn Bilder im Gebrauch in Erscheinung treten, dann sind sie performativ. Sie sind an die Bewegungen des menschlichen Körpers und an sein Begehren gebunden*': Christoph Wulf and Jörg Zirfas (eds), *Ikonologie des Performativen* (Munich, 2005), p. 17.

makes the mystery 'active'. The act of walking 'deep' into the room as the angel did, even frightening the Virgin, is repeated emotionally in us, the beholders.

But there is more. Paradoxically speaking, the incarnation takes place within a mystery that is *withdrawn from the naked eye*. Something is needed beyond, beyond the iconic interspace of pictoriality, disguised symbolism and mirror metaphors. The pictorial needs to unveil deeper dimensions that weave the Annunciation together with incarnation, on the one hand the route towards the invisible, on the other the mystery of creating something from nothing. This brings me to a specific medium as an agent of pictorial sublimation, wind.

THE OPENING TOWARDS THE INVISIBLE; WIND

'How can this be?' These words, spoken by Mary according to Luke, have intrigued readers since the Church Fathers. How could the Virgin have received a child by the Holy Spirit? Had the Most High overshadowed her, as the angel said? Did this suffice as an explanation? Certainly the Latin Church put forward a different answer, one suggested by an 'acoustic metaphor'.[24] Eve conceived the word of the serpent, whereas Mary surrendered to a different kind of persuasive power. The power of the word that entered through her ear was soon described in sensory terms: 'O blessed Virgin … made mother without cooperation of man. For here the ear was the wife, and the angelic word the husband', wrote Eleutherius of Tournai around AD500.[25] Or subsequently, in the Carolingian era, Agobard of Lyon (d. 840) said: 'He, light and God of the created universe, descends from heaven, sent forth from the breast of the Father (*missus ab arce patris*);[26] having put on the purple stole, he enters through the ear of the Virgin, and exits through the golden gate'.[27]

The notion that the voice could impregnate through the ear originated in the underlying idea of impregnating 'breath' (see the Greek *pneuma* and Hebrew *ruah*), which also means wind.[28] Wind is rarely quiet. Its sound is the roar of the force of nature, a rumbling ascribed to God (Ezekiel 3:12).[29] Hence, the Pentecostal tongues of fire were preceded by a sound like the blowing of a violent wind that came from

24 Leo Steinberg, '"How shall this be?"', *Artibus et Historiae*, 8:16 (1987), 25–44 at 26. Augustine (354–430) asserts the following in his *Sermo de Tempore*, XXII: 'Deus per angelum loquebatur et Virgo per aurem impraegnebatur'. St Ephraem of Syria (306–73) (*De divers. serm.* I, *opp. syr*, III, p. 607) says: 'Per novam mariae aurem intravit atque infusa est vita'. **25** Steinberg, '"How shall this be?"', 28. **26** *De correctione antiphonarii*, cap. VIII: 'Descendit de coelis missus ab arce patris, introivit per aurem Virginis in regionem nostram indutus stola purpurea et exivit per auream portam lux et Deus universae fabricae mundi'. In the Middle Ages, one would have recognized the etymological relationship between chest *arca* and altar *ara*: see Jeannette Kohl and Rebecca Müller (eds), *KopfBild. Die Büste in Mittelalter und früher Neuzeit* (Munich, 2007), pp 9–30, 18. **27** Steinberg, '"How shall this be?"', 28, draws attention to the play on Latin *aurem* (ear) and *auream* (gold). The golden gate is the southern eschatological gate in Jerusalem, where the Visitation supposedly occurred. A gate is also an image of a 'feminine' entrance, as in the Song of Songs. **28** On this complex etymology, see the excellent article by Robert Luyster, 'Wind and water: cosmogonic symbolism in the Old Testament', *Zeitschrift für alttestamentische Wissenschaft*, 93:1 (1981), 1–10. **29** 'Then the Spirit lifted me up, and I heard behind me a loud rumbling sound – May the glory of the Lord be praised in his dwelling place!'

heaven (Acts 2:2) (pl. 20). The association between the Godhead and wind manifested as sound is shared by different religious belief systems, including that of the ancient Greeks, for whom a voice like the roaring wind was said to belong to Zeus. The roaring wind of the father is in fact a prefiguration of a more sophisticated means of communication: speech. In Genesis, God 'speaks' things to life. In Christianity, speech – or the word – is born of God's breath and only subsequently nestles in the flesh. 'In the beginning was the word, and the word was with God' (John 1:1). St Zeno of Verona (300–71) asserts that Mary's womb swelled from words rather than semen.[30] The invisibility and immateriality of the breath and of speech form the etymological core of various words that subsequently came to express notions such as spirit, idea and mind. This association is apparent in Greek *psyche*, Hebrew *nephesh*, German *Geist* and English *ghost*, all of which originally meant 'breath'.[31] This explains the richness of the notion of *pneuma*, which means wind and breath as well as spirit. In short, from the roaring wind to the impregnating breath, the foundation is laid for an entity, the Holy Spirit, who has the power to enter the human body.

Hence scenes depicting the Annunciation often feature a dove – a symbolic representation of the Holy Spirit, usually near Mary's ear – as it 'imbues' her with the principle of life (pl. 21). The semantic history of the word 'wind' goes back to various fields: gold (radiance), the ear (sound) and the dove (bird/flight), with exceptional derivatives such as the sense of the tongue (speech), the mouth (breath), odour and moisture.[32] The questions that follow are: Why is the creative substance represented as emanating from the mouth, and why as breath in particular? Why is it a dove that conveys it? And why is the ear chosen to be the receptive organ?[33]

The mouth is a feminine attribute in that it is receptive, but as a medium for the production of saliva and breath, and as the *locus* of the tongue, it clearly has some male connotations as well. Breathing as a life-generating act also appears in the Book of Genesis, where God breathes life into Adam through his nostrils (Genesis 2:7) (pl. 22).[34] In the Qur'an, the angel Gabriel is said to have 'breathed' onto the belly of Mary, thereby impregnating her. Life-breath as a source of impregnation may be associated with the properties of the air that seeps in and out of our bodies: blowing like the wind, movement, sound, invisibility, moisture and warmth. Hera was impregnated by the wind and gave birth to Hephaestus. Zephyrus, wind of spring and of flowers, begot Euphrosyne with Aurora.[35] Ovid (43BC– AD17) describes how Chloris or Flora was raped by Zephyrus.[36] Aristotle (384–22BC) and Pliny the Elder (AD23–79) assert

---

30 Steinberg, '"How shall this be?"', 28.   **31** Ernest Jones, *Essays in applied psycho-analysis*, 2 (New York, 1964), p. 295ff.   **32** Ibid., pp 266–357.   **33** Ibid., p. 273.   **34** Ibid., pp 273ff considers the nostril to be a pendant to the ear. In the pre-modern era, the nasal cavity was regarded as highly fragile and any injury to it as life-threatening, judging by the prevalence of amulets that provided protection against nosebleeds: A.A. Barb, 'St Zacharias the prophet and martyr: a study in charms and incantations', *Journal of the Warburg and Courtauld Institutes*, 11 (1948), 35–67 at 63, 67.   **35** Jones, *Essays in applied psycho-analysis*, p. 281.   **36** Kora Neuser, *Anemoi. Studien zur Darstellung der Winde und Windgottheiten in der Antike* (Rome, 1982), passim, refers to numerous examples on Greek and Roman pottery showing winged youngsters (winds) abducting women.

that female partridges can be 'fecundated when merely standing opposite to the male, provided that the wind is blowing from him to her'. According to a German saying, the east wind makes the penis shorter, whereas the *Föhnfieber* in Switzerland is a west wind associated with warmth and fertility.[37]

The other characteristic of wind – moisture – is mirrored in bodily fluids: uterine moisture, urine, sweat and semen. The wind-breath-spirit complex coincides with notions of fluidity, much as water and spirit together are seen to have a purifying effect in Christian baptism. In a primitive conception of insemination, it is framed as the result of a fusion of wind (or gas) and water, creating a vapour that is fertile not only for the reproductive organs, but also for the brain (see the glossolalia of the Greek Sibyls at vapour baths). The moist breath that comes forth from the mouth, with a red tongue like a fluid-producing 'phallus', is sometimes compared to the element of fire (cf. the equation of the tongues of Pentecost with the descending breath/spirit/ pneuma).

The combination of these semantic associations and their profound anthropological ramifications conspired to charge the notions of breath and wind with the potentiality implied in the Annunciation. This endpoint is at once a beginning, whereby the passing of intestinal flatus forms the phantasmal basis for the associative chain outlined above. In a process of sublimation, the odour, sound, moisture and warmth of 'wind' produced by the body is de-materialized, de-sensualized and de-corporealized to the extent that it gives rise to the most abstract of notions: the impregnating breath of God, represented as golden rays of light. How we can connect incarnation and wind with beams of light will become clear below in my case study.

THE EAR, THE MOUTH AND THE EYE

In *Le détail*, the French art historian Daniel Arasse (1944–2003) draws the reader's attention to a painting of the Annunciation by Filippo Lippi (1406–69) in which the buttonhole at Mary's navel is rendered without a corresponding button (pl. 23).[38] The minuscule opening is barely discernible to the naked eye. As with the other barely visible details that Arasse discusses in his book, and which he invariably interprets as expressions of the enigmatic and intimate connection between the painter and his art, he argues that the missing button could have a symbolic significance. The small slit, at the same horizontal as the dove, the impregnator of the flesh by the word, could be seen as subtly suggestive of the navel as a paradoxically closed opening. It is virginal, as the iconography demands, yet sensual and erotic, as painting requires. Some critics recognize in the model the features of Lucrezia Buti, a nun from a convent in Prato, the Tuscan town where Mary's *cintula*, or waistband, was kept as a relic. This band,

---

37 Jones, *Essays in applied psycho-analysis*, p. 284.   38 Daniel Arasse, *Le détail. Pour une histoire rapprochée de la peinture* (Paris, 1996), p. 338.

with its knot across the navel, is a traditional symbol of the 'tying' and 'untying' of fertility.[39] As a submerged detail, it serves as a visible invisibility in Lippi's pictorial universe. As Arasse puts it, 'the longing of the painter lies contained in the actual painting'.[40]

From the barely visible hole emanate tiny golden rays that echo those emerging from the bill of the dove. The golden rays stand for the impregnating 'breath', the glow of the conception. However, this would imply that, in Lippi's rendering, the light of word become flesh is already shining from within Mary's belly. On the other hand, the dual emanation of light is in keeping with the principles of fifteenth-century optics, according to which sight results from a simultaneous physical emanation from the eye as well as the object observed.[41] The prevailing scientific definition of sight (and thus painting) becomes the definition of conception (and thus incarnation). Renaissance painting – preoccupied with *mimesis* and optical accuracy, yet not averse to the layered symbolic meaning contained in those definitions – presents itself as an incarnation and *vice versa*. This way, painting represses the sonorous senses in favour of light and sight. The peculiar consequence is that the opening at navel-height – blind and hence visionary – presents itself as a 'looking inward,' endoscopically, with a virginal uterine gaze. For the closed opening that is the navel is also a residue, a scar of the indefinable: the foetal life inside the mother.

Lippi's detailed treatment of the navel may also be seen as a virtuoso refinement of an older Tuscan tradition. In the Annunciation of Gentile da Fabriano (*c.*1421–5), a ray of light emanating from God's chest penetrates into Mary's room through a six-lobed oculus and strikes her below the heart, where the shape of the window is reflected on her lower body (pl. 24). The 'eye' of Mary's room is repeated as an optical photogram: she bears the divine light of a supernatural impregnation in an entirely pictorial fashion. The light has descended into painterly virtuosity: the subtle golden rays, the hidden energy of the dove and the optical resonance of a window on textile, which turns Mary's belly into a kind of 'receptive eye' of 'wind-ness'. In fifteenth-century Renaissance art, the auricular metaphors increasingly became ocular metaphors. Leo Steinberg calls this a 'bond passing from God to Mary, designed to neutralize sense by confounding our specialized sensory apparatus'.[42] The result is an amalgamation, a synthesis of a higher order: light that speaks, rays that evoke hearing, the voice of God

---

39 On the relationship between waistband and knot, as well as its magical implications, see also Ulriche Zischka, *Zur sakralen und profanen Anwendung des Knotenmotivs als magisches Mittel, Symbol oder Dekor. Eine vergleichende volkskundliche Untersuchung* (Munich, 1977); Douglas Q. Adams, 'Knot' in J.P. Mallory and Douglas Q. Adams (eds), *Encyclopedia of Indo-European culture* (London, 1997), p. 336.   40 'Le désir du peintre dans la peinture même'; Arasse, *Le détail*, p. 340.   41 This theory within the optica of the Renaissance is called the 'emission theory'. One would believe that the crossing beams of light 'touch' each other. According to these opinions the act of gazing is related to the act of touching: see Gezienus T. Doesschate, 'Oxford and the revival of optics in the thirteenth century', *Vision Research*, 1 (1962), 313–42; David C. Lindberg, *Theories of vision from Al-Kindi to Kepler* (Chicago, 1976); Darren Wong and Boo Hong Kwen, 'Shedding light on the nature of science through a historical study of light' (paper presented at the National Institute of Education, Nanyong Technological University; available from Darren Wong at researchgate.net).   42 Steinberg, '"How shall this be?"', 38.

7.1 Piero della Francesca (1415–92), *Madonna del Parto*, *c.*1460, Monterchi, Museo Civico.

who sees, the belly that receives and perceives, as Mary looks up at the *oculus* in her room.[43]

43 Ingeborg Zapperi Walter, *Piero della Francesca, Madonna del parto: ein Kunstwerk zwischen Politik und Devotion* (Frankfurt a. M., 1992). In 1992, the fresco was moved to its current location in the museum of Monterchi. To this day, the Madonna has a special significance to pregnant local women, and the museum is

Seen from this perspective it is apparent that the Madonna del Parto (*c.*1460) by Piero della Francesca (1415–92), showing Mary with a round belly under a piece of cloth held up by two angels, actually represents the Annunciation (fig. 7.1). The fresco originally covered a wall near the high altar of Santa Maria di Momentana (previously Santa Maria in Silvis), a chapel near the town of Monterchi in the hilly countryside of Tuscany. Opposite the high altar, there was an *oculus*. Importantly, in the month of March, when the Annunciation is celebrated (21 March), the sun would have passed high through the western sky and lit up the fresco. This intentional touch is reminiscent of paintings in which the touch of light symbolizes the conception, the parthenogenesis. The striking alignment of the sun, the window and the fresco transfers the location of the Annunciation to the Tuscan countryside, as it were. In other words, the laws of the natural cycle and the seasons are invoked, so that the Madonna del Parto assumes a cosmogonic significance. Her belly is a repository of the primeval force of creation itself. Piero della Francesca suggested this by the split along the front of Mary's dress, on which her hand rests seemingly casually. This 'vaginal' form is a reference to the 'closed opening', the paradox of the virginal conception. Moreover, it is echoed in the curtains of the canopy that are opened by the two angels, like the Holy of Holies.[44]

Let us return now to our *detail* in Lippi's painting: barely visible to the naked eye, the dove appears to be floating along on a spiral current of air. This unique and sophisticated visual representation of the wind, or of the quintessence, if you will, makes the dove – with its bill and golden rays, floating on little whirlwinds until it comes eye to eye with the navel – less of an idiosyncratic presence in the otherwise homogenous composition. Whereas the angel is the messenger of God, the dove represents God's desire or even the means of its realization.[45] As Jones argues, the bird is a rather obvious choice of phallic symbol, given the following characteristics: power of flight, a snake-like neck and head, a protruding bill, the absence of external genitalia (aphrodite), the power of song and the relation to air and the wind. But why a dove (*kolumba*) in particular?

Typologically, the dove refers to the Old Testament, in which it brings Noah a leaf after the flood. But in the deluge myth, the dove is not just the messenger of salvation: it is the genius, the inseminator, the founder of a new generation.[46] The ancients like Pliny were aware that mistletoe is propagated from tree to tree by doves.[47] Aristophanes, in his play *Omithes* (birds) from 414BC, suggests that the etymological meaning of *kolumba/-is* is 'deep' or 'dipper', given the concentric 'swimming'

---

closed to the public whenever they request a 'private conversation' with her. There is an abundance of literature on this and other examples of the Madonna del Parto in Tuscany: see especially Brendan Cassidy, 'A relic, some pictures and the mothers of Florence in the late fourteenth century', *Gesta*, 30:2 (1991), 91–9; Ermes M. Ronchi (ed.), *La Madonna nell'attesa del Parto: capalavori dal patrimonio italiano del '300 e '400* (Milan, 2001).   **44** The pomegranates on the fabric of the canopy refer to Semitic fertility symbols.   **45** Jones, *Essays in applied psychoanalysis*, p. 325.   **46** Ibid., p. 334.   **47** Ibid.

movements in the air.[48] This is reminiscent of the concentrically whirling air in Lippi's painting, and most suggestive of what is about to occur deep inside the belly of Mary.

To conclude, the archetype of the wind as a deeper visual concept and anthropological emanation in the arts 'impregnated' the Annunciation iconography on both an exterior and interior level. On the outside, it appears as the mouth or *arca* of God, as descending angels dressed in fluttering nymph-like attire,[49] as whirling doves, and as word and speech emanating as golden letters from the mouth of Gabriel. In its interior guise, the wind is invisible, the reverse of *pneuma*. It is the wind that impregnates, that penetrates the body and enables it to bring forth new life. This invisibility of the conception and incarnation is exteriorized in motifs expressing deeper affects relating to the movement of air, breathing and impregnation. Representing such 'invisible' aspects pictorially is obviously a challenge. Thus breath becomes a golden ray, a gust of air becomes the fluttering of a transparent veil, word and speech become epigraphy, and Mary herself – in the words of the Bible – is overshadowed.[50] There is one invisible element that is neatly and seamlessly interwoven with the notions of water, fire, air and earth: namely, odour.[51] Odour thus connects the four natural elements. But as the most invisible element also, it may be the most challenging pictorial emanation.

ODOUR: AN EPISTEMOLOGICAL DETOUR

Research into the impact and meaning of odour as part of a model of knowledge has long been underestimated. Nevertheless, in ancient, oral cultures – as well as in late antique and medieval epistemology – rites and models were developed in which scent occupied a prominent place.[52]

David Parkin investigated the connection between wind and breath, and the rituals surrounding odours in east Africa.[53] There the idea still persists that the wind conceals

---

48 Ibid., p. 338.   **49** I cannot go into the matter of the Quattrocento Nymph paradigm that was first developed in the sense of the wind as a *Pathosformel* for movement and *Ekphrasis* by Aby Warburg (1866–1929); for this approach, see the brilliant article by George Didi-Huberman, 'Bewegende Bewegungen. Die Schleier der Ninfa nach Aby Warburg' in Johannes Endres, Barbara Wittmann and Gerhard Wolf (eds), *Ikonologie des Zwischenraums. Der Schleier als Medium und Metapher* (Munich, 2005), pp 331–60.   **50** As previously mentioned, in the Gospel of Luke, Mary's question is answered as follows by the angel: 'The Holy Spirit will come on you, and the power of the Most High will overshadow you'. In Semitic traditions, shadow is a symbol of fertility. It is also a feminine aspect, as opposed to the male aspect of light. Up to the fifteenth century, this specific tradition was not followed in painting though. Instead, the 'preferred' route of impregnation was via the ear. However, as artists began to refine the techniques of representing light and shadow, the motif in the source text was rediscovered, which would appear to give substance to the argument that a medium must be technically mature enough to receive the motif pictorially. In other words, the shadow of the Annunciation also touches upon a turning point in the art of painting: it is realism that recuperates the fertility symbol and incorporates it as a reflection on the pictorial process itself; cf. Annick de Souzenelle, *Le symbolisme du corps humain* (Paris, 1991), p. 38; Victor I. Stoichita, *A short history of the shadow* (London, 1997), passim.   **51** Jones, *Essays in applied psychoanalysis*, p. 321.   **52** I first explored this thesis and the hermeneutics of odour (and taste) in relation to the *Noli me tangere* motif (John 20:17) in: 'An odour, a touch, a smell. Impossible to describe. Noli me tangere and the senses' in Wietse de Boer and Christine Goettler (eds), *Religion and the senses in early modern Europe: intersections* (Leiden, 2012), pp 109–52.   **53** Parkin, 'Wafting on the wind', *Journal of the Royal Anthropological Institute*, 13:1

a world of spirits who can be not only invoked on the basis of odour, but also transformed. Odour is both the essence of the wind's spirit and the means by which it can
be manipulated. Odours form sensitive mappings, the threads of the wind: they bind
the invisible to the material world. Odours can be captured; they are preserved and
invoked in pomades, fluids and burning herbs. Governing the wind overlaps interaction with scents. After all, the odour traces the identity of a facet of wind and leads
humanity to an invisible higher power, comparable to sound, which is also invisible
but is nevertheless a form of communication that makes contact with that power
possible. Music and song support the odours of the wind spirits, surrounding them
with a certain atmosphere and ceremony.

Odours constitute a transitional bridge that is shaped by the way in which odours
are created: burning (incense), steam or smoke. These techniques give odour a
difference in density and (im)materiality, and as a result differentiate between the very
spirits and demons to be invoked or driven away:

> But unlike sight, touch and hearing, odour or fragrance is always incomplete,
> reaching back and bringing forth social and sensory trails which never settle …
> And once passed: a smell cannot be re-imagined to that degree, it depends also
> on a particular context to be remembered.[54]

Odours, however, have the particular side effect of always managing to escape;
fleeting as fragrance is, its paradoxical hermeneutic is its lack of articulation. Smell is
always incomplete:

> I suggest, however, that one way in which a smell becomes completed is when it
> is so concentrated as to be a substance, an element of physical matter, such as a
> pine resin, a rotting carcass or cooked food.[55]

In addition, odour must make use of material as its medium: it is by means of this
process that wind can be 'known' and 'tamed'. This knowledge is cyclical: odour is the
point of contact between the density of the source of the smell (for example, a carcass)
and the spirit/demon.[56] Odour teaches us about the continual transformation of
substance and immateriality.

In the Greek-Western paradigm, smell and taste come fourth and fifth in the
hierarchy of the senses.[57] However, Judaeo-Christian thought shows a particular fascination with these lower senses, where nostalgic regression and an intuitive form of
episteme come into play. Let us briefly consider two medieval contexts: the twelfth-

---

(2007), 39–53. **54** Ibid., 47. **55** Ibid. **56** Ibid. **57** On the hierarchy of the senses, see Carl Nordenfalk,
'The five senses in Flemish art before 1600' in G. Cavalli-Björkman (ed.), *Netherlandish mannerism* (Stockholm,
1985), pp 135–54; Hans Jonas, 'The nobility of sight: a study in the phenomenology of the senses' in Hans Jonas
(ed.), *The phenomenology of life: towards a philosophical biology* (Chicago, 1982), pp 135–56.

century *Liber Floridus* by Lambert of Saint-Omer and the *Legend of the Rood*, on the one hand, and the mystical garden metaphors on the other.

In the prologue to the *Liber Floridus*, smell and taste appear as metaphors of knowledge.[58] The author wants to offer the reader the honey that the bees collect from flowers in the garden. He also refers to the etymology of *sapere* as *sapor*, which consequently inserts the notion of taste and smell into the heart of wisdom, or *sapientia*. The notion of the bees and the garden is of course topical: it refers to paradise. However, this reference to the *locus amoenus* defines smell and taste as primordial senses of a lost world. We can see how Lambert is interested specifically in the prototype of scent as a 'knowledge-generating sense'. This is why he refers to the *Legend of the Rood*, a story that was profoundly embedded and widely disseminated in medieval culture. It mirrors precisely the importance that odour gains in the more intuitive and cosmological realms of deeper insight.

In the legend, Seth returns to paradise to collect healing oil from the Tree of Life in order to cure the dying Adam.[59] However, the angel Michael gives him instead a branch of the Tree of Knowledge. Seth – like the aforementioned dove – becomes the carrier of a twig from which a new covenant will grow (fig. 7.2). Indeed, Jerome (347–420) recognizes in Seth the concept of *semen*, and hence a fertilizer, a future stem for the patriarchal generations until the coming of Christ.[60] As Adam smells the branch, he feels contented and falls into the deep sleep of death. In the Gnostic sources for this motif, the scent of the branch does even more: it offers him universal knowledge, the *gnosis* Adam desired and transmitted to Seth.[61] Seth would write the *gnosis* on two columns, one made of stone so as to be able to endure the test of water and one made of clay so that it could stand the test of fire. It is beyond the scope of the present contribution to develop this branch of Judaeo-Christian tradition further; suffice it to say that it lays bare traces of a belief in the exceptional power of smell as a way of acquiring access to privileged knowledge that was usually reserved for God alone. Like touching the Tree of Good and Evil, scent could apparently provide access to the ultimate knowledge, to *gnosis*. Scent creates an opening toward knowledge; a knowledge, moreover, that was regarded as a deep yearning for what had been lost.

In Christian paradigms, taste is also considered a transcendental capacity of knowledge and desire,[62] as is apparent from the motif of the infamous bite of the

58 Karen De Coene, 'Navelnacht. Regeneratie en kosmologie in de middeleeuwen' (PhD, Leuven, 2006), p. 68.
59 For details on this matter, see Barbara Baert, 'Adam, Seth and Jerusalem: the legend of the wood of the cross in medieval literature and iconography' in *Adam, le premier homme* (Firenze, 2012), pp 69–99.   **60** Jerome, *Liber interpretationis hebraicorum nominum*, 20:17 (Turnhout): 71: 'Seth positio sive positus aut poculum vel gramen aut semen seu resurrectio'. The indo-European semantic stems for 'seed' encompass the semantics of *sacerdos*, priest, but also, grass and vegetation. Moreover, in the Celtic and Russian languages there exists a common root between *semen* and to impregnate, jump upon. This brings Seth's seed and his important mission back to the wind: also a fertilizer and impregnator for new life and new generations (http://indo-european.info/pokorny-etymological-dictionary/index.htm).   **61** Baert, 'Adam, Seth and Jerusalem', pp 69–99.   **62** At the end of his *De Arrha Animae*, Hugh of Saint-Victor (1096–1141) talks about *tangere*, and *gustare*, as opposed to seeing in the context of the Song of Songs, when it comes to the visit of the bridegroom: see Hugh of Saint-Victor, 'De arrha

7.2 *Seth meets the guardian of Paradise and receives a twig*. *Eva und Adam*, Lutwin, fifteenth century, Vienna, Österreichische Nationalbibliothek, Codex Vindob. 2980, fo. 73v.

apple.[63] Taste (*gustus*, *tactus* with the tongue) can be seen as a form of tactility involving the mouth; it is also a primary element in a child's *sensorium* as it discovers the world by tasting. Both smell and taste seem to intensify the impact of the knowledge-gener-ating senses on the field of lost secrets (intuition, the archetype of the lost paradise, the unconscious etc.), an intensification that is actually translated cosmologically (initiated *gnosis*, meeting and uniting with God himself), much as the four scented winds support the cosmos.[64]

The second primary context for the epistemology of odour during the Middle Ages

animae' in H.B. Feiss and P. Sicard (eds), *L'Oeuvre de Hugues de Saint-Victor I. De institutione novitiorum. De virtute orandi. De laude caritatis. De arrha animae* (Turnhout, 1997), pp 226–300 at p. 282; PL 176, cols 951–70. **63** Karen de Coene, 'Navelnacht', p. 74.   **64** The psychoanalyst Bracha Lichtenberg considers smell and taste to be 'matrixial' senses. They are proto-verbal and even proto-birth, related to the period in the mother's womb. Also after birth, smell and taste remain very intimate signifiers of the bond between mother and child: Bracha Lichtenberg Ettinger, 'The with-in-visible screen: images of absence in the inner space of painting' in Catherine de Zegher (ed.), *Inside the visible: an elliptical traverse of 20th-century art* (Cambridge, 1996), p. 101; B. Lichtenberg Ettinger, *Artworking, 1985–99* (Brussels, 2000). However, precisely the same kind of fascination inspires a revalu-ation of tactility in the work of Luce Irigaray. According to Irigaray, the sense of touch stands for unity. The unborn child in the womb is surrounded by fluidity. Thought detached from touch, argues Irigaray, leads to the banishment of human beings from paradise: Karlijn Demasure, 'Noli me tangere: a contribution to the reading of Jn 20:17 based on a number of philosophical reflections on touch', *Louvain Studies*, 32 (2007), 304–29 at 327.

brings me to the genre of the 'garden metaphor': an influential *topos* at the beginning of modern times relating to the reception of, and sharing in, higher knowledge. Reindert Falkenburg has shown in his *Fruit of devotion* that early modernity was a pivotal moment in the mystical tradition of 'love in the garden':

> The first tractates to employ allegorical references to the spiritual garden as a central theme date from the beginning of the thirteenth century. However, the genre only became widely popular in the fifteenth and the early sixteenth centuries. In this period spiritual garden allegories appear as separate texts, but also as elements within other, mainly devotional literary forms.[65]

These tracts were also read by the laity and were stimulated by the *Devotia moderna*. One might mention *Die geestlicke boomgaert der vruchten*, printed around 1500, but also Gerard Leeu's earlier *Thoofkijn van devotien*, in which the soul and its spiritual relationship with God is expressed in the drinking (hence tasting) of the water of life in the garden of Eden (fig. 7.3).[66]

With regard to the material culture of this period in the Low Countries, I refer to the fifteenth- and sixteenth-century 'Enclosed Gardens' (pl. 25).[67] This phenomenon of Enclosed Gardens in the north, particularly in modern-day Flanders, touches a deep undercurrent. Enclosed Gardens are in fact little trays or cases in which floral and vegetal motifs are mimicked by the use of beads and paper. Often these cases also included relics or little tableaux of biblical fragments. Enclosed Gardens evoke the Garden of Paradise, but more than that they evoke nostalgia and desire for the lost garden. A sort of 'remnant art', Enclosed Gardens gave material expression to the swarming, eddying, piling up of this unconscious discourse.[68] Paradise is here an emblem of the kind of knowledge that escapes the cerebral; of the knowledge, partially lost, that builds up energetically in the cosmos, but in the human descends in the form of instinct, fertility and the urge to create – in short, through the whole *sensorium*. Enclosed Gardens appeal not only to the gaze, but also to the sense of smell and touch. For this reason Enclosed Gardens might be seen as a matrixial field, an overgrowth in which feminine sensibilities are active. Luce Irigaray links it to the haptic:

65 Falkenburg, *The fruit of devotion: mysticism and the imagery of love in Flemish paintings of the Virgin and Child, 1450–1550* (Amsterdam, 1994), p. 20. **66** Antwerp, 1487; Ghent, Universitaire Bibliotheek, Res. 169, fo. 16. This is a Middle Dutch translation of Pierre d'Ailly's *Le jardin amoureux de l'âme*; Falkenburg, *The fruit of devotion*, pp 36–7, figs 47–8. **67** Paul Vandenbroeck (ed.), *Hooglied. De beeldwereld van religieuze vrouwen in de Zuidelijke Nederlanden, vanaf de 13de eeuw* (Brussels, 1994), pp 91–104; Baert, 'The glorified body: relics, materiality and the internalized image' in P. Vandenbroeck and G. Rooiakkers (eds), *Backlit heaven* (Mechelen, 2009), pp 130–53. **68** Birgit Pelzer, 'Relicten' in P. Vandenbroeck (ed.), *Hooglied. De beeldwereld van religieuze vrouwen in de Zuidelijke Nederlanden, vanaf de 13de eeuw* (Brussels, 1994), pp 179–204 at pp 181–2.

7.3 Gerard Leeu (*c.*1445/50–92), *The souls in the garden, Thoofkijn van devotien,*
Antwerp, 1487, Ghent, university library, Res. 169, fo. 16r.

The tangible represented a divine happiness, an 'earthly paradise', until the moment it entered into the perspective of the knowledge of good and evil. Prohibition might lead to a kind of knowledge that belongs to God alone.

In Irigaray's interpretation, this is knowledge detached from touch.[69] These miniature paradises were very popular in the sixteenth century, and they were sold on the market for a broader public with private aspirations, thereby losing their original feminine significations with respect to the interpretation of the senses. They became part of a more general devotional fascination with the garden allegory and prayer.

By the end of the Middle Ages, treatises, vernacular texts and devotional objects teach us that the garden allegory grew from a specific female mysticism into a more general 'spirituality of love' to be practiced in metaphors such as smell and taste as the unique portals to the divine. It was again the merit of Falkenburg to show the deep *Wirkungsgeschichte* of the garden allegory in the pictorial Marian *Andachtsbilder* of the Low Countries. For if texts and prayers use tastes and smells as conduits of devotional experience and spiritual insight, why would looking at these motifs in the form of flowers and fruits in paintings not fulfil exactly the same spiritual function? Gerard David's (1460–1523) *Virgin and Child* expresses prayer by suggesting the divine scent of a rose that Mary presents to the child (fig. 7.4),[70] and such examples could be multiplied beyond counting. We may conclude with Falkenburg: 'In the perspective of "mirrored piety" it is possible to look to the garden tracts for greater insight into the nature of devotional attitudes associated with the consumption of fruit and flowers in the *Andachtsbilder*'.[71]

RETURNING TO THE ROOM WITH THE ANGEL

We have seen that odour penetrates an intuitive and mysterious knowledge (*gnosis*), that odour possesses the capacity to take us back to the past, to the repressed, to the source and that it thus evokes the desire for restoration (nostalgia), and that the idea of odour in the end clings to Marian mystic devotion, and thereby creates a new artistic field that extends from allegories of paradise in the enclosed gardens to the iconographic symbolism of flowers in *Andachtsbilder*. In short, one was familiar with the epistemology of odour in archetypes and legends, in devotional practice and feminine Marian intuition. A systematic study of the ramifications of odour (and by extension the element of touch) in the late Middle Ages has yet to be written. Here I propose an initial step: I defend the integration of odour as a meaningful motif in the Annunciation, albeit a subtle one – not least because scent is intrinsically inarticulate.

The Annunciation exposes two major 'scent trails'. On the one hand, we have seen

69 Irigaray, *An ethics of sexual difference* (New York, 2004), p. 137.   **70** Granada, Iglesia del Sacro Monte; Falkenburg, *The fruit of devotion*, pp 85–6, fig. 31.   **71** Falkenburg, *The fruit of devotion*, p. 83.

7.4 Gerard David (*c*.1460–1523), *Virgin and Child*, early sixteenth century (1510–23),
oil on panel, 43 x 34cm, Granada, Iglesia del Sacro Monte.

from the 'interior allegory' that devotional instructions and the *Devotio Moderna* lavished a great deal of mental and literary attention on the smell of blossoms, flowers and the like. The act of scattering, covering and decorating with scented herbs, grasses and flowers – on the floor, on the walls of the house – was considered a metaphor for virtue, for the perfect receiving room. Scented rooms extend a welcome, like the angel of the Annunciation, and they also reflect the unblemished character of the (startled) hostess, Mary.

In the second place it is typical of odour that it must make use of material in order to translate itself into the medium of intuition, memory and the mystical. In the Annunciation this 'material' is the attribute of Mary herself: the lily (branch). In the collection of fifteenth-century sermons mentioned above, based on Bernard of Clairvaux, the author says that he himself has the habit of freshening his house with the goodness of flowers, such as that of the lily. The lily is the flower of purity par excellence, and hence of bodily virtue.[72] The lily is prized for its elegance and slenderness. And the gold of the stamens symbolizes the magnificence of the divine.[73] But beneath the symbol of purity pulsates the scented connotation of the flower. The lily's position in iconography is therefore also indicative. Lilies commonly appeared at the centre of compositions (pl. 26), as if to separate the realm of heaven (the angel, the supra-time and supra-space) from the receptive universe of the living room. If the lily is indeed the compositional marker between the two worlds, or even a materialization of that imaginary threshold, then its scent in the Annunciation may be regarded as the medium of 'transgression' or 'connection' between those worlds.[74] But which worlds do we mean? In other words, what is it that needs scent? What deeper intuition, unspeakable and invisible, is pulsating here, in need of the subtlest of all senses: smell?

Because odour is a magical, adjuring element, and at the same time one of the most ephemeral substrates of the intuition, of the repressed past, odour in the Annunciation emanates the incarnation: the life that emerged from invisibility and subsequently 'collapsed' into visibility. What better way to guide this transgression of invisibility to visibility than through odour, which embraces the continual transformation of substance and immateriality? What better way to follow this path than to start with the sublimation of wind, passing through *pneuma*, *spiritus* and gold until we reach the essence of this semantic field: the precipitation of something that can only be perceived by the nose? Is not the vegetative that gives off an overwhelming scent – tree, flower, cross/crotch, seed/semen – a mirror of visible invisibility?

But first I would like to make a small detour. In the Indo-European languages, shadow – such as the shadow (of the Holy Spirit) in the biblical source that slides across Mary's body, impregnating her – has three semantic points of contact that have been developed in the course of this essay: (1) fine material, fine dust, such as pollen; (2) vegetative growth in the forest; (3) and finally wind, again.[75] The first concerns the

---

72 *Reynicheyt des herten ende reynicheyt des lichaems*; Leiden University library, Ltk 2189, fo. 199.   73 Jozef van Vlierberg, *Het symbolisme der bloemen* (Dendermonde, 1930), p. 31.   74 The threshold between the two worlds may also be expressed by the emptiness or, better still, by the perspectivistic space itself. The *perspicere* symbolizes the 'looking through' that which remains invisible: the conception or the void: for this, see Herman Parret, 'De l'invisible comme présence', *Visio*, 7:3–4 (2003), 63–91.   75 http://indo-european.info/pokorny-etymological-dictionary/index.htm.

conviction that dark shadow consists of matter (in the way that light is also supposed to be matter). Shadow is thus a substance, something material *and* immaterial, like odour. The relationship between dust and pollen connects shadow and flowers – in this case the lily – as 'impregnators'. Vegetative growth in the forest evokes the dark place as a fertility symbol, as a feminine principle (see above). Wind is related to shadow thanks to its mobility; wind brings forth shadows. Among the Navajo in particular, who cultivated a highly developed, animistic vision of countless wind spirits, shadow and wind were seen as equally phantom-like phenomena.[76]

The process of becoming flesh has installed itself as the *punctum*, as the revolution, as the knot in the Christian history of salvation. We cannot know this knot, but we can sense it in part. Only in unarticulated intuition does the knot unfold itself, untangle itself before our eyes through the vigilance of an insight that resides in the chamber of mystery. When the angel entered the room and startled his hostess, the collapsing in time and space of something that had long remained hidden took place. Only scent can evoke such deep *anamnesis*: this flash, this singular interlacing of past, present and future escapes the ocular, the auricular, the sense of touch, and binds itself to the pneumatic in humankind: its ability to breathe, to live and hence to smell.

This mysterious immaculate flower seems to be charged with all humanity's nostalgia,[77] and forms the culmination, the final step, in the sublimation of wind in the (im)possibility of grasping the mystery of all mysteries: incarnation. Now we are ready for the ultimate revelation: the dimension in the Annunciation that precedes figuration pictorially – the amorphous, the 'stain'.

TO END WITH: VEINS, STAINS

An unusual thirteenth-century Annunciation is still venerated today in the church of Santissima Annunziata in Florence. According to legend, the painter fell asleep at his task, and when he awakened an angel had miraculously completed the face of Mary (pl. 27). The legend is a variant of the so-called *acheiropoietoi*: images not made by human hands.[78] The belief in miraculously given or finished images, of which the *mandylion* is the prototype, arose in Byzantium. The cloth bears the imprint of the visage of Christ, which in his mercy he gave to an artist for the Syrian king Abgar, who suffered from leprosy (pl. 28). Another variant is the *Hodegon* icon, a half-length portrait of Mary of which the original was supposed to have been painted by the evangelist Luke himself. The Florentine miracle is related to the latter type of *acheiropoietos*.

---

76 For the American Indians, see Jan Deblieu, *Wind: how the flow of the air has shaped life, myth and the land* (New York, 1998), pp 28–9.   **77** A strong kinship is presumed between the lily (and its schematic three lobes) and the ancient Semitic symbol of the branch/tree of life; Israel Regardie, *The Tree of Life: a study in magic* (York, 1994), p. 74 and passim.   **78** Gerhard Wolf, *Schleier und Spiegel. Traditionen des Christusbildes und die Bildkonzepte der Renaissance* (Munich, 2002).

The altar in the Santissima Annunziata represents paradigms relating to the creation of images, a process known as iconogenesis. In Byzantine tradition it was believed that icon painters received divine inspiration through the ear, whispered by an angel or the Holy Spirit. Only by virtue of the grace thus granted could the icon assume its function as a gateway to the invisible: God. In Byzantium an icon was defined as a process of continual incarnation, and painting by extension as an activity that ran parallel to the Annunciation itself, in which the words in Mary's ear also led to an image: the son of God. The representation of Christ is after all legitimated by the visibility of the divine plan of salvation, which is called *oeikonomia*. Nicephore (758–828) recognizes in this theological term the word *eikon*, thereby strengthening his iconophilic position by virtue of this homonymic relationship.[79] John of Damascus (d. 749) knows that he who ignores the image, ignores the incarnation.[80] In the eighth-century psalter of Chludov, an iconoclast who pierces the portrait of Christ is compared to Longinus, who tormented the Saviour with his spear. He who denies the image, denies Salvation (pl. 29).[81]

Visuality inspired by a voice, by breath, has a cosmogonic character; it is essentially involved in the mystery of creation. To paint is to transmute: painting penetrates to the spirit, the *pneuma* of creation itself.[82] Leonardo da Vinci says (paraphrasing): 'If you look at a wall crowded with stains, or pieces of stone, then you can imagine a scene, you can recognize in it the analogy with landscape, with a backdrop of mountains, rivers, cliffs, trees, plains, valleys and various hills'.[83] Stains and stones stimulate our imagination with respect to actual scenes, and not only as a sort of *Spielerei*; it goes deeper, back to the conviction that figuration is already contained in nature, that nature is in fact pregnant with it: the so-called *pierres imagées*.[84] 'From the thirteenth to the seventeenth century some lovers of art and curiosities had a real passion for these "paintings" that nature seemed to have enclosed within the depths of agate, marble, jasper and porphyry.'[85] In artists' and collectors' inventories, one often comes across cherished stones described as *a natura depicti* (painted by nature) or *a natura sine omni artis ministerio* (natural, without the intervention of the arts).

In the most recent anthropological image analyses, the striking presence of stones and flaming marble in Annunciations is interpreted as a visual enterprise meant to explain the hidden, mysterious ground of creation itself.[86] Independently of each

79 Mondzain-Baudinet (ed.), *Nicéphore* (Paris, 1989); Mondzain-Baudinet (ed.), *Image, Icône, Economie* (Paris, 1996). **80** Julia Kristeva, *Visions capitales* (Paris, 1998), p. 60. **81** Moskou, Historical Museum, fo. 67; Marie-Christine Sepière, *L'image d'un Dieu souffrant (IXe–Xe siècle)* (Paris, 1984), pl. 1; see Kathleen Corrigan, *Visual polemics in the ninth-century psalters* (Cambridge, 1992). **82** Claire Farago, 'Exiting art history: locating "art" in the modern history of the subject', *Konsthistorisk tidskrift*, 70:1–2 (2001), 3–19. **83** André Chastel, *Léonard de Vinci par lui-même* (Paris, 1952), pp 100–1. **84** Jurgis Baltrusaitis, *Aberrations* (Paris, 1957), p. 47. **85** 'On peut dire que, du XIII au XVIIe, il existe une véritable passion chez certains amateurs d'art ou de singularités pour ces tableaux que la nature semble avoir enfermés au sein des agates, des marbres, des jaspes et des porphyre': Roger Caillois, 'Méduse et Cie' in Roger Caillois (ed.), *Oeuvres* (Paris, 2008), p. 502. **86** There is a rich tradition beginning in the early Christian and Byzantine period of viewing certain types of flamed marble as *acheiropoietoi*. Contemporaries, travellers and the faithful describe the magnificent marble slabs on the walls and floors of

other, Georges Didi-Huberman and Paul Vandenbroeck described this *marbre faux* in depictions of the Annunciation and the Incarnation as an expression of a pictorial phase that precedes figuration (pl. 30).[87] In other words, artists symbolically embed amorphous, marbled mineral drawings in iconographies that are fostered by the symbolism of 'preceding' or of 'descent into material in order to take on form'. They will also resort to the phenomenon as a reflection on their own artisthood, which follows the process of an abstract idea descending into the world of form and material.

As we have seen, according to Didi-Huberman, one of the 'openings' of the image is launched in the Judaeo-Christian paradigm that man is created in God's image. However, man lost this unity, or *ressemblance*, in the Fall: it became *défiguration* or *dissemblance*. The history of *la pensée figurée* is thus determined by an eternal quest for the restoration of this analogy. Art and iconography also characterize themselves as an endless series of traces, as a lost covenant. That restoration is closest at the moment of transition from one covenant to the next: the incarnation or *la promesse de retrouver l'image*. The incarnation itself cannot be represented, however: *l'image échappe*. It is the *circoncision de l'image* that constantly escapes its matrix. The history of images is a history of the desire to coincide with the invisible.

The integration of abstract, painted materials in the iconography of the Annunciation imposes a relationship between the pre-figurative and the figurative. The integration of the two consists in the fact that between both worlds or visual fields an energy is unleashed that continually jumps from one to the other, as if between the promise of the figure that will be created out of nothing and the figure/figuration itself. Both are experienced in the world of the *plattomenos* (forming) and the world of *mimesis* (depicting), respectively, as virtuosity. At the same time this forms, according to the Neo-Platonist Pseudo-Dionysius (fifth–sixth century), the binome upon which all visual/plastic creation rests. In other words there is a constant shifting, a *dissemblance*: 'to figure without assuming substance'[88] to take on a 'formless form' or an 'unshowable shape', and is thus oriented towards the associative, the mystery, the processual.[89] The energetic abstraction that the *plattomenos*, the dizzying flaming of marble panels – woven marble, if you will – embeds in the Annunciation bears witness to a deeper anthropological division between sub-symbolic gradations (a-figurative, abstract) and symbolic linguicity (figurative, legibility, mimetic).

In other words, the Annunciation appears to maintain a sensitivity with respect to two epistemological traces in the history of culture: the matrixial (receptive, prenatal) and the phallic (additive, formed). Or between odour and seed, between lily and dove, between a golden ray and a stain.

churches as splendid landscapes and stirring seas, as the cosmogonic elements of nature involved in creation itself: see Fabio Barry, 'Walking on water: cosmic floors in antiquity and the Middle Ages', *Art Bulletin*, 89:4 (2007), 627–56; Maria Luigia Fobelli, 'Descrizione e percezione delle immagini acheropite sui marmi bizantini' in *Immagine e Ideologia* (Milan, 2007), pp 27–32. **87** Georges Didi-Huberman, *Fra Angelico* (Paris, 1990); Paul Vandenbroeck, 'Matrix Marmorea' in Baert et al., *New perspectives in iconology*, pp 180–210. **88** Paul Vandenbroeck, 'Matrix Marmorea', p. 192. **89** Ibid., p. 193.

What does he do? How does he bring her to life? Very cautiously. He wants her to become conscious and, holding the rather simple theory that all knowledge comes from the senses, decides to open her sensorium. Slowly, slowly. He will give her, to begin with, just one of the senses. And which does he pick? Not sight, noblest of the senses, not hearing – well, no need to run through the whole list, short as it is. Let's hasten to relate that he first awards her, perhaps ungenerously, the most primitive sense, that of smell.

Susan Sontag, *The Volcano Lover*

8 Prostheses of pious perception: on the instrumentalization and mediation of the medieval sensorium

HANS HENRIK LOHFERT JØRGENSEN

Why 'instruments'? Why focus on instruments of devotion, instruments of belief, instruments of sensation, instruments of perception? Part of us – our more purist part, that is – may consider instruments peripheral and external to the very kernel of religious experience, as if they make us miss the true point of both religion and experience. Instruments may seem to be mere accessories, supplemental extras, dispensable gadgets, that is to say, exterior equipment facilitating and aiding, but not central to either the inner properties of devotion or the internal operations of human consciousness and cognition. In this essentialist view – which we have probably all endorsed in some of our weaker moments – instruments substitute for immediate, direct and unaided access to things, thus taking the place of genuine immediacy and replacing it with the mediation of tools, props and utensils. Machines, it may seem to us, take the place of the body, prostheses take the place of perception, images and screens take the place of vision and sight, outward props take the place of inward prayer. Even if we do not adhere to any such technophobic convictions, we may still from time to time find ourselves nostalgic for authenticity and pure, untainted states of mind confirming the transparency of our senses and the ontology of our world. Although acknowledging that the senses are socio-cultural systems – that is, an ideological apparatus of historically construed techniques – with an inclination to naturalize themselves and slip into the culturally subconscious, we still need to believe in them and to believe in what we see.

This ambivalence has also made itself felt in the field of academic criticism over the years. Philosophers of technology and representation, historians, sociologists and media theorists as diverse as Marx Wartofsky, Johan Huizinga, Norbert Elias, Marshall McLuhan, Paul Virilio and Friedrich Kittler have all in their own way – and, to be sure, in following their own, otherwise quite different historical agendas – argued along such lines of experiential opacity and alienation. Yet these same critics are also all curiously fascinated with the purported instruments of estrangement, be it Virilio's instruments of perception, Wartofsky's instruments of pictorial representation, Huizinga's instruments of religious expression, Elias' instruments of eating and bodily contact or Kittler and McLuhan's instruments of mediation. For Huizinga, the sincerity of belief waned with late medieval embodiment of faith in visible forms and exterior arrangements, 'hardening into mere externalism':

> all that is meant to stimulate spiritual consciousness is reduced to worldliness in other-worldly guise … pious feeling is apt to resolve itself in the image … The symbolism of spiritual love has become a mere mechanical process … Religious customs tended to multiply in an almost mechanical way.[1]

Nevertheless, despite his anxieties about outward mechanization, this skeptical historian of holy mediation was at the same time deeply mesmerized by 'the exuberant imagery of the time', saturated as it could be with 'extreme religious sensibility'.[2] The tension so sensitively felt by Huizinga between the inward saturation with religious emotion and its outward representation, mediation, and instrumentalization lies at the very core of the following considerations, opting for an instrumental reconciliation and dissolution of these assumed opposites.

For Norbert Elias it was not true spiritual feeling and sensibility but the physical and social structure of relationships between people that were at stake in the cultural use of artefacts and devices. In his view of the process of civilization, novel eating techniques and instruments took part in reforming medieval manners and hence in erecting new thresholds of feeling and bodily sensation: 'frontiers of sensibility … the invisible wall of affects which seems now to rise between one human body and another, repelling and separating'.[3] In this understanding of an unrestrained immediacy supposed to be gradually diminishing from medieval to modern codes of conduct, especially the introduction of the individual fork – a civilizing instrument – became emblematic of a new sensory and psychic distance between bodies, foods and individuals.[4] Whether image, fork or some other kind of visual, tactile or oral utensil, their mediacy has sometimes tended to be apprehended as the false snake intervening in a paradise of immediate and authentic contact with Self and Other.

But not to forget, the fork also extends the reach and grip of the hand, and at the same time media have been conceived of as projections of the senses and the body. Equally enthralled by the interdependence of media and human sensibility, McLuhan perceived the instruments of sensory media (in a very broad sense) as prosthetic *extensions of the senses* – or 'Extensions of Man' – rather than inhibitions of the senses, thus echoing a fascination with the man/machine-exchange characteristic of his own times.[5]

1 Johan Huizinga, *The waning of the Middle Ages*, trans. F. Hopman (1924; London, 1990), pp 147, 149, 192. **2** Huizinga, *The waning of the Middle Ages*, pp 184, 190. For a nuanced appreciation of Huizinga's contribution, see Bynum, *Christian materiality*, pp 29f., 295. **3** Norbert Elias, *The civilizing process*, trans. Edmund Jephcott (1939, Oxford, 1994), p. 56. **4** Elias, *The civilizing process*, pp 48 ff., 55. See also Hans Peter Duerr, *Nacktheit und Scham: Der Mythos vom Zivilisationsprozess* (Frankfurt a. M., 1988), for an opposition to this somewhat stylized and tendentious notion of uncivilized and unspoilt immediacy in earlier cultures, including the Middle Ages, which have mostly been anything but immediate, unregulated, or 'authentic' in their shame-driven discipline of social behaviour and sensory attitudes towards the body. **5** Marshall McLuhan, *Understanding media*

The ambivalent allure of mechanical man also informed the subsequent decades, however, as when media- and war-archaeologist Paul Virilio felt threatened by the prospect of synthetic perception and had his 'vision machine' simultaneously both enhance and invalidate natural perception, augment and weaken the human gaze, telescope and delimit our sensory horizon: 'le passage de la vision à la visualisation' initiated the cybernetics of sensation.[6] In a related outburst of apocalyptic techno-phobia (or is it philia?), symptomatic of such technological determinism, Friedrich Kittler raised the stakes even higher and went on to declare that 'media determine our situation', implying that our entire cognitive and epistemological infrastructure is mediatized.[7] Media constitute the basic condition and structural framework for experience and understanding, no less, and consequently the senses themselves are an historical effect of media:

> The dominant information technologies of the day control all understanding and its illusions. What remains of people is what media can store and commu-nicate … the very schematism of perceptibility. … Sound and image, voice and text are reduced to surface effects, known to consumers as interface. Sense and the senses turn into eyewash – media-produced glamor. … Media 'define what really is'.[8]

Reality collapses into mediality, senses collapse into interface properties, people and perceptibility collapse into instrumentality. In comparison with Huizinga on the wane, hierarchies of reality/mediality/ideality may have been turned upside down, but fears and fascinations subsist and still make us ask – and doubt – how real mediatized realities can really be.

(1964; London, 1997). It is hardly a coincidence that Andy Warhol – so attracted to the artificial and mechanical – at about the same time explained his machine-like mode of visualization with a celebrated claim characteristic of this period and its modernity: 'The reason I'm painting this way is that I want to be a machine'. See also Caroline A. Jones, 'The mediated sensorium' in Caroline A. Jones (ed.), *Sensorium* (Cambridge, MA, 2006), pp 5–49 at p. 6, on the 'techno aspirations' of the post-war period and beyond.   **6** Paul Virilio, *La machine de vision* (Paris, 1988), p. 39. For a medievalist's critical evaluation and correction of Virilio's take on the history of techno-logically enhanced perception, see Hans Henrik Lohfert Jørgensen, 'Synets modernisering – i senmiddelalderen, En alternativ perceptionshistorie' in Helene Illeris and Hans Dam Christensen (eds), *Visuel kultur – viden, liv, politik* (Copenhagen, 2009), pp 11–28.   **7** This is the famous and infamous opening phrase of Friedrich A. Kittler, *Gramophone, Film, Typewriter*, trans. Geoffrey Winthrop-Young and Michael Wutz (1986; Stanford, 1999), p. xxxix.   **8** Kittler, *Gramophone, film, typewriter*, pp xl, xli, 1, 3. In these passages, Kittler's war-inspired prophecies may seem to echo the oracular ethos of Virilio's futurist visions whose 'dromological' analyses of military media and perception technology appear to have been an important source of inspiration for Kittler. See also the comments of W.J.T. Mitchell and Mark B.N. Hansen, 'Introduction' in Mitchell and Hansen (eds), *Critical terms for media studies* (Chicago, 2010), pp vii–xxii at p. vii; and Caroline A. Jones, 'Senses' in Mitchell and Hansen (eds), *Critical terms for media studies*, pp 88–100 at p. 88.

THE MEDIUM OF BELIEF: PROPS AND PROSTHESES

This imbrication of the means of expression and impression, this entanglement of the realities of mediation and sensation, also apply to instruments of devotion and even to the operations of religion and faith itself, presently undergoing a re-evaluation: 'the outwardness of belief', the 'external aspect of religion', 'the mechanisms of piety and devotion'.[9] Based on the conviction that 'there is no *homo interior* without the *homo exterior*', the ENID endeavour is thus also a symptom of the current interest in processes of instrumentalization and mediation, increasingly considered fundamental to the deep history of cultures.[10] In our age of outward performativity searching for inward authenticity (or indeed producing it),[11] we are perhaps able to recognize that mechanical man has always been an intrinsic part of spiritual man. In a dialectical relationship, according to the ENID concept, instrumentality both expresses and forms spirituality so as to become an integrated and indistinguishable component of it. In a manner that is as performative and instrumental as it is constitutive and sacramental, 'signs produce what they signify' – that is, they themselves produce and engender what they may seem to be merely reproducing or representing (for instance in the medieval *praxis pietatis* of tears as a sign of internal emotion as well as an external medium for it).[12]

Our present socio-historical situation, which provides the overall framing of the ENID approach to past practices, is highlighted by contemporary art and technology theorist Caroline Jones in a recent essay on 'The mediated sensorium':

> The human sensorium has always been mediated. But over the past few decades that condition has greatly intensified. Amplified, shielded, channeled, prosthetized, simulated, stimulated, irritated – our sensorium is more mediated

---

9 Henning Laugerud and Laura Katrine Skinnebach, 'Introduction' in Laugerud and Skinnebach (eds), *Instruments of devotion* (Aarhus, 2007), pp 9–19 at pp 10, 12. This is the first publication defining the principles and research interests of *ENID: European Network on the Instruments of Devotion*. **10** Laugerud and Skinnebach, 'Introduction', *Instruments of devotion*, p. 11, referring to Henrik von Achen's contribution to the same volume (see n. 12). **11** Introducing the concept of 'perceived authenticity', the emerging field of experience economy offers an insight into 'this essential paradox: all human enterprise is ontologically fake – that is, in its very being it is inauthentic – and yet, output from that enterprise can be phenomenologically real – that is, it is perceived as authentic by the individuals who buy it', see James H. Gilmore and B. Joseph Pine II, *Authenticity: what consumers really want* (Boston, MA, 2007), p. 89. If we historicize 'what consumers really want' into a consideration of what the faithful really wanted, we may accept a holy experience as phenomenologically real and authentic to pious observers, not in spite of, but exactly because of being produced by their very observation of it. **12** Henrik von Achen, 'Piety, practice and process' in Laugerud and Skinnebach (eds), *Instruments of devotion*, pp 23–44 at p. 28. Symptomatically, von Achen also feels the need to ward off suspicion about the instrumental dimension and stress that it 'should not be seen as something secondary', but should rather be appreciated as a substantial constituent of piety. For a discussion with Huizinga and others of the medieval relationship between conventional tears and genuine emotion, see Lyn A. Blanchfield, 'Prolegomenon: considerations of weeping and sincerity in the Middle Ages' in Elina Gertsman (ed.), *Crying in the Middle Ages: tears of history* (New York, 2012), pp xxi–xxx; pp xxif.: 'Weeping constitutes a challenging intersection between emotion and behavior. In many medieval sources, tears are often described as objects that can be manipulated. … weeping, after all, is a gesture, a behavioral and performative act open to manipulation'.

today than ever before. Yet it bothers us less. The cyborg model of the 1980s and
the virtual dreams of the 1990s have evolved into a twenty-first-century 'comfort
zone', in which the prosthetic and supplemental are habitual. The microspeaker
in the ear, the drug in the blood, the nanosurgical implant, the simulated taste
in the mouth – these 'enhancements' no longer provoke the apocalyptic
excitement they did even a few years ago.[13]

As a consequence of this gradual appeasement, we are now able to take a look into
some of the most intimate workings of the human mind – those of belief and piety –
through the perspective of internalized sensory instruments and external instrumentalization of the senses. In our era of 'augmented reality', we may readily accept the
notion of prostheses of pious perception augmenting the perceived realities of faith
and structuring the religious mind-set of the faithful. Whether produced by today's
implants or yesterday's grafts, implantations of such percepts have always had the
ability to become sensations of truth, exactly because they both shape and transmit
believers' deeper world-view. David Morgan, for example, argues in favour of sensory
mediation as 'the medium of belief'. In *The sacred gaze*, he sets out to explore 'the
mediation of belief that goes to the heart of belief as a historical phenomenon'.
Maintaining that 'belief is mediated', he looks into the visual and material culture of
religion as a physical domain instrumental to belief:

> Belief happens in what people say, but also in what they do. It is embodied in
> various practices and actions, in their uses of buildings, pictures, in the taste of
> food and the smell of fragrances. … Belief happens in and through things and
> what people do with them.

By implication, instruments of seeing and sensing may be instruments of devotion:
'visual practice alongside images themselves, insofar as religion happens visually,
constitute the visual medium of belief'. In this inquiry into the operation of vision as
a religious act, Morgan seeks to understand

> how religious belief takes shape in the history of visual media. How is visual
> piety, visual belief, a function of its mediation? … A medium – whether it is
> words, food, or looking at pictures – is where belief happens.

The study of religion suggested by Morgan thus entails a history of its physical and
sensory instrumentalization.[14] Belief is propped and prosthetic.

13 Jones, 'The mediated sensorium', p. 5.   **14** David Morgan, *The sacred gaze: religious visual culture in theory
and practice* (Berkeley, CA, 2005), pp 3, 6, 8. For a different, but certainly related, definition of cultic vision and
sacred seeing, see Hans Henrik Lohfert Jørgensen, 'Cultic vision: seeing as ritual, visual and liturgical experience
in the early Christian and medieval Church' in Jeremy Llewellyn et al. (eds), *The appearances of medieval rituals:*

If this is right, instrumentalization may indeed be constitutive of human religious conception as well as human sensory perception, both mutually underpinning each other within a given world-view. It then follows that the world of man, as conceived and perceived, is always already mediatized and only accessible through some act of mediation. But it also follows that this fundamental premise need not lead to secularization, disenchantment, and alienation since it can readily enable belief and bring about suggestive sensory as well as extra-sensory experience. In other words, it is an open question to what extent the use of instruments and the resulting cognitive condition is in fact constitutive of our humanity, and has always been so – hence depending on what may be considered 'posthuman' machinery, implied by the human condition itself. If this is the case, then the 'human' has always already been 'posthuman'; an acknowledgement, which of course renders those very terms somewhat superfluous. Nevertheless, in our current situation, the ongoing acceleration of our reliance on instruments allows us to appreciate historical genealogies and parallels in past cultures, such as the Middle Ages, and in so doing we are prone to discover the pervasive importance of media and mediation to the very fabric of those cultures.

THE INSTRUMENTALITY OF HUMAN EXPERIENCE AND EXISTENCE

Accordingly, when Caroline Jones evaluates the existing state of perception (i.e. separation, bureaucratization and channeling of the modern senses) she makes sure to define the sensory apparatus in a far-reaching historical perspective:

> The resulting set of experiences can be called a sensorium: it lives only in us and through us, enhanced by our technologies and extended prosthetically but always subject to our consciousness (itself dependent on sensory formations). … our senses are instrumentalized: we are joined to the sensory tools we have made to amplify and accompany the self. Instrumentalization is always part of the mediated sensorium, it is as old as the pressure felt by a hand grasping a bone or a stick.[15]

The sensorium, socially situated and cultivated, has always already been mediatized: it has been shaped, structured and organized by the cultural and cultic practices to which it has been employed and through which its historical plasticity has been modelled. The stick grasped by our hand in effect changes our sensorium. It changes our feeling of things because we get used to feeling by and through the stick or, as it were, the fork or some other medium of touch. When we handle or manipulate things we come to

the play of construction and modification (Turnhout, 2004), pp 173–97. **15** Jones, 'The mediated sensorium', pp 8, 17.

feel them as if we touch them with the stick or the fork in the hand. Eventually, this feeling is remembered by our hand itself and internalized in our sense of touch. The stick sticks with us, so to speak, and influences our mode of grasping even when it is not there and is not actually used in the perceptual act. The prosthesis becomes part of us, inseparable from our sensory functions, implanting itself in our sensory constitution and infrastructure. It allows us to reach further and grasp more. It extends our hands and augments our reality, but it also changes that reality through its mediation of it. At the same time it expands and increases our sphere of tactility and delimits or narrows it to a certain way of sensing things. The sensitivity of the empowered hand is both augmented and domesticated, improved and restrained, boosted and curbed, in the mediation and its ensuing cultivation of the sense. Indeed, this simultaneous effect of sensory empowerment and delimitation is integral to us whether our tool is a primitive stick of old or, say, an industrial vacuum cleaner of new.

Arguing along the same lines, W.J.T. Mitchell and Mark Hansen also address the 'irreducible role of mediation in the history of human being' in their introduction to the recent, yet seminal *Critical terms for media studies*. Here, they take *media* to be 'a general mediality that is constitutive of the human as a "biotechnical" form of life'. Radicalizing their 'techno-anthropological sense of media', they even suggest its operations to have 'structured the history of humanity from its very origin'. In taking their cue from McLuhan, they insist on 'our fundamentally prosthetic mode of being', where 'the human and the technical coevolve' with 'media as a prosthesis of human agency'.[16] According to Mitchell and Hansen, the instrumentality of our existence possesses a profound archaeological dimension to be excavated by media history. Mediation by instruments has always been a premise for human action and reaction, communication and sensation, perception and reception, utterance and response. Learning about our tools we also learn about ourselves. To study the cultural history of instruments is to study the deep history of culture. But of course, not all types, modes and means of instrumentality are the same and certain differentiations are called for in such a study. Leaving aside more general areas of human production and consumption, I will venture into the domain of 'techno-spiritual' instruments central to the workings of medieval culture. In order to identify the foundational institution of this domain, though, I first need to establish a rather concrete, material and operational understanding of the 'anthro-mechanic' apparatus used for tooling devotions and implementing devoted states of mind and senses: vicarious, projected, prosthetic – yet touching, engaging and involving identification.

---

16 Mitchell and Hansen, 'Introduction', *Critical terms for media studies*, pp ix, xii, xiii.

PIOUS PERCEPTION AND PROPS OF PRAYER

This use of exterior equipment of emotion and sensation certainly also applies to the Middle Ages and to the instruments of devotion that played a vital role in the history of its media and senses. In what follows, I will attempt to provide the basic framework for an appreciation of the medieval mediation of the senses in the context of cult and devotion. This social context was arguably a crucial arena for the formation and negotiation of what we may term *pious perception:* an ideal mode of sensing and sensory apprehension aspired to by the devout in search for religious experience. The religious mode of experience required a suitable way of perception appropriate for establishing a dialogue with the divine realities. In her recent dissertation on what she terms 'devotional perception', Laura Katrine Skinnebach convincingly argues that it was built into the very fabric of devotional practice, which took advantage of various external and material aids to 'form a habitus of perception': 'the process of repeated devotional practice would lead to devotional sensing, and serve to *form* the senses as an instrument of devotional perception'. In this 'configuration of the senses into a virtuous sensory habitus', pious practices would therefore also be subject to changing notions of the sacred and percipients' access to it through the Middle Ages.[17]

In some situations, a specific modality of sacred sensation could indeed be deemed a devotional activity in itself, bordering on contemplation, meditation or prayer. Exerted through the perceptual disposition and motivation of the devotee committed to a specifically Christian state of experience, belief was also expressed in sensory habits. Sometimes the fervent intensity of these sensory solicitations may even have amounted to a kind of *corporeal credo* performed through experiential convictions, commitments and instruments. In its dedication to sensing in a faithful way, the God-directed sensorium may eventually have strived for a godly gratification of the sensory experience itself. This was for instance the case in the habitual practice of sacramental viewing or 'Augenkommunion', enjoying a popular cult in its own right during the later Middle Ages. Just seeing the enacted elevation of Christ's perceptible body at the moment of consecration was considered by many churchgoers to be a sensory variant of Eucharistic consumption believed to potentially result in the beholder's own spiritual and perceptual elevation.[18] By this time, the indulgence system had also become, among other things, an outward formalization and legitimizing sanction – a kind of official sanctification – of particular ways of sacrament and image perception,

---

17 Skinnebach, *Practises of perception*, pp 232–3. **18** By supporters of this so-called 'spiritual communion', intensely beholding the body of the Saviour in the sensory appearance of the elevated and exposed host was considered nearly as vigorous and efficacious as actually attending Holy Communion. Miri Rubin, *Corpus Christi: the Eucharist in late medieval culture* (Cambridge, 1991), pp 63–4, 150, notes a 'growing appreciation of the quasi-sacramental value of gazing at the present Christ, … a strong "vicarious" procedure [resulting in] widespread understandings entertained by the laity that gazing was as good as reception [of the Eucharist proper]'. Optical reception of the sacrament thus came to replace actual physical reception, if not always in theory then at least in practice. Édouard Dumoutet, *Le désir de voir l'hostie et les origines de la dévotion au Saint-Sacrement* (Paris, 1926), pp 18–21, discusses the respective positions on the issue of several scholastic theologians.

aimed at receiving a little trace of grace merely from praying before and beholding the appointed object of attention. Indulgences guaranteed the beneficial effect of looking devoutly at the consecrated host exhibited for that perceptual purpose or of becoming absorbed in a holy picture by seeing, holding, touching, caressing and kissing it.[19] Praying was certainly not only a habit (or *habitus*) of directing mind and words, either to God or his holy representatives, but also of directing the body and senses – and of making the entire sensory system conform to this exalted '*sensophilia*'.

Enactments of the kind just mentioned mediated and sanctified the senses by way of a number of physical and material instruments. Take another case, the one of the rosary, a tangible tool with an exquisite tactile, olfactory and auditory operation used for tooling a true meditation of faith. In this multisensory meditation, the tangibility of the touchable prop itself produced a haptic mode of prayer: a palpable prayer enacted by counting fingers and felt by feeble skin in order to touch soft hearts. The physical rosary beads were sometimes actually made from dried and deodorized rose petals with extracted oils, hence giving forth the aroma of saintly sacrifice and exaltation, like the sweet incense of prayer rising to heaven (Psalm 141:2, Revelation 8:4).[20] Amber beads were highly prized for their feel and smell. The bigger markers could even be designed to emit sweet-smelling perfumes and be scented with odoriferous substances such as musk, ambergris or perfume paste, for which recipes are still preserved. Radiated by pierced metal beads or fragrant filigree pomanders, such aromatic odours offered an external aid for the internal absorption.[21] Carefully differentiated by material, size, shape, surface and texture, the warmed-up beads would slide through the fingers and orchestrate the manual gesture of prayer, while conflating atmospheric impressions of flowery fragrance with the ethereal sound of recited prayers. This absorbing devotional instrument encoded faithful fingers with sensitive prayers, as if the digits themselves were doing the praying and performing the piety. The sense of touch was codified and engaged in a haptic modality of devotion – a tactile technique instrumentalizing the sense for sacred purposes: pleading skin, palpable devotion, touched heart. Supported by the instrumental rosary, the hands of

---

19 For a discussion of indulgence as a spiritual and sensory sanction formally rewarded to prayer accompanied by the perception of certain pictorial motifs or by the attentive observation of the elevation and exposition of the sacrament during mass, see Hans Henrik Lohfert Jørgensen, *I kroppens spejl, Krop og syn i senmiddelalderlige danske kalkmalerier* (Aarhus, 2004), pp 19ff, 56ff. For examples of indulgence given to pictures that directly presuppose 'ymaginis visionem', see Anton L. Mayer, 'Die heilbringende Schau in Sitte und Kult' in O. Casel (ed.), *Heilige Überlieferung, Festschrift für Ildefons Herwegen* (Münster, 1938), pp 234–62 at p. 251 n. 72. For further examples involving other sensory modalities as well, see Skinnebach, *Practises of perception*, p. 247ff; *Kjøbenhavns Diplomatarium*, 2 (1874), n. 68; Peter Browe, *Die Verehrung der Eucharistie im Mittelalter* (1933, Rome, 1967), p. 54; Sixten Ringbom, 'Bild och avlat, I. Veronikabilden', *ICO – Iconographisk Post*, 3 (1983), 8–18; Sixten Ringbom, 'Bild och avlat, II. Smärtomannen, Rosenkransen och Jomfrun i solinne', *ICO – Iconographisk Post*, 4 (1983), 1–16. 20 For a discussion of the rosary as an elaborate multisensory prayer form, also including a number of literary and visual examples, see Pil Dahlerup, *Sanselig Senmiddelalder, Litterære perspektiver på danske tekster, 1482–1523* (Aarhus, 2010), p. 347ff. 21 Anne Winston-Allen, *Stories of the Rose: the making of the rosary in the Middle Ages* (University Park, PA, 1997, 2005), p. 112; Ronald W. Lightbown, *Mediaeval European jewellery, with a catalogue of the collection in the Victoria & Albert Museum* (London, 1992), pp 347, 351.

the pious became an instrument for their piety. The mechanics of meditation depended on a perceptible prop for the production and promotion of prayer: a manual memory medium keeping track of the recitations and repetitions while keeping contact with the contemplating body.

Going back to at least the eleventh century and presumably beyond, chains for sequential prayer were made of pebbles, knotted strings and beads of wood, bone, horn, shell, mother-of-pearl, amber, jet, coral, crystal, glass, gems, colourful stones, pearls or precious metals. So-called 'Paternosters' (for laypeople's or lay brethren's repeated Our Fathers) came to be mass merchandise, produced in massive amounts (pl. 31). As early as the thirteenth century, they accounted for a flourishing craft and trade, a devotional industry, suggesting that this pre-existing devotional technology was in fact the precondition for the rosary devotion – rather than the other way around.[22] Used as prayer counters, according to Constance Classen, 'such mnemonic devices added a visual and tactile dimension to the vocal repetitions of prayers, allowing supplicants to see and feel the accumulation of their spiritual efforts'.[23] Anne Winston-Allen in turn insists that 'in dealing with the rosary it is even more necessary to stress that the "meaning" is not "in the text" but in the context, that is, in the performance of the ritual'. She too emphasizes the 'mnemonic devices that aid in its performance' and 'could be used as prompts in the ritual "telling" of the beads', that is, the pious practice promoted by oral, aural, visual and tactile means in conjunction with the Marian and Christological prayer texts (fig. 8.1).[24]

So saturated with holy prayer and power was the appealing palpability and materiality of rosaries that people wore them on the body as a protective amulet or talisman warding off evil, harm, illness, insanity or sin. Just wearing or carrying them sometimes earned generous indulgences. Such beneficent effects could even be reinforced by marker beads or pendants containing relics or discharging medical substances. Surely, contact with relics would add a saintly touch to the physical manipulation of the chain and the embodied chain prayer, in principle making the devotion mediate a corporeal visit to a holy grave. No wonder that many practitioners carried the efficacious chains on their limbs or slept with them around the neck as an instrument of protection. Others held them in their hands when they died, as if the bearable beads themselves would mediate the materialized prayer and act as a medium or instrument for the salvific contact to the Virgin, continued in the hereafter.[25] Significantly, in visual depictions, rosaries were often pictured in conjunction with hands, either those of devotees handling and fondling the beads while praying them or the wounded hands of Jesus himself, inserted in Paternoster beads to arouse compassion and make the devout identify with the bodily pain felt by the Saviour in

22 Winston-Allen, *Stories of the Rose*, pp 14f., 111ff; Lightbown, *Mediaeval European jewellery*, p. 342ff.
23 Constance Classen, *The deepest sense: a cultural history of touch* (Urbana, IL, 2012), p. 32. **24** Winston-Allen, *Stories of the Rose*, pp 29, 30, 32. **25** Lightbown, *Mediaeval European jewellery*, pp 351, 353; Winston-Allen, *Stories of the Rose*, p. 116 (quoting, among others, an apotropaic Danish rosary text of 1496 by Michael Nielsen).

his mesmerizing passion (as addressed in the standard psalter or prayer cycle of repeated *Ave Marias* and *Paternosters*). Pain, passion, piety, prayer – it was all mediated by a prosthetic device designed to creep under the believer's skin and configure it for a touching experience. The rosary – a practical prosthesis as well as a prosthetized practice – sought to make its users feel, smell, see and hear in a passionate and meditative mode of experience. As a tool for religious sensitivity, it installed in the practitioner that very sensitivity, or at least a tangible ideal of it.

8.1 With her sensitive fingers full of devotional instruments and media – a portable image of the Virgin and Child, a hand-size book, a string of prayer beads – St Hedwig of Silesia seems to owe her sanctity to this multisensory posture of piety. Miniature in the *Hedwig Codex*, Poland, 1353, J. Paul Getty Museum, Los Angeles, MS Ludwig XI 7, fo. 12v (detail).

CONFIGURING THE CHRISTIAN SENSORIUM: PERCEPTION <–> MEDIATION <–> INSTRUMENTALIZATION

The example of the rosary, as pious as it is perceptible, gives us a hint of how the cultivation and configuration of the sensorium took place in concrete, physical terms. How were the senses Christianized, we might ask, on both a somatic and a spiritual level of sensation? The answer to this, I believe, is *mediation*. Sacred experiences were mediated by a whole array of cultic and devotional instruments, taken in the broadest sense, which guided the perceptual act, tuned perception, and construed it according to prevailing religious norms and cultural standards. The senses were shaped and disciplined by their holy media, but also amplified and expanded, so as to become able to grasp sensory and extra-sensory properties especially relevant to the implied sanctity of their designated goal. One such property in question would be the sweet-smelling, honey-like 'odour of sanctity' purported to radiate from sacred bodies, tombs or sites visited by prepared pilgrims eager to tune their sensitivity to this 'iconic' olfactory experience.[26] Ineffable and volatile as it may seem to us today, the virtue of holiness manifested itself as a sensory feature to be reckoned with, and therefore expected, in select places or objects.[27] Imbued with sacred expectations, perhaps perfumed by incense, spiced substances or flowers, these media of sanctity framed a particular trait in the sensory environment and distinguished it for holy perception, thus tuning their percipient into a consecrated quality of experience. The whole pilgrimage site with its shrine and architectural layout took part in moulding the pilgrim's sensorium into a hallowed mode of operation, apt at differentiating a blessed impulse from the sensory continuum and perceiving it as such. The sensory site of belief became a material 'medium of belief', in David Morgan's sense, consecrating the sensorium and producing a reverent state of perception with a nose for the revered percepts of faith. The framing ceremonial environment acted not just as an instrument for the production and manifestation of sensory impulses but also as an amplifying extension of the organ of sensation: a grand prosthesis that *made* sweetness become a savour of holiness, and *made* ordinary savour become an extraordinary sensation. The physical spectacle of pilgrimage effected and enacted pilgrim perception.[28]

One salient example will have to stand for many others. One of the most important and paradigmatic scenes of pilgrimage in the Middle Ages was the grave of Bishop Nikolàus of Myra (d. *c.*343), translated – or rather abducted – from Lycia in Asia Minor to Bari in Apulia in 1087. Along from Myra was also translated an ancient cult of *myron*, a highly fragrant and consumable nectar pouring from the saintly sarcophagus, recalling evangelical myrrh or unguent. It was originally generated by wine or myrtle ointment infused into the sepulchre through a system of tubes and

---

26 As, for instance, at the cathedral of Aarhus in Denmark where the local shrine of 'Holy Niels' was known to have emitted a pleasant aroma, by then conventionalized as a sure sign of sanctity, deodorizing the vicinity of the city and its surrounding environment. When this thirteenth-century cult decreased (Niels never obtained canonization), the olfactory marker disappeared with it and vaporized like perfume in the wind: see M.Cl. Gertz (ed.), *Vitae Sanctorum Danorum* (Copenhagen, 1908–12), p. 405; quoted by Helge Paludan, 'Skt. Clemens og Hellig Niels, Fromhedsliv og politik i Århus stift omkring 1190' in Poul Enemark, Per Ingesman and Jens Villiam Jensen (eds), *Kongemagt og samfund i middelalderen, Festskrift til Erik Ulsig* (Aarhus, 1988), pp 41–53 at p. 47. **27** As vividly demonstrated by Woolgar, *The senses in late medieval England*, pp 29ff, 118ff. **28** For examples of such ritualized perceptions incited by various contexts and props of pilgrimage, see Sarah Blick and Rita Tekippe (eds), *Art and architecture of late medieval pilgrimage in northern Europe and the British Isles*, 2 vols (Leiden, 2005).

orifices to soak the buried body: a 'mechanical miracle', so to speak, allowing the extracted liquor to materialize the physical and metaphysical contact between the dead and the living. Later, the miraculous mechanics were internalized and the somatic distillate perceived as a supernatural secretion emanating from the sacred corpse itself to be collected in small vials and distributed among believers as a pharmaceutical solution.[29] This strongly scented, potable mixture is known from various early sources elsewhere as well, as in the case of St Andrew for instance, whose apostolic tomb in Patras overflowed with the wonder-working *oleum sanctorum*, embodying the perfumed power of coffin and cadaver as an instrument of devotion.[30] At the basilica of *San Nicola di Bari*, enshrined below in the pilgrims' crypt the remains of St Nicholas allegedly exuded the so-called 'manna', that is, an oily or liquid substance secreted from the holy body, gathered in ampoules and bottles to be given to aspiring visitors.[31] So appealing was this fluid manifestation of sainthood that witnesses even reported of different kinds of extraction:

> As I myself have been able to observe, two rivulets exude from that sepulcher [of Nicholas], and until this day they have never ceased to flow. From a hole, at the height of the entombed saint's head, flows an oily and shiny liquid which seems to be beneficial to those who rub it on themselves. From another hole, at the height of the feet, emanates a sweet and transparent water, which restores physical health to the infirm when they drink it.[32]

---

29 This development from funeral unction and *apomyrisma* to Byzantine *myron*, medieval *manna*, and the prolif-eration of 'saints myroblytes' is addressed by Béatrice Caseau, 'Parfum et guérison dans le Christianisme ancien et byzantin: Des huiles parfumées des médecins aux *myron* des saints byzantins' in Véronique Boudon–Millot and Bernard Pouderon (eds), *Les Pères de l'Église face à la science médicale de leur temps* (Paris, 2005), pp 141–91 at p. 174ff; and Francesco Paolo de Ceglia, 'The science of Santa Claus: discussions on the Manna of Nicholas of Myra in the Modern Age', *Nuncius*, 27 (2012), 241–69 at 246: 'when dealing with a holy body, it was thought that the liquids entering into contact with the relics would retain their medical–apotropaic–thaumaturgic properties, in some way becoming a part or expression of the body. The ointments healed because they were a means of spreading the virtue of the holy body.' **30** A plentiful profusion of sanctity expressed in vivid sensory terms by Gregory of Tours, *De gloria martyrum*, XXX; *Glory of the martyrs*, trans. Raymond van Dam (Liverpool, 1988), p. 48f.: 'On the day of his festival the apostle Andrew works a great miracle, that is, manna with the appearance of flour and oil with the fragrance of nectar which overflows from his tomb. … in some years so much oil gushed from his tomb that a torrent flowed into the middle of the church. … But when the oil flows, it offers such a strong fragrance to [people's] noses that you might think a collection of many different spices had been sprinkled there. A miracle and a blessing for the people accompany this [flow of oil]. For salves and potions are made from this oil'. Later, this legend was also summarized by Jacobus de Voragine, *Legenda aurea*, II; *The Golden Legend, readings on the saints*, trans. William Granger Ryan, 2 vols (Princeton, NJ, 1993), I, p. 18. **31** Pilgrim ampullae filled with oil or manna flowing from a venerated saint's corpse could be acquired in Bari and, for example, Eichstatt, York, Thessalonica, and possibly Noyon: see Katja Boertjes, 'Pilgrim Ampullae from Vendôme: souvenirs from a pilgrimage to the Holy Tear of Christ' in Sarah Blick and Rita Tekippe (eds), *Art and architecture of late medieval pilgrimage in northern Europe and the British Isles*, 2 vols (Leiden, 2005), I, pp 443–72 at p. 451. **32** *S. Nicolai Acta primigenia*, ed. Nicolò Carmine Falcone (Naples, 1751), p. 124; quoted after de Ceglia, 'The science of Santa Claus', 247.

This perceptible experience of a fountain of oil and a fountain of water (*fons olei et fons aquae*) gushing from the sacred sepulchre was conventionalized in the Latin West by the immensely influential Golden Legend, *Legenda aurea*, collected by Jacobus de Voragine around 1260.[33] The legendary flow was also confirmed by authorities such as St Bridget (Birgitta of Vadstena, d. 1373) during a pilgrimage to Bari in 1366, while the Beguine mystic Mary of Oignies (d. 1213) was even known to have experienced something as palatable as milk issue from Nicholas' bones, probably at an altar elsewhere with relics of his.[34]

According to Old Testament precedence, the melliferous 'manna' dispensed by an emanating corpus would be a sweet and aromatic extract, which could attract a throng of pilgrims convinced of its sensory reality as a divine remedy. What convinced them may in large measure have been the solemn grandeur of the architectural and ceremonial setting that housed and gave access to the ritual extraction in the thaumaturgical tomb (pls 32–35). On 1 October 1089 Pope Urban II laid the precious relics of the new protector of Bari – and 'Patron Saint of all the Russias' – beneath the crypt altar and consecrated the shrine. Erected between 1089 and 1197, Nicholas' majestic Romanesque building was designed to command a landmark position facing the sea, allowing for 'a strong religious identity and international visibility in the Mediterranean'.[35] It was a sanctuary of waters, both exterior – the maritime ones protected by St Nicholas – and interior – the therapeutic ones concocted in the near waterside crypt. Already in the grand internal space, it announces a higher, sensory and extra-sensory presence, parading a hieratic octagonal ciborium in the sequestered chancel above the secretive subterranean crypt with a distinct 'numinous' feel to it. Endowed with rich hangings, lamps and censers,[36] the entire shrine would have provided an awe-inspiring atmosphere of mystical presence, an ambience permeated by sanctity, which would ultimately condense into the saintly exudation – as if the holiness 'thick' in the air had liquefied and the whole scene had densified into a holy fluid, a perceptual proof of the charged character of the place. While the imposing monument was seemingly constructed there as a consequence of the saint's exuding presence, it also itself contributed to sanctifying the sensory secretion and provided percipients with a perceptual framework for savouring the sacred, even in some bottled and diluted underground moisture. The whole set-up took part in a construction of holiness worthy of veneration, from sacred bottle to sacred building.

33 Jacobus de Voragine, *Legenda aurea*, III; *the Golden Legend*, I, p. 25.   **34** According to Jacob von Vitry's *Life of Marie d'Oignies* and Bridget's *Revelations*, IV, 103. Some sources mention exudations from relics elsewhere than in Bari, such as Nicholas' finger conserved in Worms: see de Ceglia, 'The science of Santa Claus', 245 n. 17. **35** Flavia Laviosa, 'Modern routes of hope and journeys of faith in the Mediterranean: Apulia and Saint Nicholas of Bari', *Mediterranean Studies*, 18:1 (2009), 197–212 at 204.   **36** The magnificent baldachin of the high altar was even furnished with rings for a liturgical velum, according to Joseph Braun, *Der christliche Altar in seiner geschichtlichen Entwicklung*, 2 vols (München, 1924), II, p. 144. For a classical treatment of the architectural history of the building, see Kenneth John Conant, *Carolingian and Romanesque architecture, 800 to 1200* (1959, London, 1973), p. 214 ff.

It became what Alexei Lidov has termed a 'hierotopy': a space of hierophany articulated by man-made arrangements and instruments.[37]

A late medieval pilgrim, Georges Languerant, visited Bari in 1485 and reported that 'there beneath is the body of St Nicolas, which produces oil, called manna, that one gives away in an ampulla to some pilgrims; for my part, I found a way to get three of these'.[38] Thrice blessed, Georges made full use of the apparatus so instrumental to his perception of sainthood. For him, the holy man's virtues were mediated in small ampoules, the more the merrier: saint on bottle, sanctity on flask. This particular instance may perhaps seem somewhat extravagant but it does indeed exemplify the production of pious experience through at times very concrete appliances and utilities. In general, sacred sensation was an effect of its sacralizing instruments, processing and implementing the expectations of the percipient into concrete percepts of powerful presence. The sensorium was instrumentalized – and hence sanctified: sensations were produced in bottles, an ability for charismatic perception was manufactured with the aid of material and discursive props. In the current case, the sensory quality of mellifluous 'sweetness' depended on the entire physical and mythical setting of the juicy relic cult. The subterranean elixir was encoded with a perceptual value of holiness, notwithstanding its actual flavour, due to its material mediations as well as its representational framing as a divine gift. Thus, Francesco de Ceglia has drawn attention to the discursive fabrication of 'manna', based on both verbal and perceptual mediation of the concept: 'the word in the end influenced the perception of the thing, creating in the collective imagination a manna with colors and a consistency quite different from its actual qualities'.[39] Manna myth and manna medium worked together as a magic manna machine, which served to mould consumers' expectancies into privileged perceptions of power. The wondrous experience was buttressed not least by the biblical manna narratives (Exodus 16:1–36, Numbers 11:1–9), which provided the contextual backdrop and sensory matrix for St Nicholas' mediated manifestations to his followers. What the faithful would receive from their savoury mediator was a 'taste of saint' mediated by Scripture, architecture, shrine, legend, liturgy, local tradition and the implements and rituals of pilgrimage.

The point here, to repeat from above, is that instrumentalization and mediation are not opposed to sacralization and Christianization. Mediation does not necessarily entail secularization and alienation from the intimate religious experience. On the contrary, the sensation of sacred immediacy and sensory intimacy with the holy is generated by the very media producing it. Without building and Bible, without

---

37 For an introduction to the lately very influential notion of 'hierotopy', see Alexei Lidov, 'Hierotopy: the creation of sacred spaces as a form of creativity and subject of cultural history' in Alexei Lidov (ed.), *Hierotopy* (Moscow, 2006), pp 32–58. **38** 'là dessoubz est le corpz dud. St. Nicolas, lequel rend lad. huylle, laquelle s'appelle manne, de laquelle on en donne à cescun pélerin une ampoulette, dont, pour ma part, je trouvay la manière d'en avoir trois': Baron de la Fons-Mélicoq, 'Voyage archéologique au XVe siècle, Suite de l'Italie', *Annales Archéologiques*, 22 (1862), 133–41 at 140; quoted by Boertjes, 'Pilgrim Ampullae from Vendôme', p. 451 n. 33. **39** De Ceglia, 'The science of Santa Claus', 244.

basilica and officiant, without tales and bottles, St Nicholas' manna would have been perhaps just some dew on the ground, wholly deprived of curative and prophylactic powers. The mediating instrument, paradoxically, does not create distance but perceptual proximity and contact – it does not alienate the sacred but helps produce it. It emphasizes and actualizes a sensory impulse from the continuum, which would otherwise remain uncharted and insignificant. In reality, sanctity is not a powerful essence of divine origin that can only be diminished and weakened by intervening layers of sensory mediation, but rather an experiential product *of* that very mediation. The sacred is a 'techno-anthropological' feature of the cultural and sensory history of religion: a prosthetized percept. Media provide, instigate and chart our sense of sanctity – of course not as the single, reified cause, but in a continued dialectic with the human recipient and her culturally constructed sensorium, duly informed by social expectations of perception.

SENSES MEDIATIZED AND INSTRUMENTALIZED

By now, it will not have escaped the attentive reader that instrumentalization is an ample concept, which may imply quite different practices and modes of mediation, ranging from the use of instruments proper (such as the rosary) to instrumental enactments of sensory experience in complex contexts of devotion (such as pilgrim shrines). Admittedly, manifold techniques were entertained and combined in the pious codification of the senses and sanctification of sensation. Sanctity explored all available channels of mediation in order to make an impact and reach those in need. Following the principle of the incarnation, the spirited powers could condense into any kind of material intermediary and be transmitted by any sort of sensory substance. The chosen medium instructed believers in the capacity of sensory matter to carry and transmit holiness to the senses, thus engendering the conditions for pious perception. The mediation of the sacred for devotion was also a mediation of the devout mode of experience: the transaction went both ways and in the process the senses themselves were mediatized as well. A piece of cloth held out to touch a saintly tomb or statue acted as an instrument for the powerful transference from the cult object to the percipient but also as a prosthetic extension of the percipient's own hands grasping for contact with the sacred, not entirely unlike the stick in Caroline Jones' hand.[40] The texture of the fabric extended the texture of the skin in a tactile interchange between the body of the saint and the body of the believer. As we have already seen, tactility

---

40 Two prominent instances of this use of textiles as a medium for touching the sacred span the entire medieval period: drapes and other fabrics were empowered by contact with the miracle-working Madonna-statue in the pilgrimage to the chapel of *Die Schöne Maria von Regensburg* in 1519–20, and *brandea* – i.e. cloth or contact relics saturated with sanctity – were lowered onto St Peter's tomb in Rome by visitors in the late sixth century (as recorded by Gregory of Tours, *Glory of the martyrs*, p. 46; *De gloria martyrum*, XXVII; Jacques-Paul Migne (ed.), *Patrologiae Latinae, Cursus Completus* (Turnhout, 1844–65), 71, col. 729).

and haptics like other sensory domains might be instrumentalized for the mediation of sacred sentiments.

This reciprocal two-way mediation of pious perception also applied to media of representation, employing their capacities of communication to reproduce sacred sense experiences both as targeted objects of holy perception and as perceptual models to follow by their faithful viewers, readers or listeners. Holy Writ was, among other things, a paradigmatic pattern of holy perception that taught the faithful how to observe, feel and know the sacred dimensions of reality in the same way as their biblical prototypes had done: Moses on the mount, listening to God's voice; John on Patmos, seeing otherworldly visions; David in prayer, smelling the divine sacrifice of the Lord; the chosen people in the desert, tasting the manna from heaven – but also 'common' recipients like the blood-sick woman touching Christ's robe and feeling his ineffable, yet palpable powers (Mark 5:24–34; Luke 8:42–8; Matthew 9:19–22).[41] Cult images in turn provided a Christian schema of sensory perception by reproducing the charismatic conception of sanctity in concrete historical persons or occurrences of an exemplary nature. Such prototypical figures would act either as revered perceptual targets themselves or as blessed exemplars of how to sense an implied sacrosanct presence: the Mother staring affectionately at the infant Jesus, as the viewer's loving eyes should also do; an evangelist listening to divine inspiration and transmitting it to our inspired ears; an apostle at the Last Supper inviting our consumption of the bread of life; a saint following the command of 'Dextera Dei' in his actions, as our God-fearing hands must also do; an angel touching the soft skin of the suffering Saviour, as the tender skin of our compassionate fingers strive to do.

In this way, pious pictures would often not just suggest sacred sensations by depicting them but also lay out some guidelines for their percipient and her manner of perceiving the portrayed perceptual impulses. Pictorial representation instrumentalized vision by manufacturing visual experiences and mediating sacred sights, administering *what* the devotee should see and *how* to see it. Highly productive as prostheses of perception, images fabricated and conducted vision on behalf of their spectators. Through their standards and measures of visualization, they constructed an idealized visual field controlling both its contents and its optical operations. Prosthetized and propped, visual perception was very much determined by the instrument of icons, which allowed certain things to be seen in certain ways (augmenting the scope of spiritual realities, meanings and values) while omitting other possible percepts and preferences. The ideal use of sensory information was for instance laid down by an unknown Augustinian monk developing a significant theory of images and image perception in a treatise in defense of pictures – *Tractatus contra errores* – written in 1395, possibly in Prague. Advocating a more recent view of images

---

41 A topic thoroughly treated by Barbara Baert, '"Who touched my clothes?"', *Konsthistorisk tidskrift/Journal of Art History*, 79:2 (2010), 65–90; Baert, *Interspaces between word, gaze and touch*.

as prior to doctrine because of their heartfelt sensuousness, the anonymous author still relied on the old mystical topos of anagogical sensation uplifting the beatified beholder:

> Our cognition originates from our senses, through which we move from the particular to the universal, from the visible to the invisible. … Through the contemplation of images God is sweetly loved by the heart and the devout mind is moved upwards towards the invisible. … Examples and images are able to penetrate eyes and heart, because the eyesight is the primary herald of the heart. … Through looking at images the heart is moved to love of those whom they depict, either to compassion for their suffering or to prayer. … Everything seen by the eyes is more deeply impressed in the heart, more strongly held and longer remembered. For whenever we see the Passion of Christ or of the saints, he is shown to us crucified, wounded, beaten and crowned with thorns, and similarly the saints. And the vision causes the heart to tremble, the soul is wounded, the mind is touched, the spirit feels compassion and configures in itself the whole Passion of Christ and of the saints.[42]

As an anagogical apparatus for this emotional configuration of the self, pictures contributed to the shaping of mind, heart and senses, inducing in the viewer a penetrating mode of vision, a profound and passionate gaze. Able to pierce, wound, impress and touch the praying, the moving mediation of painful imagery prompted a sweet but intensely tactile transmission from devouring eyes to devout heart, in accordance with existing models of heart-based sensation and 'cardio-sensory' touch.[43] The introspective image/sight/heart-continuum heralded an interior penetration of exterior media. Highlighting his favourite instruments in this process of sensory sublimation, the same writer called images *cordium penetrativa*, that is, 'tools which are able to penetrate hearts and wound minds because nobody has such a heart of stone that looking at a tortured person would not feel compassion with him'.[44] In other words,

---

42 The treatise was published by J. Sedlák in Prague, 1915, and is part of a larger text from the *Codex no. 2*, originating in the monastery at Osek in Northern Bohemia, now in the National Library at Prague. Here, I quote from Pavel Kalina, 'Cordium penetrativa: an essay on iconoclasm and image worship around the year 1400', *Umění, Časopis Ústavu dějin umění Akademie věd České republiky*, 43:3 (1995), 247–57 at 248, 250, 256; who also gives the Latin text. In the opinion of Kalina, the treatise reflects the views of the majority of believers around 1400 and is of great importance to the study of European and Central European art and imagery. A little of it is also cited by Michael Camille, 'Mimetic identification and passion devotion in the later Middle Ages: a double-sided panel by Meister Francke' in A.A. MacDonald, H.N.B. Ridderbos and R.M. Schlusemann (eds), *The broken body: passion devotion in late-medieval culture* (Groningen, 1998), pp 183–210 at p. 197. For an exposition of how the anagogical 'a visibilibus ad invisibilia' clause became related to images during the early Middle Ages, see Herbert L. Kessler, 'Real absence: early medieval art and the metamorphosis of vision' in *Morfologie Sociali e Culturali in Europa fra Tarda Antichità e Alto Medioevo, Settimane di Studio del Centro Italiano di Studi sull'Alto Medioevo XLV, 3–9 aprile 1997* (Spoleto, 1998), pp 1157–211 at p. 1176ff. **43** See Heather Webb, 'Cardiosensory impulses in late medieval spirituality' in Stephen G. Nichols, Andreas Kablitz and Alison Calhoun (eds), *Rethinking the medieval senses: heritage, fascinations, frames* (Baltimore, MD, 2008), pp 265–85. **44** Quoted

pictures were indeed perceived as tools of penetration, as prostheses of perception and cognition, contrivances of devotion and emotion. Pictures of passion were viewed as instruments of compassion, conveying the mechanics of emotion through a tear-filled gaze of pity evoked by pitiful imagery. Late medieval piety relied heavily on its techno-anthropological foundation: a picture in the eye, a prop in the heart, Jesus in the image.

THE MAKING OF SACRED SENSES: SANCTIFYING
SENSESCAPES AND DEVOTIONAL DIDACTICS

So, in conclusion, cult images sculpted and shaped cultic vision through their representational techniques of visualization, that is, of seeing and making seen, and as such they contributed to the institution and configuration of the medieval sense system. In the words of Marx Wartofsky, philosopher of representation,

> vision is an artifact, produced by means of other artifacts – for example, by pictures. ... we *see* by way of our picturing. ... representational pictures are *didactic* artifacts. They teach us to see: they guide our vision in such a way that the seen world becomes the world scene.[45]

Without images no vision, without media no senses, without props no perception. Nevertheless, the didactic guidance of pious perception could be even more concrete and corporeal in material processes of instrumentalization working directly on the sensory operation itself. Like holy images teaching the eye what and how to see, so holy spaces contributed to sensory didactics and sought to reorganize visual, aural and nasal perception taking place in (and hence conditioned by) the spatial environment. Not wholly unlike Virilio's 'vision machine', the church building tutored the Christian gaze and instructed it to direct its faculties of observation towards a magnified object of visual scrutiny (such as sacrament, altar, grave or icon). The spectator was educated to focus on the exposed objects of cult and telescope her eyesight towards eminently visible targets of devotion and ocular desire. In this enticing spectacle, the allured viewer was presented with a sensory choreography for contemplation of perceptible realities thus invested with holiness and reverence.

Likewise, holy scents, vapours and smoke were transmitted and intensified by holy spaces to become sensory features of sanctity. Exotic, pungent odours were framed as emblematic and iconic by the use of liturgical or devotional instruments of olfaction: ampullae wafting sacrosanct aromas, perfumed relic containers and *encolpia* worn on the chest, ceremonial censers and thuribles enacting ritual and perceptual spaces of

from Kalina, 'Cordium penetrativa', 248, 256, who also emphasizes this central passage.   **45** Marx W. Wartofsky, 'Picturing and representing' in Calvin F. Nodine and Dennis F. Fisher (eds), *Perception and pictorial representation* (New York, 1979), pp 272–83 at pp 272, 273, 282.

hieratic fragrance. Such corporeal and environmental deodorizers would furnish the nasal system with a distinguishing 'motif' and redirect the entire socio-cultural *smellscape*. According to Susan Ashbrook Harvey, already during ancient Christianity smell acquired a unifying and significative function in the spatial and sensorial organization of devotion:

> The entire scene of devotional activity compelled the participant towards a paradisical encounter: the beauty of the saint's shrine, its architecture and pictorial adornment; the fragrance of incense offerings, the perfumed holy oil poured through the reliquary; the flowers, linens and ornaments hung at the tomb. Surrounded by the accoutrements of a holy place, … the odor of sanctity pervaded the [pious] experience and was its most common element; but that odor was also the means by which a believer's entire sensorium was awakened and engaged. … smell was the vehicle of power [which] permeated and worked within the body of the believer who sought divine aid or blessing.[46]

The blessed smell infused both body and space with sanctity, allowing interior and exterior processes of olfaction to interact, empower and enrich one another. Permeating both believers' interior ambience and belief's exterior surroundings, the expected and enacted odour of sanctity installed a holy 'hierotopy' in concrete space, a *sensescape* of sanctifying perceptions.[47] Whether the aromatic myrrh gushed from the sacred place, shrine, tomb, reliquary, relic carrier, jewelry or an icon exuding sweet-scented oil, these material instruments 'taught, exhorted, trained and encouraged Christians to use their senses and their bodies as instruments for gaining knowledge of God … Christian olfactory piety had as its telos the cultivation of revelatory expectation'.[48] Hence the teleological and didactic use of instruments for organizing, cultivating and choreographing the senses – hence props for perfuming pious perception with sacred significance and divine meaning.

Ultimately, this reorganization of perception also concerned the medieval *sound-scape*, subject to a similar intensification of sensory experience. The perceptual transmission of sound was thoroughly affected by the domed and vaulted spaces so singular and characteristic of church architecture and cult environments, giving a distinctive sonic shape to audible perception. Here, sounding instruments of angelic music evoked the heavenly city as well as the listener's aural ability to hear it in the appropriate mode of serene sensation, elevating the ear towards higher spheres of celestial music. Correspondingly, the acoustics of the vaulted stone building

---

46 Susan Ashbrook Harvey, *Scenting salvation, ancient Christianity and the olfactory imagination* (Berkeley, CA, 2006), p. 228f. (on the aromatic experience of relic devotion and what she terms 'olfactory piety'). See also the historical considerations of changing ideas of smell during early Christianity by Mark M. Smith, *Sensing the past* (Berkeley, CA, 2008), p. 62f. **47** On the concept of 'hierotopy', see above, n. 37. **48** Harvey, *Scenting salvation*, p. 229.

8.2 The reverberating acoustics of hagiophonic space makes of the human voice a grand instrument and of the resonant ear a hagiophonic listener. The sonic effect is especially grandiose and awe-inspiring in domed or vaulted spaces enclosed by the vibrantly echoing walls of a circular plan, like the so-called 'round church' of Thorsager, Jutland, Denmark, *c.*1200. According to one straightforward phenomenological witness (aged 6), 'it makes one's voice very big and makes one sound like God'. The brick-built hagiophone is an instrument of divinity and divine experience.

reverberated, augmented and extended the sound, acting as a phonic instrument ready to implant its resonant ideals in the auditor: a sacred amplifier or magnifier reorganizing human vocals as well as human audition into an experience of what we may term *hagiophony* – or 'holy phonics' (from Greek, *hagios*, 'holy', and *phōnē*, 'sound, voice'). As an exterior organ of sacred sound and ritual resonance, the sonorous space promoted a solemn and ceremonious mode of listening, instrumentalizing both the production and the perception of sound. The exterior organ of the building offered an extension of the interior organ of the ear, an auditory prosthesis, which processed earthly voices into a sensation of divine beatitude. The vaulted amplifier acted as a prolongation of the inner aural vault, enhancing its listening faculties and tuning it into the blissful experience of melodic melismas and hagiophonic perception.[49] Whether it harboured the hallowed hymns of mass or the rosy recitation of private prayers, this grandiose instrument acted as a 'hagiophone': a machine for hearing the holy, a pervasive medium integrating percept and percipient into an experience of holiness perceived, holiness mediatized and holiness instrumentalized (fig. 8.2). Still today, the sonic solemnity and awestruck atmosphere created by this kind of space may strike us as a very suggestive instrument indeed for installing in the listener an attention to inner states of mind and senses. It exemplifies to us what the instrumentalization of pious perception is all about – that is, the creation of an exterior organ for interior piety, an external mechanism of sensation to be internalized and absorbed in the internal mechanisms of mediatized man.

---

49 To some extent, treatments of this experiential aspect of the soundscape provided by medieval architecture have been eclipsed by an abstract interest in principles of composition common to music and architecture, such as the harmonic proportions identified by Otto von Simson, *The Gothic cathedral: origins of Gothic architecture and the medieval concept of order* (1956, Princeton, NJ, 1989). See the well-placed comments by Peter Vergo, *That divine order: music and the visual arts from antiquity to the eighteenth century* (London, 2005), p. 95ff.

Bibliography

Aavitsland, Kristin B., 'Incarnation: paradoxes of perception and mediation in medieval liturgical art' in Henning Laugerud et al. (eds), *The saturated sensorium* (Aarhus, 2015).

Aavitsland, Kristin B., *Imagining the human condition in medieval Rome: the Cistercian fresco cycle at Abbazia delle Tre Fontane* (Burlington, 2012).

Abbot Suger on the abbey church of St Denis and its art treasures, ed. and trans. E. Panofsky and G. Panofsky-Soergel (Princeton, NJ, 1979).

Achen, Henrik von, 'Piety, practise and process' in Henning Laugerud and Laura Katrine Skinnebach (eds), *Instruments of devotion: the practices and objects of religious piety from the late Middle Ages to the 20th century* (Aarhus, 2007), pp 23–44.

Adams, Douglas Q., 'Knot' in J.P. Mallory and Douglas Q. Adams (eds), *Encyclopedia of Indo-European culture* (London, 1997), p. 336.

Addis, William and Thomas Arnold, *A Catholic dictionary*, 15th ed. (London, 1951).

Anchoritic spirituality: Ancrene Wisse and associated works, ed. and trans. Anne Savage and Nicholas Watson (Mahwah, NJ, 1991).

Angenendt, Arnold et al. (eds), 'Gezählte Frömmigkeit', *Frühmittelalterliche Studien*, 29 (1995), 1–71.

Arasse, Daniel, *Le detail: pour une histoire rapprochée de la peinture* (Paris, 1996).

Arblaster, John and Rob Faesen (eds), *A companion to Ruusbroec* (Leiden, 2014).

Arndt, Hella and Renate Kroos, 'Zur Ikonographie der Johannesschüssel', *Aachener Kunstblätter*, 38 (1969), 243–328.

Augustine, *Confessions*, trans. Maria Boulding OSB (New York, 1997).

Augustine, *The Confessions of St Augustine* (New York, 2002).

Augustine, *De doctrina Christiana*, ed. and trans. R.P.H. Green (Oxford, 1995).

Baert, Barbara, Ann-Sophie Lehmann and Jenke van den Akkerveken (eds), *New perspectives in iconology: visual studies and anthropology* (Brussels, 2012).

Baert, Barbara, '"Who touched my clothes?": the healing of the woman with the haemorrhage (Mark 5:24–34; Luke 8:42–8 and Matthew 9:19–22) in early medieval visual culture', *Konsthistorisk tidskrift/Journal of Art History*, 79:2 (2010), 65–90.

Baert, Barbara, 'Adam, Seth and Jerusalem: the legend of the wood of the Cross in medieval literature and iconography' in *Adam, le premier home* (Firenze, 2012), pp 69–99.

Baert, Barbara, 'An odour, a touch, a smell. Impossible to describe. Noli me tangere and the senses' in Wietse de Boer and Christine Goettler (eds), *Religion and the senses in early modern Europe, intersections* (Leiden, 2012), pp 109–52.

Baert, Barbara, 'The glorified body: relics, materiality and the internalized image' in P. Vandenbroeck and G. Rooiakkers (eds), *Backlit heaven* (Mechelen, 2009), pp 130–53.

Baert, Barbara, *Caput Joannis in Disco: {essay on a man's head}* (Leiden, 2012).

Baert, Barbara, *Interspaces between word, gaze and touch: the bible and the visual medium in the Middle Ages, collected essays on 'Noli me tangere', the woman with the haemorrhage, the Head of John the Baptist, Annua Nuntia Lovaniensia*, vol. 62 (Leuven, 2011).

Baert, Barbara, 'Saint-John's head on a plate by Andrea Solario (1507, Louvre): transmisson and

168

transformation of an "Andachtsbild" between Middle Ages and Renaissance, between North and South', *Critica d'arte*, 3 (2007), 62–86.

Baert, Barbara, 'The head of St John the Baptist on a tazza by Andrea Solario (1507): the transformation and the transition of the *Johannesschüssel* from the Middle Ages to the Renaissance' in Annette de Vries (ed.), *Cultural mediators: artists and writers at the crossroads of tradition, innovation and reception in the Low Countries and Italy, 1450–1650* (Leuven, 2008), pp 87–107.

Bagnoli, Martina et al. (eds), *Treasures of heaven: saints, relics and devotion in medieval Europe* (London, 2011).

Bagnoli, Martina, 'The stuff of heaven: materials and craftsmanship in medieval reliquaries' in Bagnoli, *Treasures of heaven*, pp 137–47.

Baltrusaitis, Jurgis, *Aberrations* (Paris, 1957).

Barb, A.A., 'St Zacharias the prophet and martyr: a study in charms and incantations', *Journal of the Warburg and Courtauld Institutes*, 11 (1948), 35–67.

Barnay, Sylvie, 'Vision, visionary' in Andre Vauchez (ed.), *Encyclopedia of the Middle Ages* (Cambridge, 2000), pp 1526–7.

Barry, Fabio, 'Walking on water: cosmic floors in antiquity and the Middle Ages', *Art Bulletin*, 89:4 (2007), 627–56.

Bartlett, Robert, *Why can the dead do such great things? Saints and worshippers from the martyrs to the Reformation* (Princeton, NJ, 2013).

Bauer, Christian, *Geistliche Prosa im Kloster Tegernsee. Untersuchungen zu Gebrauch und Überlieferung deutschsprachiger Literatur im. 15. Jahrhundert* (Tübingen, 1995).

Becker, Hans Jakob et al. (eds), *Geistliches Wunderhorn. Große deutsche Kirchenlieder* (Munich, 2001).

Bedaux, Jan Baptiste, 'The reality of symbols: the question of disguised symbolism in Jan van Eyck's Arnolfini portrait', *Simiolus*, 16 (1986), 5–26.

Belting, Hans, *Bild und Kult: Eine Geschichte des Bildes vor dem Zeitalter der Kunst* (Munich, 1990).

Belting, Hans, *Bild-Anthropologie. Entwürfe für eine Bildwissenschaft* (Munich, 2001).

Belting, Hans, *Likeness and presence: a history of the image before the era of art* (Chicago and London, 1994).

Belting, Hans, *Das Bild und sein Publikum im Mittelalter. Form und Funktion früher Bildtafeln der Passion* (Berlin, 2000).

Bennett, Jill, 'Stigmata and sense memory: St Francis and the affective image', *Art History*, 24:1 (2001), 1–16.

Bennett, Kirsty, 'The book collections of Llanthony Priory from foundation until dissolution (*c.*1100–1538)', 2 vols (PhD, University of Kent, 2006).

Bhreathnach, Edel, 'The mendicant orders and vernacular Irish learning in the late medieval period', *Irish Historical Studies*, 37:147 (May 2011), 357–75.

The Bible. The Harper Collins Study Bible, new revised standard version, rev. ed. (2006).

Biernoff, Suzannah, *Sight and embodiment in the Middle Ages* (Basingstoke, 2002).

Biernoff, Suzannah, 'Carnal relations: embodied sight in Merleau-Ponty, Roger Bacon and St Francis', *Journal of Visual Culture*, 4:1 (London, 2005), 39–52.

Binski, Paul, *Medieval death: ritual and representation* (London, 1996).

Binski, Paul, 'The Northern Master at Assisi', *Proceedings of the British Academy*, 117 (2002), 73–138.

Blanchfield, Lyn A., 'Prolegomenon: considerations of weeping and sincerity in the Middle Ages' in Elina Gertsman (ed.), *Crying in the Middle Ages: tears of history* (New York, 2012), pp xxi–xxx.

Blick, Sarah and Rita Tekippe (eds), *Art and architecture of late medieval pilgrimage in northern Europe and the British Isles*, 2 vols (Leiden, 2005).

Boehm, Barbara Drake, '"A brilliant resurrection": enamel shrines for relics in Limoges and Cologne, 1100–1230' in Bagnoli, *Treasures of heaven*, pp 149–61.

Boertjes, Katja, 'Pilgrim ampullae from Vendôme: souvenirs from a pilgrimage to the holy tear of Christ' in Blick and Tekippe (eds), *Art and architecture of late medieval pilgrimage* (2005), I, pp 443–72.

Bollmann, Anne, 'Een vrauwe te sijn op mijn selfs handt. Alijt Bake (1413–1455) als geistliche Reformerin des innerlichen Lebens', *Ons Geestelijk Erf*, 76 (2002), 64–98.

Bonaventure, *Mystical Opuscula* (Paterson, NJ, 1960).

Boncompagno da Signa, *Rhetorica novissima* in A. Gaudentio (ed.), *Bibliotheca Iuridica Medii Aevi*, II (Bologna, 1892).

Bott, Gerhard (ed.), *Martin Luther und die Reformation in Deutschland – Ausstellung zum 500. Geburtstag Martin Luthers im Germanischen Nationalmuseum Nürenberg 1983* (Frankfurt a. M., 1983).

Boynton, Susan and Diane J. Reilly (eds), *The practice of the Bible in the Middle Ages: production, reception and performance in western Christianity* (New York, 2011).

Bozóky, Edina and Anne-Marie Helvétius, *Les reliques: objets, cultes, symboles* (Turnhout, 1999).

Bradley, Ritamary, 'Julian of Norwich: writer and mystic' in Paul Szarmach (ed.), *An introduction to the medieval mystics of Europe* (Albany, NY, 1984), pp 195–216.

Braun, Joseph, *Der christliche Altar in seiner geschichtlichen Entwicklung*, 2 vols (München, 1924).

Braun, Joseph, *Die Reliquiare des Christlichen Kultes und ihre Entwicklung* (Freiburg i. Br., 1940).

Bredekamp, Horst, *Theorie des Bildakts* (Berlin, 2010).

Breeze, Andrew, 'The Charter of Christ in medieval English, Welsh and Irish', *Celtica*, 19 (1987), 111–20.

Breeze, Andrew, 'The Virgin's tears of blood', *Celtica*, 20 (1988), 110–22.

Breuil, Auguste, 'Du culte de saint Jean Baptiste et des usages profanes qui s'y rattachent', *Mémoires de la Société des Antiquaires de Picardie*, 8 (1845), 155–244.

Browe, Peter, *Die Verehrung der Eucharistie im Mittelalter* (1933, Rome, 1967).

Browe, Peter, 'Die Elevation in der Messe', *Bonner Zeitschrift für Theologie und Seelsorge*, 8 (1931), 20–66; repr.: *Die Eucharistie im Mittelalter. Liturgiehistorische Forschungen in kulturwissenschaftlicher Absicht. Mit einter Einführung hg. von Hubertus Lutterbach und Thomas Flammer* (Münster, 2003).

Buettner, Brigitte, 'From stones to bones: reflections on jeweled reliquaries' in Reudenbach and Toussaint, *Reliquiare im Mittelalter* (2011), pp 43–60.

Burger, Christoph, 'Auf dem Wege ins himmlische Vaterland. Ein neu entdeckter Zyklus von Liedtexten aus dem niederrheinischen Chorherrenstift Gaesdonck' in Rudolf Suntrup and

Jan R. Veenstra (eds), *Himmel auf Erden/Heaven on Earth* (Frankfurt a. M., 2009), pp 89–105.

Burger, Christoph, 'Late medieval piety expressed in song manuscripts of the Devotio Moderna' in Ulrike Hascher-Burger and Hermina Joldersma (eds), *Music in the spiritual culture of the Devotio Moderna*. Theme-issue *Church History and Religious Culture*, 88:3 (Leiden, 2009), pp 329–45.

Burger, Christoph, 'Mystische Vereinigung – erst in Himmel oder schon auf Erden? Das Doppelgesicht der geistlichen Literatur im 15. Jahrundert' in Berndt Hamm and Voker Leppin (eds), *Gottes Nähe unmittlebar erfahren. Mystik im Mittelalter und bei Martin Luther* (Tübingen, 2007), pp 97–110.

Busa, Roberto, SJ, *Sancti Thomae Aquinatis opera omnia*, 7 vols (Stuttgart, 1979).

Büttner, Frank O., *Imitatio Pietatis. Motive der christliche Ikonographie als Modelle zur Verähnlichung* (Berlin, 1983).

Bynum, Caroline Walker and Paul Freedman (eds), *Last things: death and the Apocalypse in the Middle Ages* (Philadelphia, 1999).

Bynum, Caroline Walker, 'Seeing and seeing beyond: the Mass of St Gregory in the fifteenth century' in J. Hamburger and A. Bouché (eds), *The mind's eye: art and theological argument in the Middle Ages* (Princeton, NJ, 2006).

Bynum, Caroline Walker, *Christian materiality: an essay on religion in late medieval Europe* (New York, 2011).

Bynum, Caroline Walker, *Fragmentation and redemption: essays on gender and the human body in medieval religion* (New York, 1992).

Bynum, Caroline Walker, *Holy feast and holy fast: the religious significance of food to medieval women* (London, 1987).

Bynum, Caroline Walker, *Jesus as mother: studies in the spirituality of the High Middle Ages* (Los Angeles, CA, 1982).

Bynum, Caroline Walker, *Wonderful blood: theology and practice in late medieval Northern Germany and beyond* (Philadelphia, PA, 2007).

Byrne, Aisling, 'The earls of Kildare and their books at the end of the Middle Ages', *The Library*, 7th ser., 14:2 (June 2013), 129–53.

Byrne, Niall, *The register of St Saviour's Chantry of Waterford* (Dublin, 2013).

Caillois, Roger, 'Méduse et Cie' in R. Caillois (ed.), *Oeuvres* (Paris, 2008), p. 502.

The Cambridge companion to medieval English mysticism, ed. Samuel Fanous and Vincent Gillespie (Cambridge, 2011).

Camille, Michael, 'Mimetic identification and passion devotion in the later Middle Ages: a double-sided panel by Meister Francke' in A.A. MacDonald, H.N.B. Ridderbos and R.M. Schlusemann (eds), *The broken body: passion devotion in late-medieval culture* (Groningen, 1998), pp 183–210.

Camille, Michael, *Gothic art, glorious visions* (Chicago, 1996).

Camille, Michael, 'Him whom you have ardently desired you may see: Cistercian exegesis and the Prefatory Pictures in a French Apocalypse' in M.P. Lillich (ed.), *Studies in Cistercian art and architecture*, 3 (Kalamazoo, MI, 1987), pp 137–60.

Caplan, Harry, 'The four senses of scriptural interpretation and the mediaeval theory of preaching', *Speculum*, 4 (1929), 282–90.

Carruthers, Mary, *The book of memory: a study of memory in medieval culture* (Cambridge, 1990).

Carruthers, Mary, 'Boncompagno da Signa at the cutting-edge of rhetoric: rhetorical *Memoria* and the craft of memory', *The Journal of Medieval Latin*, 6 (Turhout, 1996), 44–64.

Carruthers, Mary, *The craft of thought: meditation, rhetoric and the making of images, 400–1200* (Cambridge, 1999).

Carruthers, Mary and Jan M. Ziolkowski, *The medieval craft of memory: an anthology of texts and pictures* (Philadelphia, PA, 2002).

Carruthers, Mary, *The experience of beauty in the Middle Ages* (Oxford, 2013).

Caseau, Béatrice, 'Parfum et guérison dans le Christianisme ancien et byzantin: Des huiles parfumées des médecins aux *myron* des saints byzantins' in Véronique Boudon–Millot & Bernard Pouderon (eds), *Les Pères de l'Église face à la science médicale de leur temps* (Paris, 2005), pp 141–91.

Caspers, Charles, 'Het Sint Jansfeest in kerk- en volksgebruik' in Leo Janssen and Karel Loeff (eds), *Getuigenis op straat: De Larense Sint Janstraditie* (Laren, 2005), pp 121–35.

Cassidy, Brendan, 'A relic, some pictures and the mothers of Florence in the late fourteenth century', *Gesta*, 30:2 (1991), 91–9.

Catalogue of Irish manuscripts in the British Library (formerly British Museum), ed. Robin Flower, vol. ii (repr. Dublin, 1992).

Catherine of Siena, *The dialogue: the classics of western spirituality*, trans. Suzanne Noffke OP (Mahwah, NJ, 1980).

Ceglia, Francesco Paolo de, 'The science of Santa Claus: discussions on the Manna of Nicholas of Myra in the Modern Age', *Nuncius*, 27 (2012), 241–69.

Cervone, Cristina Maria, *Poetics of the Incarnation: Middle English writing and the leap of love* (Philadelphia, PA, 2012).

Chastel, André, *Léonard de Vinci par lui-même* (Paris, 1952).

Cheetham, Francis W., *English medieval alabasters: with a catalogue of the collection in the Victoria and Albert Museum* (Woodbridge, 2005).

Cicero, Marcus Tullius, *De oratore (Loeb Classical Library)*, 1, trans. E.W. Sutton and H. Rackham (London, 1979 (1942)).

Classen, Constance, *The deepest sense: a cultural history of touch* (Urbana, IL, 2012).

Cleven, Esther, 'Man and image: Hans Belting's anthropology of the image and the German Bildwisschenschaften' in Baert et al. (eds), *New perspectives in iconology: visual studies and anthropology* (Brussels, 2012), pp 143–60.

Combs Stuebe, Isabel, 'The "Johannisschüssel": from narrative to reliquary to "Andachtsbild"', *Marsyas: Studies in the History of Art*, 14 (1968–9), 1–16.

Conant, Kenneth John, *Carolingian and Romanesque architecture, 800–1200* (1959; London, 1973).

Corrigan, Kathleen, *Visual polemics in the ninth-century psalters* (Cambridge, 1992).

Cousins, Ewert, *Bonaventure: the souls journey into God, the Tree of Life, the Life of St Francis* (New York, 1978).

Dahlerup, Pil, *Sanselig Senmiddelalder, Litterære perspektiver på danske tekster, 1482–1523* (Aarhus, 2010).

Davies, Olivier, 'Late medieval mystics' in G.R. Evans (ed.), *The medieval theologians* (Oxford, 2001), pp 221–31.

de Cock, Alfons, *Volksgeneeskunde in Vlaanderen* (Ghent, 1891).

de Coene, Karen, 'Navelnacht. Regeneratie en kosmologie in de middeleeuwen' (PhD, Leuven, 2006).

de Souzenelle, Annick, *Le symbolisme du corps humain* (Paris, 1991).

Deblieu, Jan, *Wind: how the flow of the air has shaped life, myth and the land* (New York, 1998).

Demasure, Karlijn, 'Noli me tangere: a contribution to the reading of Jn 20:17 based on a number of philosophical reflections on touch', *Louvain Studies*, 32 (2007), 304–29.

Despres, Denise L., 'Ecstasy, intimacy and Middle English contemplative culture' in Robert de Maria Jr, Heesok Chang and Samantha Zacher (eds), *A companion to British literature, 1: medieval literature, 700–1450* (Chichester, 2014).

Dhanens, Elisabeth, *De artistieke uitrusting van de Sint-Janskerk te Gent in de 15de eeuw*, Mededelingen van de Koninklijke Academie voor wetenschappen: letteren en schone kunsten van België: Klasse der Schone Kunsten 44/1 (Brussel, 1983).

Dhanens, Elisabeth, *Sint-Baafskathedraal Gent* (Ghent, 1965).

Didi-Huberman, Georges, 'Bewegende Bewegungen. Die Schleier der Ninfa nach Aby Warburg' in Johannes Endres, Barbara Wittmann and Gerhard Wolf (eds), *Ikonologie des Zwischenraums. Der Schleier als Medium und Metapher* (Munich, 2005), pp 331–60.

Didi-Huberman, Georges, *Ce que nous voyons, ce qui nous regarde* (Paris, 1992).

Didi-Huberman, Georges, *Fra Angelico. Dissemblance et figuration* (Paris, 1990).

Didi-Huberman, Georges, *L'image ouverte* (Paris, 2007).

Diedrichs, Christof L., *Vom Glauben zum Sehen: Die Sichtbarkeit der Reliquie im Reliquiar: Ein Beitrag zur Geschichte des Sehens* (Berlin, 2001).

Dinzelbacher, Peter, 'Religiöses Erleben vor bildener Kunst in autobiographische und biographische Zeugnisse des Hoch- und Spätmittelalters' in Søren Kaspersen (ed.), *Images of Kult and devotion: function and reception of Christian images in medieval and post-medieval Europe* (Copenhagen, 2004).

Doesschate, Gezienus T., 'Oxford and the revival of optics in the thirteenth century', *Vision Research*, 1 (1962), 313–42.

du Fresne, Charles, sieur du Cange, *Traité historique du chef de S. Jean-Baptiste* (Paris, 1665).

Duerr, Hans Peter, *Nacktheit und Scham: Der Mythos vom Zivilisationsprozess* (Frankfurt a. M., 1988).

Duffy, Eamon, *The stripping of the altars: traditional religion in England, 1400–1580* (London, 1992).

Dumoutet, Édouard, *Le Désir de voir l'Hostie et les Origines de la Dévotion au Saint-Sacrement* (Paris, 1926).

Dupeux, Cecile et al. (eds), *Bildersturm: Wahnsinn oder Gottes Wille? Exhibition catalogue* (Bern, 2000).

Eisermann, Falk, 'Medienwechsel-Medienwandel. Geistliche Texte auf Einblattdrucken und anderen Überlieferungsträgern des 15. Jahrhundert' in Wolfgang Harms and Michael Schilling (eds), *Das illustrierte Flugblatt in der Kultur der Frühen Neuzeit. Wolfenbütteler Arbeitsgespräch 1997* (Frankfurt a. M., 1998), pp 35–58.

Eisermann, Falk, 'The indulgence as a media event: developments in communication through broadsides in the fifteenth century' in Robert Swanson (ed.), *Promissory notes on the treasury of merits: indulgences in late medieval Europe* (Leiden, 2006), pp 309–30.

Eisermann, Falk, *Verzeichnis der typographischen Einblattdrucke des 15. Jahrhunderts im Heiligen Römischen Reich deutscher Nation*, 3 vols (Wiesbaden, 2004).

Elias, Norbert, *The civilizing process: the history of manners and state formation and civilization*, trans. Edmund Jephcott (1939; Oxford, 1994).

Erickson, Carolly, *The medieval vision: essays in history and perception* (New York, 1978).

Evans, R.B. (ed.), 'History of psychology', *American Journal of Psychology*, 106:4 (Urbana, IL, 1993).

Faesen, Rob, 'Was Hadewijch a Beguine or a Cistercian? An annotated hypothesis', *Cîteaux: Commentarii Cistercienses/revue d'histoire Cistercienne/a Journal of Historical Studies*, 55 (2004), 47–64.

Faesen, Rob, *Begeerte in het werk van Hadewijch* (Leuven, 2000).

Falkenburg, Reindert L., 'The household of the soul: conformity in the "Mérode Triptych"' in Maryan A. Ainsworth (ed.), *Early Netherlandish painting at the crossroads: a critical look at current methodologies* (New York, 2001), pp 2–17.

Falkenburg, Reindert L., *The fruit of devotion: mysticism and the imagery of love in Flemish paintings of the Virgin and Child, 1450–1550* (Amsterdam, 1994).

Farago, Claire, 'Exiting art history: locating "art" in the modern history of the subject', *Konsthistorisk tidskrift*, 70:1–2 (2001), 3–19.

Fawtier, Robert, *Sainte Catherine de Sienne. Essai de critique des Sources. Sources Hagiographiques* (Paris, 1922).

Field, Richard, 'Der frühe Holzschnitt: Was man weiß und was man nicht weiß' in Peter W. Parshall and Rainer Schoch (eds), *Die Anfänge der europäischen Druckgraphik: Holzschnitte des 15. Jahrhunderts und ihr Gerauch* (Nürnberg, 2005), pp 19–35.

Finucane, R.C., *Miracles and pilgrims: popular beliefs in medieval England* (London, 1977; New York, 1995).

Fisher, Annika Elisabeth, 'Cross altar and crucifix in Ottonian Cologne: past narrative, present ritual, future resurrection' in Kaspersen and Thunø (eds), *Decorating the Lord's table* (2006), pp 43–62.

Flavius Josephus, *The complete works of Josephus*, ed. William Whiston (Grand Rapids, MI, 1981).

Freise, Dorothea, *Geistliche Spiele in der Stadt des ausgehenden Mittelalters. Frankfurt – Friedberg – Alsfeld* (Göttingen, 2002).

Frye, Northrop, *The great code: the bible and literature* (San Diego, CA, 1983).

Gecser, Otto (ed.), *Promoting the saints: cults, and their contexts from late antiquity until the early modern period* (Budapest, 2011).

Geml, Georg, 'Frühe Johannesschüsseln' (MA, University of Vienna, 2009).

Gertrude of Helfta, *Le Héraut. Oeuvre spirituelles, tome II–V. Source Chrétienne*, nos 139, 143, 255, 331 (Paris, 1968–86).

Gertrude of Helfta, *The herald of divine love*, ed. and trans. Margaret Winkworth (New York, 1993).

Gilmore, James H. and B. Joseph Pine II, *Authenticity, what consumers really want* (Boston, MA, 2007).

Goodich, Michael E., *Miracle and wonders: the development of the concept of miracle, 1150–1350* (London, 2007).

Gormans, Andreas and Thomas Lentes (eds), *Das Bild der Erscheinung. Die Gregorsmesse im Mittelalter* (Berlin, 2007).

Gregory of Tours, *Glory of the martyrs*, trans. Raymond van Dam (Liverpool, 1988).

Griese, Sabine, 'Bild, Text, Betracher: Kommunikationsmöglichkeiten von Einblatt-Druckgraphik im 15. Jahrhundert' in Nikolaus Henkel et al. (eds), *Dialoge. Sprachliche Kommunikation in und zwischen Texten im deutschen Mittelalter* (Tübingen, 2003), pp 315–35.

Griese, Sabine, 'Das Andachtsbuch als symbolische Form. Bertholds Zeitglöcklein und verwandte Texte als Laien-Gebetbücher' in Rudolf Suntrup, Jan R. Venstra, Anne Bollmann (eds), *The mediaton of symbol in late medieval and early modern times: Medien der Symbolik in Spätmittelalter und Früher Neuzeit* (Frankfurt a. M., 2005), pp 3–36.

Griese, Sabine, '"Dirigierte Kommunikation". Beobachtungen zu xylographischen Einblattdrucken und ihren Textsorten im 15. Jahrhundert' in Wolfgang Harms and Michael Schilling (eds), *Das illustrierte Flugblatt in der Kultur der Frühen Neuzeit: Wolfenbütteler Arbeitsgespräch 1997* (Frankfurt a. M. et al., 1998), pp 75–99.

Griese, Sabine, *Text-Bilder und ihre Kontexte. Medialität und Materialität von Einblatt-Holz- und -Metallschnitten des 15. Jahrunderts* (Zürich, 2011).

Grootens, Petrus L.M. and Johannes Brugman, *Onuitgegeven sermoenen van Jan Brugman* (Tielt, 1948).

Gui, Bernard, *The Life of Saint Thomas Aquinas: biographical documents*, ed. and trans. Kenelm Foster OP (London, 1959).

Guibertus de Novigentus, *Quo ordine sermo fieri debeat: de bucella Iudae data et de veritate Dominici corporis: de sanctis et eorum pigneribus*, ed. Robert B.C. Huygens (Turnhout, 1993).

Guillelmi a Sancto Theoderico opera omnia VI, ed. Paul Verdeyen (Turnhout, 2010).

Guillelmus de Ockham, *Scriptum in librum primum sententiarum ordinatio*, ed. Stephanus Brown and Gedeon Gál (New York, 1970).

Habig, Marion A., *St Francis of Assisi: writings and early biographies. English omnibus of the sources for the Life of St Francis* (Chicago, 1973).

Hadewijch, *Brieven*, ed. Jozef van Mierlo, I: *Tekst en commentaar* (Antwerpen, 1947).

Hadewijch, *Das Buch der Visionen*, I. *Einleitung, Text und Übersetzung*, II. *Kommentar*, ed. Gerald Hofman (Stuttgart, 1998).

Hadewijch, *The complete works: the classics of western spirituality*, trans. and intr. Columba Hart (New York, 1980).

Hadewijch, *Visioenen*, ed. Jozef van Mierlo, I: *Tekst en commentaar* (Leuven, 1924).

Hahn, Cynthia, *Strange beauty: issues in the making and meaning of reliquaries, 400–c.1204* (University Park, 2012).

Hahn, Cynthia, 'The spectacle of the charismatic body: patrons, artists and body-part reliquaries' in Bagnoli, *Treasures of heaven*, pp 163–72.

Hamburger Jeffrey and Susan Marti (ed.), *Crown and veil: female monasticism from the fifth to the fifteenth centuries* (New York, 2008).

Hamburger, Jeffrey, *Nuns as artists: the visual culture of a medieval convent* (London, 1997).

Hamburger, Jeffrey and Anne-Marie Bouché, *The mind's eye: art and theological argument in the Middle Ages* (Princeton, NJ, 2006).

Hamburger, Jeffrey, *The visual and the visionary: art and female spirituality in late medieval Germany* (New York, 1998).

Hamm, Berndt and Michael Welker, *Die Reformation. Potentiale der Freiheit* (Tübingen, 2008).

Hamm, Berndt, '"Gott berühren": Mystische Erfahrung im ausgehenden Mittelalter. Zugleich ein Beitrag zur Klärung des Mystik-begriffs' in Berndt Hamm and Voker Leppin (eds), *Gottes Nähe unmittelbar erfahren. Mystik im Mittelalter und bei Martin Luther* (Tübingen, 2007), pp 111–38.

Hamm, Berndt, 'Die Nähe des Heiligen im ausgehenden Mittelalter: Ars moriendi, Totenmemoria, Gregorsmesse' in Berndt Hamm, Klaus Herbers, Heidrun Stein-Kecks (eds), *Sakralität zwischen Antike und Neuzeit* (Stuttgart, 2007), pp 185–221.

Hamm, Berndt, 'Naher Zorn und nahe Gnade: Luthers frühe Klosterjahre als Beginn seiner reformatorischen Neuorienterung' in Christoph Bultmann, Volker Leppin, Andreas Lindner (eds), *Luther und das monastische Erbe* (Tübingen, 2007), pp 111–51.

Hamm, Berndt, 'Wollen und Nicht-Können als Thema der spättmittelalterlichen Bußseelsorge' in Berndt Hamm and Thomas Lentes (eds), *Spätmittelalterliche Frömmigkeit zwischen Ideal und Praxis* (Tübingen, 2001), pp 112–46.

Hamm, Berndt, 'Theologie und Frömmigkeit im ausgehenden Mittelalter' in Gerhard Müller, Horst Weigelt and Wolfgang Zorn (eds), *Handbuch der Evangelischen Kirche in Bayern. Bd. 1: Von den Anfängen des Christentums bis zum Ende des 18. Jahrhundert* (St Ottilien, 2002), pp 159–212.

Hamm, Berndt, *Frömmigkeitstheologie am Anfang des 16. Jahrhunderts. Studien zu Johannes von Paltz und seinem Umkreis* (Tübingen, 1982).

Hamm, Berndt, *Promissio, pactum ordinatio, Freiheit und Selbstbindung Gottes in der scholastischen Gnadenlehre* (Tübingen, 1977).

Harvey, Susan Ashbrook, *Scenting salvation, ancient Christianity and the olfactory imagination* (Berkeley, 2006).

Hascher-Burger, Ulrike, *Gesungene Innigkeit. Studien zu einer Musikhandschrift der Devotio moderna (Utrecht, Universiteitsbibliotheek, MS 16 H 34, OLIM B 113). Mit einer Edition der Gesänge* (Leiden/Boston, 2002).

Head, Thomas, 'Guibert of Nogent: on saints and their relics' in Thomas Head (ed.), *Medieval hagiographies: an anthology* (New York, 2000), pp 399–427.

Heller-Roazen, Daniel, 'Common sense: Greek, Arabic and Latin' in Stephen G. Nichols, Andreas Kablitz and Alison Calhoun (eds), *Rethinking the medieval senses: heritage, fascinations, frames* (Baltimore, MD, 2008).

Heller-Roazen, Daniel, *The inner touch: archaeology of a sensation* (New York, 2007).

Henderiks, Valentine, *Albrecht Bouts (1451/5–1549)* (Turnhout, 2011).

Hendrix, Guido (ed.), *Hugo de Santo Caro's traktaat 'De doctrina cordis'*, 2 (Leuven, 1995).

Henschen, Godfried and Daniel van Papenbroeck, *Acta Sanctorum: Junius*, 5 vols (Antwerp, 1707).

Heszler, Esther, *Der mystische Prozeß im Werk Hadewijchs: Aspekte der Erfahrung – Aspekte der Darstellung*, Dissertation Neuphilologische Fakultät – Universität Tübingen: 1992 (Ulm, 1994).

Heynck, Valens, 'Zur Lehre von der unvollkommenen Reue in der Skotistenschule des ausgehenden 15. Jahrhunderts', *Franziskanische Studien*, 24 (1937), 18–58.

Hieronymus, 'Apologia Adversos Libros Rufini' in *Sancti Eusebii Hieronymi stridonensis presbyteri opera omnia*, ed. Jacques-Paul Migne (Paris, 1845).

Hill, Edmund, *The works of St Augustine: a translation for the 21st century* (New York, 1993).

Hilton, Walter, *The Goad of Love*, ed. Clare Kirchberger (repr. Whitefish, MT, 1995).

Honemann, Volker, 'Bergbau in der Literatur des Mittelalters und der frühen Neuzeit' in Karl Heinrich Kaufhold and Wilfried Reininghaus (eds), *Stadt und Bergbau* (Köln, 2004), pp 239–61.

Horn, Eva and Manfred Weinberg, 'Aby Warburg's "Ikonologie des Zwischenraums" im Horizont der Allegorie' in E. Horn and M. Weinberg (eds), *Allegorie. Konfigurationen von Text, Bild und Lektüre* (Wiesbaden, 1998), pp 233–47.

Hugh of Saint-Victor, 'De arrha animae' in H.B. Feiss and P. Sicard (eds), *L'Oeuvre de Hugues de Saint-Victor I. De institutione novitiorum. De virtute orandi. De laude caritatis. De arrha animae* (Turnhout, 1997), pp 226–82.

Huizinga, Johan, *The waning of the Middle Ages: a study of the forms of life, thought and art in France and the Netherlands in the fourteenth and fifteenth centuries*, trans. F. Hopman (1924, London, 1990).

Hull, Vernam, 'Celtic tears of blood', *Zeitschrift für celtische Philologie*, 25 (1952), 226–36.

Hörsch, Markus, 'Johannesschüssel' in Holger Kunde (ed.), *Der Naumburger Domschatz: Sakrale Kostbarkeiten im Domschatzgewölbe* (Petersberg, 2006), pp 90–7.

Höver, Werner, *Theologia Mystica in altbairischer Übertragung: Bernhard von Clairvaux, Bonaventura, Hugo von Balma, Jean Gerson, Bernhard von Waging und andere. Studien zum Übersetzungswerk eines Tegernseer Anonymus aus der Mitte des 15. Jahrhunderts* (Munich, 1971).

Innitzer, Theodor, *Johannes der Täufer: Nach der Heiligen Schrift und der Tradition dargestellt* (Vienna, 1908).

Irigaray, Luce, *An ethics of sexual difference* (New York, 2004).

Isidore of Seville, *Etymologiarvm sive Originvm*, II, ed. W.M. Lindsay (Oxford, 1951 (1911)).

Isidore of Seville, *The etymologies of Isidore of Seville*, ed. and trans. Barney et al. (Cambridge, 2006).

Jacapone da Todi, *The Lauds*, trans. Serge Hughes and Elizabeth Hughes (New York, 1982).

Jacob-Friesen, Holger et al. (eds), *Spätmittelalter am Oberrhein, Maler und Werkstätten, 1450–1525. Ausstellungskatalog* (Stuttgart, 2001).

Jacobus de Voragine, *The Golden Legend: readings on the saints*, trans. William Granger Ryan, 2 vols (Princeton, NJ, 1993).

Jan van Ruusbroec, *Spiritual espousals*, ed. Joseph Alaerts (Turnhout, 1988).

Jerome, *Liber interpretationis hebraicorum nominum*, 20, 17 (Turnhout, no date given), 71.

Joannis Calvini, *Opera selecta*, ed. Petrus Barth and Guilelmus Niesel, 5, 3rd ed. (München, 1974).

Johannes von Paltz, *Coelifodina* in Christoph Burger and Friedhelm Stasch, *Johannes von Paltz: Werke 1, Coelifodina* (Berlin, 1983).

Johannes von Paltz, 'Die himmlische Fundgrube' in Christoph Burger, Horst Laubner et al. (eds), *Johannes von Paltz: Werke 3, Opuscule* (Berlin, 1989), pp 155–284.

Johannes Von Paltz, 'Supplementum Coelifodinae', ed. Berndt Hamm: *Johannes von Paltz: Werke 2* (Berlin, 1983).

Jonas, Hans, 'The nobility of sight: a study in the phenomenology of the senses' in Hans Jonas (ed.), *The phenomenology of life: towards a philosophical biology* (Chicago, 1982), pp 135–56.

Jones, Caroline A., 'Senses' in W.J.T. Mitchell and Mark B.N. Hansen (eds), *Critical terms for media studies* (Chicago, 2010), pp 88–100.

Jones, Caroline A., 'The mediated sensorium' in Caroline A. Jones (ed.), *Sensorium: embodied experience, technology and contemporary art* (Cambridge, MA, 2006), pp 5–49.

Jones, Ernest, *Essays in applied psycho-analysis*, 2 (New York, 1964).

Julian of Norwich, *Showings: the classics of western spirituality*, trans. E. Colledge and J. Walsh (Mahwah, NJ, 1978).

Jütte, Robert, *A history of the senses, from antiquity to cyberspace* (Cambridge, 2005).

Jørgensen, Hans Henrik Lohfert, 'Sensorium: a model for medieval perception' in Henning Laugerud, Hans Henrik Lohfert Jørgensen and Laura Katrine Skinnebach (eds), *The saturated sensorium* (Aarhus, 2015).

Jørgensen, Hans Henrik Lohfert, 'Cultic Vision – seeing as ritual, visual and liturgical experience in the early Christian and medieval Church' in Jeremy Llewellyn et al. (eds), *The appearances of medieval rituals: the play of construction and modification* (Turnhout, 2004), pp 173–97.

Jørgensen, Hans Henrik Lohfert, 'Synets modernisering – i senmiddelalderen, En alternativ perceptionshistorie' in Helene Illeris and Hans Dam Christensen (eds), *Visuel kultur – viden, liv, politik* (Copenhagen, 2009), pp 11–28.

Jørgensen, Hans Henrik Lohfert, *I kroppens spejl, Krop og syn i senmiddelalderlige danske kalkmalerier* (Aarhus, 2004).

Kalina, Pavel, 'Cordium penetrativa: an essay on iconoclasm and image worship around the year 1400', *Umění, Časopis Ústavu dějin umění Akademie věd České republiky*, 43:3 (1995), 247–57.

Kammel, Frank Matthias (ed.), *Spiegel der Seligkeit. Privates Bild und Frömmigkeit in Spätmittelalter. Exhibition catalogue: Germanisches Nationalmuseum* (Nuremberg, 2000).

Karnes, Michelle, *Imagination, meditation and cognition in the Middle Ages* (Chicago, 2011).

Kaspersen, Søren and Erik Thunø (eds), *Decorating the Lord's table: on the dynamics between image and altar in the Middle Ages* (Copenhagen, 2006).

Kemp, Simon and Garth J.O. Fletcher, 'The medieval theory of the inner senses', *American Journal of Psychology*, 106:4 (winter 1993), 559–76.

Kessler, Herbert L., 'Real absence: early medieval art and the metamorphosis of vision' in *Morfologie Sociali e Culturali in Europa fra Tarda Antichità e Alto Medioevo, Settimane di Studio del Centro Italiano di Studi sull'Alto Medioevo XLV, 3–9 aprile 1997* (Spoleto, 1998), pp 1157–211.

Kieckhefer, Richard, *Unquiet souls: fourteenth-century saints and their religious milieu* (Chicago, 1984).

Kiening, Christian (ed.), *Mediale Gegenwärtigkeit* (Zurich, 2007).

Kittler, Friedrich A., *Gramophone, film, typewriter*, trans. Geoffrey Winthrop-Young and Michael Wutz (1986; Stanford, 1999).

Klinkenberg, Emanuel S., '"Wil diin herte bereeden gheliic eenen huze." de binnenhuisallegorie in de geestelijke letterkunde', *Queeste. Tijdschrift over middeleeuwse letterkunde*, 2:14 (2007), 126–53.

Kohl, Jeanette and Rebecca Müller (eds), *Kopf/Bild. Die Büste in Mittelalter und früher Neuzeit* (Munich, 2007).

Kornrumpf, Giesela, 'du uzvliezender brunne' in *Die deutsche Literatur des Mitelalters. Verfasserlexikon*, 6 (Berlin, 1987).

Kramer, Heinrich, *The Malleus Malificarum of Heinrich Kramer and James Sprenger*, trans. Montague Summers (1928; New York, 1971).

Kristeva, Julia, *Visions capitales* (Paris, 1998).

Kruger, Steven F., *Dreaming in the Middle Ages* (Cambridge, 1993).

Kühne, Hartmut, *Ostensio reliquiarum. Untersuchungen über Entstehung, Ausbreitung, Gestalt und Funktion der Heiltumsweisungen im römisch-deutschen Regnum* (Berlin, 2000).

L'oeuvre de Hughes de Saint-Victor, 1, ed. H.B. Feiss and P. Sicard (Turnhout, 1997).

Ladner, Gerhart B., 'Medival and modern understanding of symbolism: a comparison', *Speculum*, 54:2 (1979), 223–56.

Lanz, Hanspeter, 'Johannesschüssel aus St Katharinenthal' in Jutta Frings et al. (eds), *Krone und Schleier: Kunst aus mittelalterlichen Frauenklöstern* (Munich, 2005), pp 418–19.

Laugerud, Henning and Laura Katrine Skinnebach, 'Introduction' in Henning Laugerud and Laura Katrine Skinnebach (eds), *Instruments of devotion: the practices and objects of religious piety from the late Middle Ages to the 20th century* (Aarhus, 2007), pp 9–19.

Laugerud, Henning, 'Polysemi og den dynamiske tradisjon', *Passepartout. Skrifter for kunsthistorie*, 25 (Aarhus, 2005), 94–103.

Laugerud, Henning, 'Visuality and devotion in the Middle Ages' in Henning Laugerud and Laura Katrine Skinnebach (eds), *Instruments of devotion: the practices and objects of religious piety from the late Middle Ages to the 20th century* (Aarhus, 2007), pp 173–88.

Laugerud, Henning, 'Memory: the sensory materiality of belief and understanding in late medieval Europe' in Henning Laugerud, Hans Henrik Lohfert Jørgensen and Laura Katrine Skinnebach, *The saturated sensorium* (Aarhus, 2015).

Laviosa, Flavia, 'Modern routes of hope and journeys of faith in the Mediterranean: Apulia and Saint Nicholas of Bari', *Mediterranean Studies*, 18:1 (2009), 197–212.

Leclercq, Jean, OSB, *The love of learning and the desire for God: a study of monastic culture* (New York, 2003 (1961)).

Legner, Anton, *Reliquien in Kunst und Kult zwischen Antike und Aufklärung* (Darmstadt, 1995).

Lentes, Thomas, 'Nur der geöffenete Körper schafft Heil. Das Bild der Verdoppelung des Körpers' in Christoph Geissmar-Brandi and Eleonora Louis (eds), *Glaube, Hoffnung, Liebe, Tod. Von der Entwicklung religiöser Bildkonzepte. Exhibition catalogue* (Klagenfurt, 1996), pp 152–5.

Leppin, Volker, 'Mystische Frömmigkeit und sakramentale Heilsvermittlung im späten Mittelalter', *Zeitschrift für Kirchengeschichte*, 112 (2001), 189–204.

Leppin, Volker, 'Christus nachfolgen – Christi Nähe erfahren – Christus repräsentieren: zur Glaubenswelt Elisabeths von Thüringen', *Zeitschrift für Kirchengeschichte*, 118 (2007), 320–35.

Leppin, Volker, 'Repräsentationsfrömmigkeit. Vergegenwärtigung des Heiligen in der Frömigkeit des späten Mittelalters und ihre Transformation in der Wittenberger Reformation' in Mario Fisher and Margarethe Drewson (eds), *Die Gegenwart des Gegenwärtigen. Festschrift for Gerd Haeffner* (Freiburg i. Br., 2006), pp 376–91.

Leslie, Shane, *Saint Patrick's Purgatory* (London, 1932).

Lewis, Suzanne, *Reading images: narrative discourse and reception in the thirteenth-century illuminated Apocalypse* (Cambridge, 1995).

Lichtenberg Ettinger, Bracha, 'The with-in-visible screen: images of absence in the inner space of painting' in C. de Zegher (ed.), *Inside the visible: an elliptical traverse of 20th-century art* (Cambridge, 1996).

Lichtenberg Ettinger, Bracha, *Artworking, 1985–1999* (Brussels, 2000).

Lidov, Alexei, 'Hierotopy: the creation of sacred spaces as a form of creativity and subject of cultural history' in Alexei Lidov (ed.), *Hierotopy: the creation of sacred spaces in Byzantium and medieval Russia* (Moscow, 2006), pp 32–58.

Lightbown, Ronald W., *Mediaeval European jewellery, with a catalogue of the collection in the Victoria & Albert Museum* (London, 1992).

Lindberg, David C., *Theories of vision from Al-Kindi to Kepler* (Chicago, 1976).

Lindberg, Erika L., *Sensual encounters: monastic women and spirituality in medieval Germany* (New York, 2009).

Litz, Gudrun, *Die reformatorische Bilderfrage in den schwäbischen Reichsstädten* (Tübingen, 2007).

Lubac, Henri de, *Medieval exegesis: the four senses of Scripture (Exégèse médiévale: les quatre sens de l'écriture)* (Grand Rapids, MI, 1998 (1959–64)).

Lucas, Angela, *Anglo-Irish poems of the Middle Ages* (Dublin, 1995).

Luigia Fobelli, Maria, 'Descrizione e percezione delle immagini acheropite sui marmi bizantini' in *Immagine e Ideologia. Studi in onore di Arturo Carlo Quintavalle* (Milan, 2007), pp 27–32.

Lutz, Gerhard, *Schüssel mit dem Haupt Johannes des Täufers* in Hartmut Krohm and Holger Kunde (eds), *Der Naumburger Meister: Bildhauer und Architekt im Europa der Kathedralen*, 3 vols (Petersberg, 2011), i, pp 689–91.

Luyster, Robert, 'Wind and water: cosmogonic symbolism in the Old Testament', *Zeitschrift für alttestamentische Wissenschaft*, 93:1 (1981), 1–10.

Mac Aingil, Aodh, *Scáthán Shacramuinte na hAithridhe*, ed. Cainneach Ó Maonaigh (Baile Átha Cliath [Dublin], 1952).

Manghani, Sunil, Arthur Piper and Jon Simons (eds), *Images: a reader* (London, 2006).

Mangrum, Bryan D. and Guiseppe Scavizzi (eds and trans.), *A Reformation debate: Karlstadt Emser, and Eck on sacred images: three treatises in translation* (Toronto, 1998).

Marchal, Guy P., 'Das vieldeutige Heiligenbild, Bildersturm im Mittelalter' in Peter Blickle, André Holenstein et al. (eds), *Macht und Ohnmacht der Bilder. Reformatorischer Bildersturm im Kontext der europäischen Geschichte* (Munich, 2002), pp 307–32.

Margry, Peter Jan, 'Grubbenvorst' in Peter Jan Margry and Charles Caspers (eds), *Bedevaartplaatsen in Nederland*, iii: *Provincie Limburg* (Amsterdam, 2000), pp 258–66.

Marks, Richard, *Image and devotion in late medieval England* (Stroud, 2004).

Marrow, James H., 'Symbol and meaning in northern European art of the late Middle Ages and the early Renaissance', *Simiolus*, 16 (1986), 150–69.

Martin Luther Studienausgabe, ed. Hans-Ulrich Delius (Berlin, 1979).

Matter, E. Ann and Jeanne E. Krochalis, 'Manuscrips of the Liturgy' in Thomas J. Heffernan and E. Ann Matter (eds), *The Liturgy of the medieval Church* (Kalamazoo, MI, 2005).

Mayer, Anton L., 'Die heilbringende Schau in Sitte und Kult' in O. Casel (ed.), *Heilige Überlieferung, Festschrift für Ildefons Herwegen* (Münster, 1938), pp 234–62.

McGinn, Bernard, *The flowering of mysticism: men and women in the new mysticism, 1200–1350* (New York, 1998).

McGinn, Bernard, 'Meister Eckhart: an introduction' in Paul Szarmach (ed.), *An introduction to the medieval mystics of Europe* (Albany, NY, 1984), pp 237–57.

McGinn, Bernard, *The growth of mysticism* (London, 1995).

McGinn, Bernard, *Die Mystik im Abendland*, 2 (Freiburg, 1996).

McGinn, Bernard, *The harvest of mysticism in medieval Germany* (New York, 2006).

McGuire, Brian Patrick, '*c*.1080–1215: culture and history' in Samuel Fanous and Vincent Gillespie (eds), *The Cambridge companion to medieval English mysticism* (Cambridge, 2011).

McKechnie, John (ed.), *Instructio pie vivendi et superna meditandi* (Dublin, 1933 and 1946).

McKenna, Lambert (ed.), 'Our salvation', *Studies*, 38 (1949), 463–9.

McKenna, Lambert (ed.), 'Christ our Saviour', *Studies*, 38 (1949), 183–8.

McKenna, Lambert (ed.), 'Sorrow for sin', *Irish Monthly*, 56 (1928), 437–40.

McKenna, Lambert (ed.), 'To the Blessed Virgin', *Irish Monthly*, 58 (1930), 467–71.

McKenna, Lambert (ed.), *Aithdioghluim Dána*, 2 vols (Dublin, 1939–40).

McKenna, Lambert (ed.), *Dán Dé* (Dublin, 1922).

McLuhan, Marshall, *Understanding media: the extensions of man* (1964; London, 1997).

Mechthild von Magdeburg, *Das fliessende Licht der Gottheit*, ed. Margot Schmidt (Stuttgart, 1995).

Meier, Christel, *Gemma Spiritualis: Methode und Gebrauch der Edelsteinallegorese vom frühen Christentum bis ins 18. Jahrhundert* (Munich, 1977).

Meier, Esther, *Die Gregorsmesse: Funktionen eines spätmittelalterliche Bildtypus* (Köln, 2006).

Mennemeyer, Franz, *Kult und Brauchtum Johannis des Täufers in Westfalen: Ein Beitrag zur Kult- und Brauchtumsforschung* (Emsdetten, 1940).

Mens, Alcantara, *Oorsprong en betekenis van de Nederlandse begijnen- en begardenbeweging. Vergelijkende studie XII^{de}–XII^{de} eeuw* (Antwerp, 1947).

Meyer, Erich, 'Reliquie und Reliquiar im Mittelalter' in Erich Meyer (ed.), *Eine Gabe der Freunde für Carl Georg Heise zum 28.VI.1950* (Berlin, 1950), pp 55–67.

Miedema, Nine Robijntje, *Die römishcen Kirchen im Spätmittelalter nach den 'Indulgentiae ecclesiarum urbis Romae'* (Tübingen, 2001).

Migne, Jacques-Paul (ed.), *Patrologiae Latinae, Cursus Completus* (Turnhout, 1844–65).

Mitchell, W.J.T. and Mark B.N. Hansen, 'Introduction' in W.J.T. Mitchell and Mark B.N. Hansen (eds), *Critical terms for media studies* (Chicago, 2010), pp vii–xxii.

Mitchell, W.J.T., 'Interdisciplinarity and visual culture', *Art Bulletin*, 77:4 (1995), 540–4.

Mondzain-Baudinet, Marie-José (ed.), *Image, icône, economie: les sources byzantines de l'imaginaire contemporain* (Paris, 1996).

Mondzain-Baudinet, Marie-José (ed.), *Nicéphore. Discours contre les iconoclastes* (Paris, 1989).

Mondzain-Baudinet, Marie-José, *L'image naturelle* (Paris, 1995).

Mone, Franz Xaver, *Lateinische Hymnen des Mittelalters*, 1 (Freiburg i. Br., 1854, repr. Aalen, 1964).

Montgomery, Scott B., 'Golden flesh, radiant bones: the unity of relic and reliquary in medieval perception' in Akira Akiyama (ed.), *The interrelationship of relics and images in Christian and Buddhist culture* (Tokyo, 2007), pp 59–74.

Montgomery, Scott B., *St Ursula and the eleven thousand virgins of Cologne: relics, reliquaries and the visual culture of group sanctity in late medieval Europe* (Bern, 2010).

Moran, Josephine, 'The shattered image: archaeological evidence for painted and stained glass in medieval Ireland' in Rachel Moss, Colmán Ó Clabaigh and Salvador Ryan (eds), *Art and devotion in late medieval Ireland* (Dublin, 2006), pp 121–41.

Morgan, David, *The Sacred Gaze: religious visual culture in theory and practice* (Berkeley, CA, 2005).

Moro, Gotbert, 'Das Tafelngehen in Plessnitz', *Carinthia I: Zeitschrift für geschichtliche Landeskunde von Kärnten*, 128 (1938), 75–85.

Morton, Karena, 'Aspects of image and meaning in Irish medieval wall paintings' in Rachel Moss, Colmán Ó Clabaigh and Salvador Ryan (eds), *Art and devotion in late medieval Ireland* (Dublin, 2006), pp 51–71.

Neuhausen, Christiane, *Das Ablaßwesen in der Stadt Köln vom 13. bis zum 16. Jahrhundert* (Köln, 1994).

Neumann, Bernd, *Geistliches Schauspiel im Zeugnis der Zeit. Zur Aufführung mittelalterlicher religiöser Dramen im deutschen Sprachgebiet*, 2 vols (Munich, 1987).

Neuser, Kora, *Anemoi. Studien zur Darstellung der Winde und Windgottheiten in der Antike* (Rome, 1982).

Nichols, Stephen G., Andreas Kablitz and Alison Calhoun (eds), *Rethinking the medieval senses: heritage, fascinations, frames* (Baltimore, MD, 2008).

Niehr, Klaus, *Die mitteldeutsche Skulptur der ersten Hälfte des 13. Jahrhunderts*, Artefact 3 (Weinheim, 1992).

Nielsen, Karl Martin, *Middelalderens Danske Bønnebøger, 1–5* (Copenhagen, 1946–82).

Nielsen, Niels, *Sjælens Trøst (Sjæla trøst)*, 2 vols (Copenhagen, 1937–52).

Nolan, Barbara, *The Gothic visionary perspective* (Princeton, NJ, 1977).

Nordenfalk, Carl, 'The five senses in Flemish art before 1600' in G. Cavalli-Björkman (ed.), *Netherlandish mannerism* (Stockholm, 1985), pp 135–54.

Ó Clabaigh, Colmán, 'Anchorites in medieval Ireland' in Liz Herbert McAvoy (ed.), *Anchoritic traditions of medieval Europe* (Woodbridge, 2010).

Ó Clabaigh, Colmán, *The Franciscans in Ireland, 1400–1534* (Dublin, 2002).

Ó Clabaigh, Colmán, *The friars in Ireland, 1224–1540* (Dublin, 2012).

Ó Cuív, Brian, *Catalogue of manuscripts in the Bodleian Library at Oxford and Oxford College Libraries* (Dublin, 2001).

Oberman, Heiko A., 'Facientibus quod in se est deus non denegat gratiam. Robert Holcot OP and the beginnings of Luther's Theology', *Harvard Theological Review*, 55 (1962), 317–42.

Ozment, Steven E., *Mysticism and dissent: religious ideology and social protest in the sixteenth century* (New Haven, CT, 1973).

Palmer, Nigel F., *Bibelübersetzung und Heilsgeschichte, Studien zur Freiburger Perikopenhandschrift von 1462 und zu den deutschsprachigen Lektionaren des 15. Jahrhunderts* (Berlin, 2007).

Paludan, Helge, 'Skt. Clemens og Hellig Niels, Fromhedsliv og politik i Århus stift omkring 1190' in Poul Enemark, Per Ingesman and Jens Villiam Jensen (eds), *Kongemagt og samfund i middelalderen, Festskrift til Erik Ulsig* (Aarhus, 1988), pp 41–53.

Panofsky, Erwin, 'Zum Problem der Beschreibung und Inhaltsdeutung von Werken der bildenden Kunst', *Logos. Internationale Zeitschrift für Philosophie der Kultur*, 21 (1932), 103–19.

Panofsky, Erwin, *Early Netherlandish painting: its origin and character* (Cambridge, MA, 1953).

Parkin, David, 'Wafting on the wind: smell and the cycle of spirit and matter', *Journal of the Royal Anthropological Institute*, 13:1 (2007), 39–53.

Parret, Herman, 'De l'invisible comme présence', *Visio*, 7:3–4 (2003), 63–91.

Parshall, Peter W. and Rainer Schoch (eds), *Die Anfänge der europäischen Druckgraphik*: *Holzschnitte des 15. Jahrhunderts und ihr Gerauch* (Nürnberg, 2005).

Paulus, Nikolaus, *Geschichte des Ablasses am Ausgang des Mittelalters* (Darmstadt, 2000).

Pelzer, Birgit, 'Relicten' in P. Vandenbroeck (ed.), *Hooglied. De beeldwereld van religieuze vrouwen in de Zuidelijke Nederlanden, vanaf de 13de eeuw* (Brussels, 1994), pp 179–204.

Pietsch, Paul, *Ewangely und Epistel Teutsch. Die gedruckten hochdeutschen Perikopenbücher (Plenarien), 1473–1523. Ein Beitrag zur kenntnis der Wiegendrucke, zur Geschichte des deutschen Schrifttums, insbesondere der Bibelverdeutschung und der Bibelsprache* (Göttingen, 1927).

Platelle, Henri, 'Guibert de Nogent et le "De pignoribus sanctorum": Richesses et limites d'une critique médiévale des reliques' in Bozóky and Helvétius, *Les reliques: objets, cultes, symboles* (Turnhout, 1999), pp 109–21.

Prozesky, Maria, 'Imitatio in Julian of Norwich: Christ the knight, fruitio and the pleasures of courtesy', *Parergon*, 30:1 (2013), 141–58.

Prüm monastery, *Historia translationis reliquiarum Chrysanti et Dariae ex urbe Roma in Galliam*, in *Ratramni Corbeiensis Monachi, Aeneae, Sancti Remigii … opera omnia*, ed. Jacques-Paul Migne (Paris, 1852), cols 673–82.

Raff, Thomas, *Die Sprache der Materialien: Anleitung zu einer Ikonologie der Werkstoffe* (Munich, 1994).

Raymond of Capua, *The Life of Catherine of Siena (Legenda Maior)* (Dublin, 1980).

Réau, Louis, *Iconographie de l'art chrétien*, 2 vols (Paris, 1956).

Regardie, Israel, *The tree of life: a study in magic* (York, 1994).

Reinitzer, Heimo and Olaf Scwekcke in *Die deutsche Literatur des Mittelalters. Verfasserlexikon*, Bd. 7 (Berlin and New York, 1989), cols 737–63.

Renevey, Denis, '1215–1349: texts' in Samuel Fanous and Vincent Gillespie (eds), *The Cambridge companion to medieval English mysticism* (Cambridge, 2011).

Reudenbach, Bruno and Gia Toussaint (eds), *Reliquiare im Mittelalter* (Berlin, 2011).

Reudenbach, Bruno and Gia Toussaint, 'Die Wahrnehmung und Deutung von Heiligen: Überlegungen zur Medialität von Reliquiaren', *Das Mittelalter*, 8:2 (2003), 34–40.

Reudenbach, Bruno, '"Gold ist Schlamm": Anmerkungen zur Materialbewertung im Mittelalter' in Monika Wagner and Dietmar Rübel (eds), *Material in Kunst und Alltag* (Berlin, 2002), pp 1–12.

Reudenbach, Bruno, 'Reliquiare als Heiligkeitsbeweis und Echtheitszeugnis: Grundzüge einer problematischen Gattung' in Bruno Reudenbach et al. (eds), *Reliquiare als Heiligkeitsbeweis und Echtheitszeugnis* (Berlin, 2000), pp 1–36.

Reudenbach, Bruno, 'Heil durch Sehen. Mittelalterliche Reliquiare und die visuelle Konstruktion von Heiligkeit' in Markus Mayr (ed.), *Vom Goldenen Gebeinen. Wirtschaft und Reliquie im Mittelalter* (Innsbruck, 2001), pp 135–47.

Reynaert, Joris, *De beeldspraak van Hadewijch* (Tielt and Bussem, 1981).

Ridderbos, Bernhard, 'Objects and questions' in Bernhard Ridderbos, Anne van Buren and Henk Van Veen (eds), *Early Netherlandish paintings: rediscovery, reception and research* (Amsterdam, 2005), pp 16–23.

Riehle, Wolfgang, *The Middle English mystics*, trans. Bernard Standring (London, 1981).

Ringbom, Sixten, 'Bild och avlat, I. Veronikabilden', *ICO – Iconographisk Post*, 3 (1983), 8–18.

Ringbom, Sixten, 'Bild och avlat, II. Smärtomannen, Rosenkransen och Jomfrun i solinne', *ICO – Iconographisk Post*, 4 (1983), 1–16.

Ronchi, Ermes M. (ed.), *La Madonna nell'attesa del Parto: capalavori dal patrimonio italiano del '300 e '400* (Milan, 2001).

Roth, Gunhild, 'Die Gregoriusmesse und das Gebet "*Adoro te in cruce pendentem*" im Einblattdruck. Legendenstoff, bildliche Verarbeitung und Texttradtition am Beispiel des Monogrammisten' in Volker Honemann et al. (eds), *Einblattdrucke des 15. und frühen 16. Jahrhunderts. Probleme, Perspektiven, Fallstudien* (Tübingen, 2000), pp 277–324.

Rubin, Miri, *Corpus Christi: the Eucharist in late medieval culture* (Cambridge, 1991).

Rubin, Miri, *Emotion and devotion: the meaning of Mary in medieval religious culture* (Budapest, 2009).

Rudolph, Conrad, *The "things of greater importance": Bernard of Clairvaux's Apologia and the medieval attitude towards art* (Philadelphia, 1990).

Ruh, Kurt, *Geschichte der Abendländischen Mystik*, Band II, *Frauenmystik und Franziskanische Mystik der Frühzeit* (München, 1993).

Ryan, Salvador, 'A slighted source: rehabilitating bardic religious poetry in historical discourse', *Cambrian Medieval Celtic Studies*, 48 (winter 2004), 75–99.

Ryan, Salvador, 'Penance and the privateer: handling sin in the bardic religious verse of the Book of the O'Conor Don (1631)' in Tadhg Ó hAnnracháin and Robert Armstrong (eds), *Christianities in the early modern Celtic world* (Basingstoke, 2014), pp 124–34.

Ryan, Salvador, 'Signed in blood: the crucified Christ as document' in Salvador Ryan and Brendan Leahy (eds), *Treasures of Irish Christianity, 2: a people of the Word* (Dublin, 2013), pp 85–7.

Ryan, Salvador, 'The devotional landscape of medieval Irish cultural Catholicism *inter hibernicos et inter anglicos*' in Oliver Rafferty (ed.), *Irish Catholic identities* (Manchester, 2013), pp 62–76.

Ryan, Salvador, 'The most traversed bridge: a reconsideration of elite and popular religion in late medieval Ireland' in K. Cooper and J. Gregory (eds), *Elite and popular religion* (Suffolk, 2006), pp 120–9.

Ryan, Salvador, 'Wily women of God in Breifne's devotional collections' in Brendan Scott (ed.), *Culture and society in early modern Breifne/Cavan* (Dublin, 2009), pp 31–47.

Ryan, Salvador, 'Windows on late medieval devotional practice: Máire Ní Mháille's "Book of Piety" (1513) and the world behind the texts' in Rachel Moss, Colmán Ó Clabaigh and Salvador Ryan (eds), *Art and devotion in late medieval Ireland* (Dublin, 2006), pp 1–15.

Salmon, Charles, *Histoire du chef de saint Jean Baptiste* (Amiens, 1876).

Sancti Bernardi opera omnia IV, ed. J. Leclercq and H.M. Rochais (Rome, 1963).

Sancti Hilarii Episcopi Pictavensis Tractatus Super Psalmos, ed. Antonius Zingerle (Vienna, 1891).

Schildgen, Brenda Deen, 'Rhetoric and the Body of Christ: Augustine, Jerome and the classical *Paideia*' in B.D. Schildgen (ed.), *The Rhetoric Canon* (Detroit, 1997), pp 151–73.

Schmidt, Peter, 'Beschreiben, bemalt, zerschnitten: Tegernseer Mönsche interpretieren einen Holzschnitt' in Volker Honemann et al. (eds), *Einblattdrucke des 15. und frühen 16. Jahrhunderts. Probleme, Perspektiven, Fallstudien* (Tübingen, 2000), pp 245–76.

Schmidt, Peter, 'The multiple image: the beginnings of printmaking, between old theories and new approaches' in Peter Parshall et al. (eds), *Origins of European printmaking: fifteenth-century woodcuts and their public. Exhibition catalogue: National Gallery of Art* (Washington, DC, 2005), pp 37–56.

Schmidt, Peter, 'Das vielfältige Bild: Die Anfänge des Mediums Druckgraphik; zwischen alten Thesen und neuen Zugängen' in Peter Parshall et al. (eds), *Die Anfänge der europäischen Druckgraphik. Holzschnitte des 15. Jahrhunderts und ihr Gebrauch. Ausstellungskatalog, Germanisches Nationalmuseum* (Nürnberg, 2005), pp 37–56.

Schmitt, Jean-Claude, 'Les reliques et les images' in Edina Bozóky and Anna Marie Helvétius (eds), *Les reliques: objets, cultes, symboles* (Turnhout, 1999), pp 145–59.

Schnitzler, Norbert, *Ikonoklasmus – Bildersturm. Theologischer Bilderstreit und ikonoklastisches Handeln während des 15. und 16. Jahrhunderts* (Munich, 1996).

Schoch, Johann Carl, 'Kurtze Nachricht von denen Merckwürdigkeiten der hohen Stiffts-Kirche zu Naumburg', Stadtarchiv Naumburg, Sa 50 (unpublished manuscript, 1773).

Schreiner, Klaus (ed.), *Frömmigkeit im Mittelalter: Politisch-Soziale, visuelle Praxis, körperliche Ausdruchforme* (Munich, 2002).

Schumacher, Jan, 'Breaking the bread of Scripture: on the medieval interpretation of the Bible', *Collegium Medievale*, 6:2 (Oslo, 1993), 107–32.

Seegets, Petra, *Passionstheologie und Passionsfrömmigkeit im ausgehenden Mittelalter. Der Nürnberger Franziskaner Stephan Fridolin (gest. 1498) zwischen Kloster und Stadt* (Tübingen, 1998).

Sepière, Marie-Christine, *L'image d'un Dieu souffrant (IXe–Xe siècle). Aux origines du crucifix* (Paris, 1984).

Seuse, Heinrich, *Horologium spaientiae*, ed. Pius Künzle OP (Freiburg, 1977).

Simson, Otto von, *The Gothic cathedral: origins of Gothic architecture and the medieval concept of order* (1956; Princeton, NJ, 1989).

Skemer, Don C., *Binding words: textual amulets in the Middle Ages* (University Park, PA, 2006).

Skinnebach, Laura Katrine, 'Devotion: perception as practice and body as devotion in late medieval piety' in Henning Laugerud et al. (eds), *The saturated sensorium* (Aarhus, 2015).

Skinnebach, Laura Katrine, 'Practices of perception: devotion and the senses in late medieval northern Europe' (PhD, University of Bergen, 2013).

Smalley, Beryl, *The study of the Bible in the Middle Ages* (1951; Notre Dame, 1978).

Smith, Jonathan Z., *To take place: towards a theory in ritual* (Chicago, 1992).

Smith, Mark M., *Sensing the past: seeing, hearing, smelling, tasting and touching in history* (Berkeley, CA, 2008).

Smoller, Laura A., 'Of earthquakes, hail, frogs and geography: plague and the investigation of the Apocalypse in the later Middle Ages' in Caroline Walker Bynum and Poul Freedman (eds), *Last things: death and the Apocalypse in the Middle Ages* (Philadelphia, 2000).

Steinberg, Leo, '"How shall this be?" Reflections on Filippo Lippi's *Annunciation* in London, pt I', *Artibus et Historiae*, 16 (1987), 25–44.

Steinke, Barbara, *Paradiesgarten oder Gefängnis? Das Nürnberger Katharinenkloster zwischen Klosterreform und Reformation* (Tübingen, 2006).

Steinke, Barbara, '"Den Bräutigam nehmt euch und habt ihn und verlasst ihn nicht, denn er verlässt euch nicht." Zur Moral der Mystik im Nürnberger Katharinenkloster während des 15. Jahrhundets' in Berndt Hamm and Voker Leppin (eds), *Gottes Nähe unmittelbar erfahren. Mystik im Mittelalter und bei Martin Luther* (Tübingen, 2007), pp 139–64.

Stoichita, Victor I., *A short history of the shadow* (London, 1997).

Strider, Peter, *Tafelmalerei in Nürnberg, 1350–1550* (Nürnberg, 1993).

Sunil Manghani, Arthur Piper and Jon Simons (eds), *Images: a reader* (London, 2006).

Tammen, Silke, 'Dorn und Schmerzensmann: Zum Verhältnis von Reliquie, Reliquiar und Bild in spätmittelalterlichen Christusreliquiaren' in Reudenbach and Toussaint (eds), *Reliquiare im Mittelalter*, pp 187–208.

Taubert, Johannes and Fritz Buchenrieder, 'Der Forstenrieder Kruzifixus', *Deutsche Kunst und Denkmalpflege*, 20 (1962), 81–102.

The Malleus Maleficarum of Heinrich Kramer and James Sprenger, trans. Montague Summers (New York, 1971 [1928]).

'The Wooing of Our Lord' in Anne Savage and Nicholas Watson (eds and trans.), *Anchoritic spirituality* (Mahwah, NJ, 1991).

Thiofrid of Echternach, *Thiofridi Abbatis Epternacensis Flores epytaphii sanctorum*, ed. M.C. Ferrari (Turnhout, 1993).

Thiofridus Epternacensis, *Goffridi Abbatis Vindocinensis opera omnia … Thiofridi Abbatis Efternacensis, Petri Alphonsi …*, ed. Jacques-Paul Migne (Paris, 1854).

Thomas Aquinas, *The Summa Theologica of St Thomas Aquinas*, ed. and trans. Fathers of the English Dominican Province (London, 1920).

Thomas Aquinas, *A commentary on Aristotle's De Anima*, trans. Robert Pasnau (New Haven, CT, and London, 1999).

Thomas Aquinas, *Summa Theologica*, I–V (Allen, TX, 1981 (1948)).

Thomas of Celano, *Saint Francis of Assisi*, ed. and trans. Placid Hermann OFM (Chicago, 1988 (1963)).

Thulin, Oskar, *Johannes der Täufer im geistlichen Schauspiel des Mittelalters und der Reformationszeit* (Leipzig, 1930).

Thunø, Erik, 'The golden altar of Sant'Ambrogio in Milan: image and materiality' in Kaspersen and Thunø, *Decorating the Lord's table*, pp 63–78.

Tobin, Frank, *Henry Suso: the exemplar with two German sermons* (New York and Mahwah, NJ, 1989).

Toussaint, Gia, 'Heiliges Gebein und edler Stein: Der Edelsteinschmuck von Reliquiaren im Spiegel mittelalterlicher Wahrnehmung', *Das Mittelalter*, 8:2 (2003), 41–66.

Tripps, Johannes, *Das handelnde bildwerk in der Gotik: Forschungen zur Symbolik des Kirchengebäudes und seiner Ausstattung in der Hoch-und Spätgotik* (Berlin, 2000).

van Bockstaele, Geert, *Hemelveerdegem: De kerk en het Sint-Jansretabel ca 1015 tot heden* (Lierde, 1998).

van den Berg, Dirk J., 'What is an image and what is image power', *Image & Narrative*, 8 (2004) (electronic journal).

van Knippenberg, Carla Dauven, Christian Kiening and Cornelia Herberichs (eds), *Die Medialität des Heils im späten Mittelalter* (Zürich, 2010).

van Vlierberg, Jozef, *Het symbolisme der bloemen* (Dendermonde, 1930).

Vandenbroeck, Paul (ed.), *Hooglied. De beeldwereld van religieuze vrouwen in de Zuidelijke Nederlanden, vanaf de 13de eeuw* (Brussels, 1994).

Vandenbroeck, Paul, 'Matrix Marmorea' in Baert et al. (eds), *New perspectives in iconology: visual studies and anthropology* (Brussels, 2012), pp 180–210.

Vergo, Peter, *That divine order: music and the visual arts from antiquity to the eighteenth century* (London, 2005).

Vettori, Alessandro, *Poets of divine love: Franciscan mystical poetry of the thirteenth century* (New York, 2004).

Virilio, Paul, *La machine de vision* (Paris, 1988).

Vita Beate Virginis Marie et Salvatoris Rhythmica, ed. Adolf Vögtlin, *BLVS*, 180 (Tübingen, 1880).

Walker, Alicia and Amanda Luyster (eds), *Negotiating secular and sacred in medieval art* (Farnham, 2009).

Walter, Ingeborg Zapperi, *Piero della Francesca, Madonna del parto: ein Kunstwerk zwischen Politik und Devotion* (Frankfurt a. M., 1992).

Warburg, Aby, *Einleitung Bilderatlas Mnemosyne*, ed. Martin Warnke and Claudia Brink (Berlin, 2000).

Wartofsky, Marx W., 'Picturing and representing' in Calvin F. Nodine and Dennis F. Fisher (eds), *Perception and pictorial representation* (New York, 1979), pp 272–83.

Webb, Heather, 'Cardiosensory impulses in late medieval spirituality' in Stephen G. Nichols, Andreas Kablitz and Alison Calhoun (eds), *Rethinking the medieval senses: heritage, fascinations, frames* (Baltimore, MD, 2008), pp 265–85.

Wéber, Edouard-H., 'Elements néoplatoniciens en théologie mystique au XIIIème siècle' in Kurt Ruh (ed.), *Abendländische Mystik im Mittelalter. Symposion Kloster Engelberg 1984* (Stuttgart, 1986), pp 196–217.

Wieland, Wolfgang, 'Kontinuum und Engelzeit bei Thomas von Aquino' in E. Scheibe and G. Süssmann, *Einheit und Vielheit. Festschrift für Carl Friedrich v. Weizsäcker zum 60 geburtstag* (Göttingen, 1973), pp 77–90.

Wiener Heiligthumbuch, Das Wiener Heiligthumbuch, nach der Ausgabe vom Jahre 1502 sammt den Nachträgen von 1514 (Vienna, 1882).

Williams, George Hunston, *The radical reformation* (Philadelphia, PA, 1962).

Williams-Krapp, Werner, '"Dise ding sint dennoch nit ware zeichen der heiligkeit" Zur Bewertung mystischer Erfahrungen im 15. Jahrhundert', *Zeitschrift für Literaturwissenschaft und Linguistik*, 20, Heft 80 (1990), 61–71.

Wilung, Antje, *Literatur und Ordensreform im 15. Jahrhundert. Deutsche Abendmahlsschriften im Nürnberger Katharinenkloster* (Münster, 2004).

Winston-Allen, Anne, *Stories of the Rose: the making of the rosary in the Middle Ages* (University Park, PA, 1997, 2005).

Winterhager, Wilhelm Ernst, 'Ablasskritik als Indikator historischen Wandels vor 1517. Ein Beitrag zu Vorraussetzungen und Einordnung der Reformation', *Archiv für Reformationsgeschichte*, 90 (1999), 6–71.

Wolf, Gerhard, *Schleier und Spiegel. Traditionen des Christusbildes und die Bildkonzepte der Renaissance* (Munich, 2002).

Wolf, Gerhard, 'Das Paradox des wahren Bildes' in Christoph Geissmar-Brandi and Eleonora

Louis (eds), *Glaube, Hoffnung, Liebe, Tod. Von der Entwicklung religiöser Bildkonzepte. Exhibition catalogue* (Klagenfurt, 1996), pp 430–3.

Woolf, Rosemary, 'The theme of Christ the lover-knight in medieval English literature' in Heather O'Donoghue (ed.), *Art and doctrine: essays on medieval literature* (London, 1986).

Woolgar, C.M., *The senses in late medieval England* (New Haven, CT, 2006).

World, Gerhard, *Salus Populi Romani. Die Geschichte römischer Kultbilder im Mittelalter* (Weinheim, 1990).

Wulf, Christoph and Jörg Zirfas (eds), *Ikonologie des Performativen* (Munich, 2005).

Zinn, Grover A. Jr, 'Hugh of Saint Victor and the Art of Memory', *Viator*, 5 (1974), 211–34.

Zischka, Ulrike, *Zur sakralen und profanen Anwendung des Knotenmotivs als magisches Mittel, Symbol oder Dekor. Eine vergleichende volkskundliche Untersuchung* (Munich, 1977).

Zunker, Maria Magdalena, 'Spämittelalterliche Nonnenmalereien aus der Abtei St Walburg. Versuche einer Deutung' in Franziska Bachner, Doris Gerstel and Georg Ulrich Großmann (eds), *Spiegel der Seligkeit. Privates Bild und Frömmigkeit in Spätmittelalter. Germanishes Nationamuseum, Nürnberg 31 Mai–8 Oktober 2000* (Nürnberg, 2000), pp 97–116.

Index